Memi

May the cultural mirror
help us to understanding
many things better — including
organizations —

Clinton BA
October 1993

Understanding Organizations

Studies in Communication Processes
Editor, Richard D. Rieke

Communication in Legal Advocacy
by Richard D. Rieke and Randall K. Stutman

Understanding Organizations: Interpreting Organizational Communication Cultures
by Charles R. Bantz, with a case study by Gerald Pepper

Understanding Organizations

Interpreting Organizational Communication Cultures

by Charles R. Bantz

with a case study by Gerald Pepper

UNIVERSITY OF SOUTH CAROLINA PRESS

Copyright © 1993 University of South Carolina

Published in Columbia, South Carolina, by the
University of South Carolina Press

Manufactured in the United States of America

Library of Congress Cataloging-in-Publication Data

Bantz, Charles R.
   Understanding organizations : interpreting organizational
communication cultures / Charles R. Bantz, with a case study by
Gerald Pepper.
      p.   cm. — (Studies in communication processes)
   Includes bibliographical references and index.
   ISBN 0–87249–879–4 (hard cover, acid-free)
   1. Communication in organizations.   I. Pepper, Gerald.
II. Title.   III. Series.
HD30.3.B37   1993
302.3′5 — dc20   92-44328

CONTENTS

EXAMPLES, FIGURES, AND TABLES

PREFACE

A truism of contemporary life is that organizations are inescapable—whether one is working or playing, living or dying. While the omnipresence of organizations make them an important phenomenon, it is their character, however, that makes them intriguing.

Organizations are symbolic realities constructed by humans in communication. Those symbolic realities are *organizational communication cultures* (OCC). Organizations are creations, and both organizational members and observers need to comprehend them as such. To understand organizations, I propose that one analyzes organizational communication messages and then infers organizational communication culture by identifying the organizational patterns of meanings and expectations.

The organizational communication culture method has been used in more than 200 analyses of "real-world" organizations (e.g., a legal services office, a cooperative food store, an engineering unit of a major corporation, a rock band) and organizations presented in literature (e.g., the U.S. Army of Joseph Heller's *Catch-22*). By using the OCC method interpreters come to understand the symbolic world of the organization they study as well as the process by which members construct, maintain, and transform organizations.

By presenting the method and presenting Gerald Pepper's case study illustration of the method (chap. 10), the book seeks three sets of readers. First, the role of communication in the construction of symbolic realities is an important intellectual question that is receiving a great deal of scholarly attention (e.g., witness the impact of Fisher's 1987 book *Human Communication as Narration*); this book will contribute to those discussions. Second, the OCC method has been valuable for helping students analyze organizations; the book makes the OCC method available to students of organizational communication and organizational theory. Third, given the intense practical interest in organizational culture in the 1980s (e.g., Peters's and Waterman's *In Search of Excellence* [1982]), managers of organizations and those studying to be managers will find a systematic approach to understanding organizational culture helpful. The book is useful, then, to scholars, students, and managers of organizations.

ACKNOWLEDGMENTS

The length of this project's gestation means the intellectual and practical debts I have accrued in developing the OCC method and writing this book are substantial. My intellectual debts began in graduate school when studying with Ernest Bormann, Leonard Hawes, David Smith, and Robert L. Scott and mounted rapidly as I read, taught, and did research. These later debts are owed to many, including Wayne Brockriede, Bonnie McDaniel Johnson, and Karl Weick, but especially to Mike Pacanowsky, whose workshop in 1980 drew me into the organizational culture, and the participants at the 1981 and 1987 Alta conferences. Having the opportunity to present these ideas at two Alta conferences on interpretive approaches to organizations, at the Seventh International Conference on Culture and Communication, and at the 1989 Speech Communication Association conference in San Francisco (after the earthquake) provided me with needed opportunities to gain feedback from numerous colleagues. And then there is Dr. Pepper. Without Jerry Pepper I would know very little about metaphor and this book would have no chapter 10, with its effective illustration of the OCC method.

In the 11 years I have worked on a statement of the OCC method, the bulk of my debt is to the hundreds of students whose projects helped me to better understand both organizations and the method. To select any for mention risks overlooking equally significant contributors; I would be remiss, however, if I didn't mention Dean Scheibel for his seven years of work on the method, Bob Krizek for his creative use of the method, and the authors of several studies that significantly influenced my thinking—Dawn Ohlendorf Braithwaite, Jim Branen, Shannon Grenz, and Brian Matlock.

My practical debts are significant. John Baldwin's commitment to making the manuscript clear, grammatically correct, and complete has made this a much better read. Dean Scheibel contributed not only Figure 9.1 but also made numerous comments on the text. Kay Pepper's artistry created Figure 10.1 and made publishable Figure 9.1. The reviewers for the University of

South Carolina Press were extremely thorough and perceptive, contributing both to the intellectual substance and the form of the book. Series editor Rick Rieke, press director Ken Scott, and acquisitions editor Warren Slesinger helped bring this project to print. Lori Adler, my administrative assistant, through her efficiency, encouragement, and gatekeeping, has made it possible for me to finish a book while serving as department chair.

Finally, I must acknowledge my inspirational debts. From my mother and father, Harriet Dowdell Bantz and Douglas Bantz, I realized a commitment to understanding our world. From my love, Sandra Petronio, I gained a scholarly companion, who helps me see more of life, love, and ideas.

Understanding Organizations

CHAPTER ONE

Introduction:
The Organizational Communication
Culture Method

Practically all the reality we wake up facing is a human construct left
over from yesterday.

—Northrop Frye

Our days in organizations are days of communicating. We send
and use messages to accomplish the work and play of organizational life. If we listen, really listen, to the talk around us and
attend the documents we see, we are apt to hear a maze of mundane, serious, obscene, cryptic, even important messages.
Those messages may be dramatic and enduring or routine and
transient. They can be simple and direct or complex and subtle.
We create and use a rich and varied mosaic of messages as we
engage in organizational communication.

A useful avenue for understanding organizations is the analysis of organizational communication. By defining organizational communication as the collective creation, maintenance,
and transformation of organizational meanings and organizational expectations through the sending and using of messages
(cf. Johnson, 1977, p. 4), communication is the medium through
which organizations, as symbolic realities, are constructed by
humans. Examining messages sent and used in organizations is
the main route to understanding organizations as symbolic entities constituted by their members. To label the symbolic entity
that *is* an organization, I propose the term *organizational communication culture* (OCC). The organizational communication culture method is a strategy for understanding organizations
founded on the analysis of messages (chap. 2 details the argument supporting these claims).

This book presents the organizational communication culture
approach by detailing the elements in the method. This chapter

1

provides an overview of the method, thus providing the framework for each of the chapters that follow. The interpretation of organizational communication cultures is a methodology that (1) gathers messages; (2) analyzes the messages for four major elements—vocabulary, themes, architecture, and temporality; (3) analyzes the symbolic forms in the messages—metaphors, fantasy themes, and stories; (4) infers patterns of expectations from the elements, symbolic forms, and the messages themselves; (5) infers patterns of organizational meanings from these same elements, symbolic forms, expectations, and messages; and (6) weaves the patterns of meanings and expectations into a tapestry that represents the organizational communication culture. Table 1.1 presents a summary of the method. This chapter will sketch the elements of the method presented in Table 1.1, which the remainder of the book will elaborate.

Table 1.1
The Organizational Communication Culture Method

Source of Messages	Analysis of		Inference of	
	Messages	Symbolic Forms	Organizational Expectations	Meanings
Communicative interactions	Vocabulary	Metaphors	Norms	Constructs
	Themes	Stories	Roles	Relations among
Documents				constructs
	Temporality	Fantasy themes	Motives	
	Architecture		Agenda	
			Style	

Sources of Messages

Organizational communication messages can be characterized as being either *communicative interactions* or *documents* (cf. Johnson, 1977, chap. 3). Communicative interaction is the simultaneous creation, exchange, and use of messages with others, such as face-to-face conversation and telephone talk. Communicative interaction includes both the verbal and non-verbal messages exchanged. Documents are messages with some relative permanence, such as memos, letters, procedure manuals, and buildings (the distinctions are detailed in chap. 3).

Given that the analysis of messages is central to understanding an organization, one must gather messages together for analysis, inference, and interpretation. The process of gathering messages, discussed at length in chapters 4 and 5, is taken for granted in this chapter. Here I focus on analyzing and interpreting messages. Two excerpts from observational notes illustrate the analysis and interpretation process. In presenting these examples, I am explicating the method, not providing an interpretation of the organizations' cultures. A few examples are not adequate to infer an organizational communication culture. In a complete OCC study, such as Pepper's analysis of "New Public Utility" in chapter 10, the researcher would have gathered a plethora of messages for analysis.

Each of these two examples illustrates a different type of message. Example 1.1 illustrates an organizational document. It is an item from a police chief's newsletter, which was gathered in Caddow's (1986) study of a suburban police department. Example 1.2 illustrates a communicative interaction that Olson (1985) observed between two evening-shift telephone collectors at an urban collection agency.

Message Analysis

These two examples are rich illustrations of messages in organizational life. The police chief's column in the newsletter dramatically tells a story of the department's success, while emphasizing the process of putting the criminal in his place. The collection agency conversation is typical of informal talk among coworkers, which includes talk about "clients," complaints about management, and concern about their jobs.

These two examples serve to demonstrate how message analysis focuses on identifying and interpreting four aspects of mes-

Example 1.1
Police Chief's Newsletter

VERY GOOD POLICE WORK

Members of the Patrol and Criminal Investigations Bureau combined to arrest a local armed robber on Tuesday of this week. It was an example of good police work and intradepartment cooperation. The local would-be tough guy was armed with an automatic pistol at the time. Our people showed excellent restraint from firing at him on crowded [*blank*] Road.

Unfortunately, in addition to his own, he damaged one of our patrol cars and four vehicles in an auto dealership. He was wanted for eight armed robberies between here and [*blank*].

In accord with the previous item, this guy was first arrested by our department for armed robbery in 1974 and sentenced to 12 years. He was paroled and again quickly arrested for engaging in a shootout with some other local bums and sent back to prison. He was again paroled just a few weeks ago and now, thankfully, is returning to his natural habitat.

(Signature)

_____

Chief of Police

(Caddow, 1986)

sages: *vocabulary, themes, architecture,* and *temporality.* Further, the examples show how message analysis provides the basis for inferring organizational expectations and meanings. As these examples illustrate, vocabulary, themes, architecture, and temporality are interrelated and synergistic, for vocabulary is essential to thematic development, temporality can be thematic, structures are frequently temporal, and other combinations of these elements are common.

VOCABULARY

Analyzing the vocabulary of an organization is essential to developing an understanding of its OCC. This means establishing the commonplace usages of everyday language (who is "we"?), of technical terms (*RFP*), and specialized language in context (is *IBM* good or bad around here?). This task necessitates becoming aware of the organizationally specific use of familiar terms as well as understanding the unfamiliar.

The vocabulary of police is distinctive. When police talk

Example 1.2
Collection Agency Conversation

Ann: That'll teach her [*a borrower*]. Some of these people are so
      stupid. But then they think we're pretty dumb, too.
Meg: Well, to tell the truth, with some of the things I've seen here,
      you can't blame borrowers for thinking that we have no clue.
Ann: Like what?
Meg: Well, remember Shawn Slack? She had this special project to do
      for her manager, I forget just what it was, but she found that
      she couldn't get it all done, so she started to hide some of it.
Ann: You're kidding. Where did she hide it?
Meg: Remember in the old building? There was a false ceiling. She
      took out some of the tiles and put it up there, then put the tiles
      back in.
Ann: Incredible! Maybe we should try that. [*Laughter*]
Ann: I know there were lots of stories about that kind of thing before
      the holocaust. I guess that when those efficiency experts fired
      all 30 people in one day, they knew what they were doing.
Meg: Yeah, they got rid of some troublemakers like Shawn and
      Heather. Remember Heather? Boy was she a gem.
Ann: I'm just glad that we survived that mess.
Meg: They never did fire anyone from our unit did they?
Ann: Nope. They knew better, we are the only unit that can get our
      work done. I think management knows that.
Meg: Well, not so much anymore. There are too many new people
      who don't know anything yet. I spend so much time answering
      questions that I hardly have time to do my work.
Ann: Me too. Speaking of which . . .

                                    (Olson, 1985)

among themselves they frequently use obscene labels for criminals (see Pacanowsky, 1983; Van Maanen, 1988, chap. 5, for examples). In the police chief's column, however, the chief used
polite irony referring to the "would-be tough guy," "local
bums," and "returning to his natural habitat." The irony implicitly suggests the same judgment that an obscene label makes explicit. Thus, the chief implied a strong negative opinion without
using obscene labels, which would be inappropriate in a public
document, such as a newsletter.

In the collection agency Ann and Meg's conversation is constructed with familiar words, but the words take on organizationally specific denotation and connotation in this context. For

example, while *borrower* is a common word, in a collection agency a borrower is a person Ann and Meg must call in pursuit of payments. Collectors compete with borrowers each night on the phone, and therefore *borrower* carries a negative connotation. Other common words are references to *our unit, troublemakers,* and the *old building,* terms that have specific referents for Ann and Meg. The most striking term in the conversation is *the holocaust.* Given that it commonly refers to the destruction of European Jews, using the term marks the significance of the firings to the people of the collection agency.

THEMES

Identifying repetitive and interconnected topics in messages locates themes. For example, even though he used irony, the police chief wrote about important topics: acknowledgment of good work, concern for citizens' safety, disappointment over property damage, and the risks of recidivism. If these topics appear frequently in the police department's messages, they may become organizational themes (e.g., we do good work, we protect civilians, we attack crime).

Meg and Ann's conversation is built around several "inside" topics: borrowers are always wrong, "slack" workers, the holocaust, and management knows. The topic that initiates the conversation—that borrowers are always wrong—in fact does appear in several different interactions Olson observed, suggesting that Meg and Ann's discussion of it is not unique and that it is a theme in the collection agency.

ARCHITECTURE

Analyzing messages for their structural arrangements—their architecture—entails not only looking for patterns in speaking and writing but also the arrangement of space in documents. Architecture, then, will include the arrangement of words on the page of a memo, the physical architecture of buildings, and the ordering of arguments.

The structure of the chief's column focused first on the job done well, detailed the events, then reinforced the importance of that job by showing that the would-be tough guy was a real "animal." Thus, the reader sees not only a compliment to the officers, but also how the job was done and the value of doing the job (measured by the evil of the perpetrator). The structure of the column follows a "lesson" format, including specifics of the desired behavior and the importance of the "reward."

In the collection agency conversation each of the topics is developed within a particular message structure—as a ministry. Ann and Meg move from one story to the next, telling of the dumb borrower, Shawn Slack, the devastation of the holocaust, and that newcomers are slowing down their unit's productivity. Similar to the police chief's approach, each story has a chronological structure telling events in sequential order.

TEMPORALITY

Temporality refers to the role of time in the messages. Temporality will include the pacing, flow, and frequency of messages as well as the temporal aspects of structure.

The police chief's column is a chronology ordered by the sequence of events in the chase and the accused's criminal career (a contrasting use of time would have placed all the events in the present—e.g., he is in jail; everyone has recovered). The chronological pattern followed the course of events as officers experienced them and is common in police organizations.

The collection agency conversation illustrates the interconnection of architecture and temporality, for the stories told by Ann and Meg operate chronologically, yet the overall conversational structure is episodic—moving from customer complaint to criticism of other employees to description of mass firings and back to work. Temporality of messages appears in the rapid pace of the movement among topics, in the internal chronology of stories, and even as a theme in those stories (e.g., the strong use of times past—"Remember when . . . ," "They never did fire anyone," "Remember Shawn Slack?").

Even a cursory analysis of these two messages provides the basis for interpretation of the organizational cultures. The audience for the police department newsletter, police officers and other departmental employees, thus read a message that presents an argument for good work: not only was a creep put back where he belongs, but "we" did it together, and "we" did it right.

Contrast the positive and supportive character of the chief's commentary to the interchange between Ann and Meg, employees of a collection agency. In spite of Ann's positive note about the effectiveness of their unit, the overall tone of the conversation is hardly positive. The conversation flows from Ann's anger with a borrower, shifts to the poor quality of work at the collection agency, the "holocaust" that the efficiency experts wrought, and the difficulty they are having in doing their work.

Symbolic Form Analysis

There is a substantial literature on the importance of metaphor, fantasy themes, and stories in communication. These symbolic forms may help understanding the patterns of meanings and expectations in an OCC (Scheibel, 1990). The OCC analyst must identify the use of the symbolic forms *in messages* and interpret them within the context of the organization's culture. Symbolic form analysis will build on the message analysis by exploring vocabulary, themes, architecture, and temporality. Symbolic form analysis will make a major contribution to the inference of expectations and meanings. While chapter 7 will detail symbolic form analysis, here I will only suggest the value of analyzing those symbolic forms in providing the basis for understanding an organizational communication culture.

METAPHOR ANALYSIS

The analysis of metaphor examines the relationship implied between two concepts, such as "boy" and "fish" in the sentence "the boy is a fish." The relationship between the focus (*boy*) and the frame (*fish*) is a simple metaphor (Pepper, 1987). Metaphors are important symbolic forms found in organizational messages such as the police chief's newsletter column.

The police chief describes the criminal as "returning to his natural habitat." The chief is equating the criminal with an animal (animals, not people, have habitats). Furthermore, since criminals are members of the public, the chief is labeling a member of the public in a disparaging manner. An analysis of this metaphorical usage points to a paradox of police work—that police officers work for and protect the public by arresting and jailing members of that public. While speculative, this metaphor and that paradox may help explain how police make sense of their work; they sharply differentiate between themselves, the public, and crooks / local bums / would-be-tough guys.

FANTASY THEME ANALYSIS

People interacting in groups frequently dramatize events in another time and place, telling of past victories and defeats, future achievements and failures, reveling in the joys of yesteryear and tomorrow. Through these dramatizations, common themes often emerge. These themes are labeled fantasy themes and can be analyzed in order to gain insight into the character of the group (Bales, 1970; Bormann, 1972, 1983, 1990).

The collection agency conversation illustrates the potential value of fantasy theme analysis for interpreting the symbolic reality of an organization (see Bormann, 1983). When Meg and Ann dramatize the mass firings at the collection agency they exemplify how group members dramatize events in the there and then to relieve tension in the here and now. The collection agency holocaust appears to have the elements of a fantasy theme: it is set in the past, involves strong characterizations of individuals and dramatic events, and can be labeled with a powerful and representative term (*holocaust*). By identifying fantasies that become thematic and the interrelationship among those fantasy themes, one begins to understand the symbolic formations of the organizational communication culture, formations that help members to make sense of their everyday activities.

STORIES

Stories are an extremely common symbolic form in social collectives, a form integral to the development of the symbolic realities of organizational life (M. H. Brown, 1985, 1990; Kreps, 1990; McMillan, 1990). The collection agency conversation also illustrates storytelling both in the dramatization of the layoffs (stories and fantasy themes are interrelated symbolic forms) and in the story of Shawn Slack. The telling of stories is an important part of the communal fabric of organizational life. The interpretation of stories frequently contributes significantly to understanding an OCC. The Shawn Slack story, for example, not only is used to demonstrate incompetence, but also represents the high level of performance expected of members.

Symbolic forms, built out of message elements, contribute significantly to organizational expectations and meanings. Careful consideration of metaphors, fantasy themes, and stories will provide essential information for understanding an organization. At the same time, because symbolic forms are so rich, one of the principal difficulties of OCC analysts is to resist the seductive temptation of devoting all their energy to the analysis of symbolic forms. It is seductive because symbolic forms are typically very interesting and their analysis may be very profitable. The temptation should be resisted because symbolic form analysis, while very useful for understanding OCC, is not sufficient.

Inference of Organizational Expectations

Organizational expectations are created, maintained, and transformed by sending and using messages. That is, communication involves creating, maintaining, and transforming the coorientation of behavioral expectations (Chaffee & McLeod, 1968). Members develop commonly understood patterns of organizational expectations. Those organizational expectations may be that subsequent behavior is harmonious or acrimonious, highly coordinated or highly uncoordinated, but patterns of expectations do develop. Thus, members may come to expect organizational meetings to be socially pleasant and highly task productive or socially punishing and moderately task productive. Such expectations develop as members create, maintain, and transform expectations. There are five general patterns of expectations (norms, roles, agenda, motives, and style) that emerge in organizational communication. Inferring organizational expectations builds upon the analysis of messages and symbolic forms and is dependent upon the inference of organizational meanings.

Scheibel's study of two rock bands (1986) illustrates how an observer infers organizational *norms* (expectations of appropriate behavior) from band members' talk. A particularly powerful expectation was the norm that band members would individually rehearse agreed-upon songs at home before coming to group rehearsal sessions. A related norm was that members would remember where the band had left off in the previous rehearsal, so the group would not have to "reorient" in every session. To be a member of the band meant that one should practice and be prepared. Individuals who failed to meet those norms would be criticized and would be subject to expulsion from the band.

When organizational members assume a *role*, they are expected to fulfill the role's differential rights and responsibilities. Different roles (e.g., supervisors and line workers) have different rights and responsibilities. Role differentials are commonly identified by elements of messages (vocabulary is often a signal of roles—e.g., that of chief executive officer [CEO], sales associate, or accountant II). Caddow (1986), for example, inferred differential role expectations in the police department for secretaries and records clerks (e.g., answering phones, filing) and officers (e.g., writing citations, making arrests). Further, since those jobs were highly segregated by gender (all secretaries and clerks were female and only 1 of 40 officers was female), the role expectations were built upon gender stereotypes (e.g., women are good secretaries).

Expectations about time—its structure and pace—are encompassed under the label *agenda*. Both message analysis and symbolic form analysis will help infer temporal expectations, with the analysis of message temporality being the most helpful. Thus, in the collection agency example temporality is apparent in the episodic flow of the messages from topic to topic, in the substance of the discussions about doing quality work, and in the termination of the conversation (*Meg:* "I hardly have time to do my work." *Ann:* "Me too. Speaking of which . . ."). In the brief collection agency conversation it appears that the organizational expectations for the structuring of time are that management sets parameters that are violated only at the risk of one's job, but within those parameters employees structure much of their time. Not surprisingly, identifying the agendas of an OCC requires a substantial pool of messages across time.

Probably the most difficult type of expectations for an observer to infer is *motives.* Inferring motives is difficult because identifying *organizational* expectations about *why* people behave as they do focuses only on the publicly articulated reasons for behavior and *not* on internal motivation. The concept of motives in the OCC method is limited to the organizationally communicated reasons for behavior that are attributed to self

Example 1.3
Collection Agency Motives

Ann: Hey Randy, how'd that poly-sci test go?
Randy: Oh, I don't know. I should have taken a night off from work
to study, but I can't afford it.
Terry: Yeah, I know the feeling. I can't afford to do anything on
Friday or Saturdays, so I guess it's good that I just work
those nights anyway.
Betty: Everyone fired up to work tonight?
[*This comment is met with moans and some negative comments.*]
Betty: Maybe the terminals will go down.
[*This comment got mixed responses. They like the idea of not having to
work, but didn't like not getting paid if they are sent home early. They
finally decided that it would be perfect if the computers went down for an
hour so they could stay and get paid.*]

(Olson, 1985)

and others (the OCC method is communicative analysis, not psychological analysis). To identify motives it is necessary to look for "why" statements in messages and to infer them from messages. Another section of Olson's (1985) collection agency data (ex. 1.3) illustrates the notion of motives and their inference. Olson infers from the conversation of Ann, Randy, Terry, and Betty that within the organization it is expected that people are working to make money, that they do not want to work too much but cannot afford not to work. Such an inference of motive is not unusual in an organization, yet in certain organizations, such as convents, where working to get rich is clearly not a collectively constituted motive, it is not typical.

The final expectations inferred by the OCC analyst concern *style*, specifically organizational expectations about the style of communication. Johnston (1985), in a study of a luxury car dealership, infers expectations of communicative style that relate to differential organizational roles. Johnston characterizes the new car manager as a person who never smiles and who does not seem to be "pals with the people under him"; the salespeople do not talk to him "on the very informal level that all the others talk" to one another. Organizations differ dramatically in their expectations regarding communicative style. The analyst may find the style brutal, collaborative, respectful, or aggressive (e.g., former ITT chairman Harold Geneen reportedly brought senior executives to tears by badgering them).

The inference of patterns of organizational expectations will not only build on the analysis of messages and symbolic forms, but will also contribute to additional consideration of the message elements and symbolic forms.

Inference of Organizational Meanings

The most difficult stage of an OCC analysis is the inference of organizational patterns of meaning. These patterns will include *organizational constructs* and *relationships among organizational constructs* (cf. Donnellon, Gray, & Bougon, 1986; Gray, Bougon, & Donnellon, 1985; Weick, 1979, chaps. 3, 5, 7). The collective creation of meaning involves both "creating" constructs through the collective definition of individual concepts (e.g., success, the company) and through the collective definition of the relationship between constructs (e.g., how to succeed in this company). The two patterns of organizational meaning are (1) constructs, which may or may not be forged together under another single construct, and (2) skeins of relationships among constructs, which may subsume simple relationships or complex values. The constructs and relationships among constructs—that is, the meanings collectively constituted by organizational members— are labeled *organizational meanings* to emphasize their collective character. In the OCC method, then, the focus is on organizational meanings inferred from the messages directly, from the analysis of the messages, from the analysis of symbolic forms, and from the inference of organizational expectations.

The distinction between an individual's meaning (one's personal concept of hard work) and the organizational meaning (an organization's construct of hard work) highlights the emergence of collective meanings in organizational life. Individuals have personal sets of relationships among concepts (you may assume hard work is positively related to success but negatively related to the quality of family life), but organizations may develop collective sets of relationships among constructs (in your organization appearing to work too hard is interpreted as inability to manage time, and thus there is a curvilinear relationship between effort and success: as effort increases from low to moderate, success increases proportionately; as effort increases from moderate to very high, success decreases proportionately). These sets of relationships among constructs (what Weick, 1979, chap. 3, calls causal maps) are essential to meanings as they are understood within an organization.

The collective constructs and collective relationships may be relatively simplistic and superficial, or they may be complex and profound. Caddow's (1986) analysis of her police department data, for example, identified "patrol" as a construct that reified the officers on the street. This construction was accomplished by repeated references to *patrol* on radio, by the existence of a Patrol and Criminal Investigation Bureau (ex. 1.1), and by the officers' own talk. Such simple constructs are quite prevalent in organizational communication cultures and are quite easy to infer from the analyses of messages and the inference of expectations (an example from the collection agency is the construct "borrowers").

More complex constructs are often derived from analyses of symbolic forms, as, for example, drawing the construct of "good work" from Olson's (1985) collection agency data. In the holocaust fantasy theme, the Shawn Slack story, and Ann and Meg's talk about getting work done, the boundaries of acceptable work are marked. One hears what happens when "good work" is not done as well as an interpretation of why Meg and Ann were not fired. A thorough analysis of the organizational meanings in the collection agency would suggest the interrelationships among both simple and complex constructs, such as connecting good work, borrowers, and supervision.

The inference of organizational meanings involves going beyond the pieces identified in the analysis of messages and symbolic forms and beyond the inference of organizational expectations to building an interpretation of the organizational communication culture in its complexity and contradictions. Thus, the inference of organizational meanings necessitates going back and reconsidering one's earlier analyses and developing an understanding of the organization as a whole symbolic reality, a whole that is neither unitary nor seamless, but which expresses the meaningful confusion of organizational life. The OCC exists in the pattern of organizational meanings and expectations.

The Organizational Communication Culture Report

The OCC method can be used to provide interpretive entré to an organization (e.g., Krizek, 1990, could help baseball rookies understand professional training camp), to aid one's personal understanding of her or his organization, or to represent the OCC to an audience (e.g., chap. 10). In the latter case the interpretation of the OCC can be presented in writing, film, or another medium. The majority of such reports to date have been accomplished in writing by following the form suggested in Table 1.1. Van Maanen (1988), however, suggests there are many ways to bring tales of the field into print. A researcher using the method can create a description of the OCC that is rich, textured, and understandable by creatively using the method not as a recipe (one part norms, one part temporality), but as an interpretive guide, a suggestive foil to be played against the conversation of organizational life. Pepper's description of "New Public Utility" (chap. 10) demonstrates how interpreters select focal aspects of the OCC to facilitate an understanding of the organization.

Conclusion

The OCC method is designed to guide an interpretation of an organization developed from its communicative life. The OCC method has been used, in this form and earlier versions, by more than 200 students of organizations involved in both brief and intensive studies (e.g., chap. 10; Krizek, 1990; Scheibel, 1986, 1991). In introducing the method this chapter previews the remainder of the book. Chapter 2 presents the theoretical foundations of the OCC perspective. Chapter 3 develops the concept of message in the OCC approach, establishing the foundation for subsequent chapters. Chapter 4 presents the basic conceptual questions a researcher needs to answer before gathering organizational messages in the OCC method. Chapter 5 is a detailed guide to techniques for actually gathering organizational messages. (For those readers less interested in the actual process of conducting research in organizations or those who are experienced qualitative researchers or ethnographers, chaps. 4

and 5 may be less necessary on a first read.) Chapter 6 details the analysis of messages. Chapter 7 explores the analysis of symbolic forms. Chapter 8 presents the inference of organizational expectations. Chapter 9 demonstrates the inference of organizational meanings. Chapter 10 is Gerald Pepper's report of his OCC analysis of the organizational development unit in a large utility company, New Public Utility.

CHAPTER TWO

Organizational Communication Culture

Human organizing is a complex undertaking, an alchemy wherein individuals become socialized, develop interpersonal relationships, systematize their activities, and make sense of their surroundings.
— E. M. Eisenberg and P. Riley

The organizational communication culture perspective characterizes organizations as collectively constructed symbolic realities. Those symbolic realities are labeled "cultures" because they are conceived as patterns of meanings and expectations (Allaire & Firsirotu, 1984; Geertz, 1973, chaps. 1, 15; Kessing, 1974). They are labeled "communicative" because they are constituted in communication (Hawes, 1974; Pacanowsky & O'Donnell-Trujillo, 1982; Smircich, 1983). Because they are communicatively constituted, they are social, public, and interpretable from messages (or texts [see R. H. Brown, 1987, chap. 6; Cheney & Tompkins, 1988; Geertz, 1973, pp. 448–453]). The term *OCC* specifies a focus that is organizational, communicatively constituted, and cultural. Thus, by referring to organizations as organizational communication cultures, this perspective focuses on the processes of creating, maintaining, and transforming organizational symbolic reality through communication. This chapter presents the conceptual elements of the OCC perspective by detailing the concepts of organizational communication, culture, and their intersection.

Organizational Communication

Writers present definitions of communication or organizational communication for their specific scholarly or pedagogical purpose. Sometimes they focus on the *setting* where communication occurs (dyadic, small group, organizational, public); on the *channels* through which communication occurs (face-to-face, mediated); on the *relationship of the persons involved* (marital, family, intercultural, intergroup); or on the *purpose* (persuasion, oral interpretation) for communicating. I offer a definition of organizational communication (an extension of that put forth by Johnson, 1977) that is broad enough to apply to all types of communication within an organizational setting (i.e., no matter what channels are involved, what relationship, or for what purpose):

> Organizational communication is the collective creation, maintenance, and transformation of organizational meanings and organizational expectations through the sending and using of messages.

ELEMENTS OF THE DEFINITION

The critical elements in this definition of organizational communication begin with the term *collective*. First, *collective* signals that more than one person must be involved to generate communication; this definition is not concerned with intrapersonal communication, but rather communication as a social activity. Second, *collective* suggests that communication involves interdependent activity (see Watzlawick, Beavin, & Jackson, 1967). The operative verbs for *communication* include *collaborating, coordinating,* and its root, *communing*. The collective nature of communication involves the interdependence of persons. Whether it is a CEO chatting with an assistant, an employee reading a newsletter, or individuals involved in a sedate business meeting or an intense negotiation session, communicating is accomplished by people together (even when they are not face to face, as with a newsletter). Interdependence suggests neither agreement nor success; rather, interdependence means that persons accomplish activities in concert. The activity of communication is collective, involving people who construct meanings and expectations with one another through the use and creation of messages.

By focusing on organizational communication, we are looking at a specific genre of interdependent social activity: organizing. The activity of organizing involves three or more people, who would define themselves as an organization, acting in concert to accomplish a common activity. Thus, while four drivers at a four-way stop might be acting in concert to accomplish a common activity, it is unlikely they would define themselves as an organization. On the other hand, when four sandlot basketball players form a team to play another four players, they are very likely to meet the definition of organizing used here. While this definition is far broader than some definitions of organization (cf. Etzioni, 1964; Jablin & Sussman, 1983), it is built upon those by Bernard (1968) and Weick (1969, 1979).

The *creation, maintenance, and transformation of meanings and expectations* suggest that communication is involved in the life cycle of meanings and expectations. People create organizational meanings and organizational expectations through communication (Carbaugh, 1985; Johnson, 1977; Schneider, 1976). Organizational members not only create, but also maintain and transform organizational meanings and organizational expectations.

Conceiving of this tripartite process of creation, maintenance, and transformation allows us to reconsider the notion of permanence in the patterns of organizational meanings and expectations (thus, avoiding the much criticized "conservative," or "static," view of organizations [see Gray, Bougon, & Donnellon, 1985; Poole & McPhee, 1983]). This threefold conception accomplishes four things: (1) it locates the creation of meanings and expectations in the collective process of communication; (2) it reminds us that for meanings and expectations to persist they must be maintained; (3) it suggests meanings and expectations are modified by organizational members through communication; and (4) it implies that the combination of the dynamic character of this process and the multiplicity of people involved means that organizational meanings and expectations may be equivocal, fragmented, contradictory, and confusing as well as unequivocal, unitary, consistent, and clear (see Frost, Moore, Louis, Lundberg, & Martin, 1991). Communication need not produce permanent or universal meanings and expectations. Transformation encompasses both relatively sedate incremental modification and traumatic destruction of existing meanings and expectations (cf. Gray et al., 1985). The fact that meanings are created, maintained, and transformed reminds us that communication is a dynamic, ongoing, ever-changing process (Berlo, 1960; Smith, 1972).

The most difficult aspect of this conception of communication is defining *meaning*. Since meaning is dealt with in detail in chapter 9, here I define it only as involving constructs and relationships among constructs (Donnellon, Gray, & Bougon, 1986; Gray et al., 1985; Weick, 1979, chap. 3). The collective creation of meaning involves both "creating" constructs through the collective definition of individual concepts (e.g., success, the company) and through the collective definition of the relationship between constructs (i.e., how to succeed in the particular company).

The possible difference between your meaning of success and your organization's meaning of success illustrates that organizations develop collective meanings. These meanings, which organizational members collectively constitute, are labeled *organizational meanings* to emphasize their collective character.

These organizational meanings may be confusing or clear, superficial or profound. Organizational meanings can range from the ordinary (clock "time" equals time) to the exceptional. In fact, organizational meanings sometimes become so complex and profound that they may be best labeled values (cf. Gray et al., 1985). Thus Peters and Waterman (1982, chap. 6) describe how "customer service" is a central value in IBM. No matter how superficial or profound the meanings, the vehicles to inferring organizational meanings are always messages, the "traces" of communication (see chap. 3 for a detailed discussion of messages).

The collective creation, maintenance, and transformation process includes not only meanings, but also concomitant expectations for subsequent behavior and messages (Schneider, 1976). Communication involves creating, maintaining, and transforming common behavioral expectations (Chaffee & McLeod, 1968). Members develop commonly understood patterns of expectations for organizational action. There may be organizational expectations that messages be simple and direct or complex and indirect. There may be organizational expectations that when certain individuals speak, all others listen or that several people may speak at the same time. There may be organizational expectations that all employees wear uniforms everyday (e.g., as in most airlines) or that Fridays are casual, "fun clothes" days (e.g., as at Southwest Airlines). Numerous expectations are created, maintained, and transformed in the lives of organizations. The five general patterns of expectations that emerge in organizational communication are: norms, roles, agendas, motives, and styles. Chapter 8 describes the five general patterns and how to identify them from messages.

Central to communication, particularly the analysis of organizational communication culture, are messages. Briefly, messages are defined as the observable traces of communication— that is, words uttered, nonverbal expressions, memos written, annual reports published, audiotapes recorded, and buildings built (see chap. 3).

Finally, in decomposing this definition of *communication*, note that messages are both sent and used. The sending of messages has been a continuing concern in the study of communication, from Aristotle's *Rhetoric* to contemporary texts on public speaking. The sending of messages involves the creator in the collective process of communication. The collective nature of communication necessitates considering messages created by senders and messages used by receivers. As individuals select available messages and utilize those messages, they participate in the collective process of creating, sustaining, and transforming meanings and expectations. The use of messages, while a major stream in mass media research (Katz, Blumler, & Gurevitch, 1974; Rosengren, Wenner, & Palmgreen, 1985), has not been central to organizational communication (exceptions include Bantz, Scheibel, & Harrell, 1990; Cheney, 1991; Geist & Chandler, 1983; Hawes, 1976). The concept of "use" is that people make choices about which messages they will attend to and that those choices involve a variety of motives (Bantz et al., 1990). In the context of this definition of *communication*, people are collectively using—selecting messages, responding to messages, and integrating messages within other messages.

CONSTRAINT AND RESOURCE

As communicators create and use them, messages serve as both a resource for and constraint on the communicators' message construction and the communicators' creation, maintenance, and transformation of meanings and expectations (cf. Tuchman, 1978, chap. 10; Weick, 1979, chap. 8). The messages created in the past can be used as a resource in current message construction—for example, drawing upon last year's memo or finding the right phrase in a previous annual report. Those messages also can constrain current message construction—for example, knowing a speech will be compared to one given last year may constrain the speaker's choices. Communicative genre will influence the current creation of messages as well as the interpretation of those messages (see Campbell & Jamieson, 1978).

Not only the messages but also the meanings created in the past can serve as both a resource and constraint in current meaning creation. For example, communicators can use existent meanings as a resource to help define current creating. Thus, a budget evaluator may use last week's definition of organizational goals to help in creating this week's definition of the areas of budget that are least important (and easiest to cut), while organizational members may use the construct of "holocaust" to help dramatize the possible effects of cuts the budget evaluator proposes. Prior meaning creations can simultaneously serve as a constraint on current communication by restricting the collectivity to past patterns of interpretation. Thus, this week's budget proposal is denied because it is not central to the organization's goals (by the prior definition of organizational goals), while the budget evaluators disagree with labeling the proposed cuts a holocaust since the size of the layoffs "aren't that serious" (per a previous construction of the term *holocaust*). This dynamic of resource and constraint reminds us that communication, in this view, is developmental; each "instance" of communication is not created completely "new," but neither is it simply a repetition of the past. Instead, meanings develop across time and space as members use past meanings and are also constrained by past meanings.

Communication is a process in which people collectively create and use messages as resources and constraints in the creation, maintenance, and transformation of meanings and expectations. Such a definition does not inherently limit communication to any particular setting, any particular channel, or any particular purpose. The definition does signal that communication is a process people accomplish through the use and creation of messages.

CONCEPTUAL FOUNDATION OF THE DEFINITION

The definition's immediate ancestor is Johnson's (1977) suggestion that "communication is the process of constructing meanings and expectations through the exchange of messages" (p. 4). My definition differs from Johnson's by (1) its focus on the collective; (2) its explicit characterization of "construction" as involving creation, maintenance, and transformation; and (3) its expansion of *exchange* to specifically include both creation and use of messages (cf. Pearce & Cronen, 1980).

The conceptual core of my definition of *communication* is that, by communicating, persons constitute symbolic realities. This argument is founded on the three premises of *symbolic interactionism* (Blumer, 1969): (1) people "act toward things on the basis of the meanings that the things have for them" (p. 2); (2) meanings are "social products, . . . creations that are formed in and through the defining activities of people as they interact" (p. 5); and (3) "the use of meanings by the actor occurs through a process of interpretation" (p. 5). These premises make meaning central. Meanings arise through social activity and are used interpretively. Blumer (1969) explains the concept of social activity (interpreted here as communication) by presenting six "root images" of symbolic interactionism:

1. "Human groups or society *exists in action* and must be seen in terms of action" (p. 6).
2. "Social interaction is a process that *forms* human conduct instead of being merely a means or a setting for the expression or release of human conduct" (p. 8).
3. "Objects (in the sense of their meaning) must be seen as social creations—as being formed in and arising out of the process of definition and interpretation as this process takes place in the interaction of people" (pp. 11–12).
4. Symbolic interaction characterizes people as acting organisms that not only respond nonsymbolically, but also act and interpret (p. 12).
5. Human action is a construction by an individual "taking into account" those things she or he notes and then "forging a line of conduct on the basis of how [she or] he interprets them" (p. 15).
6. Groups involve the fitting together of individuals' lines of action so that "joint action has a distinctive character in its own right," making it unnecessary to break down the joint action into the separate acts that comprise it (p. 17).

Taken as a whole, these images provide a foundation for viewing communication as formative social action that constructs meanings of people and objects, in which people interpret and act together based on those interpretations (see Faules & Alexander, 1978; Shibutani, 1966, chap. 6). Similarly, these images are congruent with understanding the process of people coming to share a common symbolic world, as suggested by symbolic convergence theory (Bormann, 1982, 1983, 1988, 1990).

Culture

Geertz (1973) agrees with Max Weber that "man is an animal suspended in webs of significance he himself has spun," adding that "I take culture to be those webs" (p. 5). By taking culture to be webs of meaning, Geertz locates culture both as a process that is accomplished by participants and as something public, because meanings are public (p. 12). For Geertz "cultural analysis is (or should be) guessing at meanings, assessing the guesses, and drawing explanatory conclusions from the better guesses" (p. 20). To study culture, then, is to study codes of meaning.

Kessing (1974) classifies Geertz's perspective as an *ideational* view of culture, that is, one that conceives of culture as a system of ideas. In particular, Geertz's (1973) approach is a symbolic, or *semiotic*, one in its emphasis on the interpretation of shared meanings and symbols. Geertz builds this perspective upon Talcott Parsons's distinction between social and cultural structures. Geertz argues that "culture is the fabric of meaning in terms of which human beings interpret their experience and guide their action" (p. 145). Given the centrality of symbols and meanings to communication, adopting a semiotic perspective on culture will provide us with an effective basis for examining organizational communication.

Pacanowsky and O'Donnell-Trujillo's (1982) explication of Geertz's web metaphor demonstrates how meaning is central to culture. They suggest that three aspects of the metaphor undergird organizational culture research. First, webs are both confining (the spider travels only on the web) and facilitative (with the web the spider can travel). Similarly, cultural meanings both confine and facilitate as they simultaneously limit us to our social reality and make it possible for us to function in our social reality. Second, webs not only exist; they are also spun, just as cultures exist and are created in persons' activities. Thus, webs, cultures, and meanings are both things and processes. Third, webs, cultures, and meanings are contexts, not causes. They do not cause behavior. Instead, they provide the context for behavior. To understand patterns of significance one must interpret those patterns. Hence, the method to understand cultures and meanings is interpretation.

Culture, thus, is an outcome and a process that arises in the meaningful activity of people. As action become meaningful, members of a culture develop expectations about the activities of members (Johnson, 1977; Schneider, 1976). These patterns of expectations include norms, roles, agendas, motives, and styles. The development of cultural activity reflects the development of meanings and expectations.

Carbaugh (1988a) provides a guide to recognizing when symbols and meanings are cultural. He argues that cultural patterns of symbolic action and meaning are: "a) deeply felt, b) commonly intelligible, and c) widely accessible" (p. 38). These characteristics may help the student of culture recognize cultural symbols, meanings, and expectations.

During the 1980s merger mania, for example, Texaco Oil bought Getty Oil, even though Pennzoil had had a contract to purchase Getty. Pennzoil sued Texaco. During the subsequent four years Texaco lost the suit, owed Pennzoil an $11.2 billion judgment, sought bankruptcy court protection, had to fend off a takeover by investor Carl Ichan, settled with Pennzoil for $3 billion, and sold off numerous properties to pay the settlement (Texaco, 1988). Even without observational data at Texaco, I suspect that "Pennzoil" is a deeply anchored, powerful, and painful symbol in Texaco's culture. In fact, it would be extremely interesting to assess the places the symbols "Pennzoil," "Getty," and "Ichan" have in Texaco's culture.

The question of the intelligibility of cultural symbols speaks to the need for those symbols to be interpretable within the collective that is being labeled as a culture. In the U.S. national culture the flag is clearly an intelligible symbol. On the other hand, the term *zoomies* would not be intelligible in U.S. national culture, while it may be within a smaller collective (such as the U.S. Air Force Academy, in which it referred at one time to cadets who bought fast cars). It is important to note, as Carbaugh (1988a) and others have, that intelligibility is not agreement; one can understand yet disagree with a cultural symbol (Bantz, 1987). Nor must intelligibility mean absolute clarity; without fully understanding them, members can coordinate the symbols they use (Weick, 1979).

The need for a cultural symbol to be widely accessible dictates that it must be possible for all persons in a collective to see, hear, or use such a cultural symbol. The cultural status of "Pennzoil" within Texaco is evidenced by the extensive media coverage of the controversy and the frequent letters and documents sent to employees and shareholders.

In this perspective culture is a system of meanings and expectations; cultural forms are deeply felt, intelligible, and accessible. Random phrases, incoherent remarks, and narrowly bound expressions are not the foci of culture. Rather, the foci are the influential symbols of meanings and expectations.

Organizational Culture

Beginning in the late 1970s, the concept of organizational culture has been examined to such an extent that it has been labeled a "fad" for its facile application in organizational consulting (Uttal, 1983). Beyond such faddish applications, however, the substantive conceptual basis for defining organizations as cultures is rich (see Allaire & Firsirotu, 1984; Barnett, 1988; Carbaugh, 1985, 1986; Eisenberg & Riley, 1988; Fine, 1984; Pacanowsky & Putnam, 1982; Riley, 1983; Schein, 1985).

Applying the semiotic conception of culture to organizations puts the focus on the cultural forms within a collectivity. As suggested above, organizing involves three or more people who would define themselves as an organization, acting in concert to accomplish a common activity. The collectivity is thus defined as an organization through the members' symbolic representation of that organization. Members frequently mark their organizations in symbolic action; they talk about working for Motorola, wear Digital or DEC T-shirts, say they are in "sales" or "purchasing," or label themselves "Microkids" or "Hardy Boys" (Kidder, 1981, pp. 59–60).

A semiotic perspective on organizational culture would seek to define the organizational parameters through the members' symbolic representations of meanings and expectations. The boundaries of the collectivity are established through the cultural analysis. Thus, Carbaugh's (1988a) suggestions of what characterizes that which is cultural point to the parameters of an organizational culture.

In *The Soul of a New Machine* Kidder (1981) presents a fascinating account of the development of a new computer by Data General Corporation. Kidder's description illustrates how the identification of cultural forms can be used to mark organizational cultures. A reading of Kidder's book suggests that there are at least three concentric levels of organizational culture at Data General. There are cultural symbols that mark the corporation (e.g., Data General ran an advertisement that said, "And we intend to make a lot of money," p. 20). There are cultural symbols that mark the Massachusetts facility as a collectivity (e.g., Kidder describes Building 14A/B as sparse and designed without an architect, chap. 1). Finally, Kidder devotes much of the book to demonstrating the cultural character of Tom West's Eclipse Group, which was charged with building a new computer under an absurd deadline with insufficient resources. There are cultural symbols marking each of these collectivities, some of which carry over from the smaller to the larger collectivity, some of which do not.

Kidder's portrait also demonstrates that organizational cultures can be contradictory, conflictive, and confusing. Employees are kept in the dark; one engineering group (West's) is competing against another, better funded group (North Carolina); and clear direction is sometimes lacking. An observer of organizational cultures may find within them conflict, division, and inconsistency that need to be examined (Frost et al., 1991; Martin & Meyerson, 1988).

COROLLARIES OF ORGANIZATIONAL CULTURE

Characterizing organizations as cultures yields four corollaries. The first corollary is that *the student of organizations is interested in all the activities of organizational members,* not simply certain types of activity. The study of organizational culture cannot solely be based on the study of official documents or formal task assignments any more than one can understand an ethnic culture solely on the basis of official records. The cultural metaphor implies that to study an organization necessitates being open to, aware of, and interested in the rich variety of organizational activities. These should include the comic and tragic, formal and informal, written and oral, work and play, conflict and romance

(Deal & Kennedy, 1982; Goodall, 1990; Louis, 1980; Pacanowsky & O'Donnell-Trujillo, 1982). Without a commitment to such a detailed study, viewing organizations as cultures is both inappropriate and unwise.

The second corollary is that *the student of organizations defines organizations as processes as well as things.* Given the dynamic nature of culture, in order to label organizations as cultures it is necessary to conceive of organizations as not simply things but also as processes. Weick (1969) introduced the concept of "organizing" to replace "organizations" in order to highlight the importance of viewing organizations as activities (see Bantz, 1975a; Bantz & Smith, 1977). A commitment to acknowledging the processual nature of organizations entails awareness that organizations develop in time, that the regularities of social life are transient, and that organizations are activities.

The third corollary, apparent by now, is that *the student of organizations sees symbols and meaning as basic to organizational life.* To the extent that cultures are characterized as symbolic, characterizing organizations as cultures is based on the centrality of symbols and meaning to organizations. Much of the management literature that takes a cultural perspective is predicated on the organizational importance of symbols (see Deal & Kennedy, 1982; Frost, Moore, Louis, Lundberg, & Martin, 1985; Morgan, 1980; Pettigrew, 1979; Pondy, Frost, Morgan, & Dandridge, 1983). The link between symbols and meaning is apparent in numerous writings on organizational culture (e.g., Conrad, 1983; Deetz, 1982, 1988; DeWine, 1988; Pacanowsky & O'Donnell-Trujillo, 1982; Pilotta, Widman, & Jasko, 1988; Smircich, 1985; Tompkins, 1985).

The fourth corollary necessary for viewing organizations as cultures is that *organizations be characterized as being socially constituted,* since culture is socially constituted. The subtlety of this point is made apparent in the distinction between culture as something that an organization *has* and culture as something an organization *is* (Smircich, 1983). Founded on the symbolic interactionist perspective (Blumer, 1969) and related to the social construction of reality perspective (Berger & Luckmann, 1967), characterizing organizations as socially constituted means the researcher is committed to viewing organizational culture as the organization. That is, what we constitute is not something attached to an objective phenomenon (the organization), but, rather, what we constitute is an intersubjective phenomenon (the organization as a culture).

Organizational Communication Culture

The use of the term *organizational communication culture* marks the intersection of organizational communication and organizational culture and represents the perspective that organizational culture is constituted in communication. Pacanowsky and O'Donnell-Trujillo (1982) define the purpose of organizational culture research as "coming to understand how organizational life is accomplished communicatively" (p. 121). Deetz (1982) argues that viewing organizations as cultures "focuses analysis on the processes by which the meanings of organizational events are produced and sustained through communication" (p. 132). Three lines of research support the argument that communication constitutes organizational culture: (1) the analysis of speech as it constitutes collective action and culture, (2) symbolic convergence theory, and (3) structurational and critical approaches to organizational communication.

SPEECH AS CONSTITUTIVE

Hawes's characterizations of organizations as collectivities (1974) and speech communities (1976) explores communicative activities as constitutive of organizations. Hawes suggests a social collectivity (organization) *"is* patterned communicative behavior; communicative behavior does not occur *within* a network of relationships but *is* that network" (1974, p. 500). Paraphrasing Garfinkel (1967), Hawes (1974) argues that communication is how organizations are transformed. He extends this argument to a specific focus on communication as constitutive, arguing that "talking and writing *constitute* as well as *reflect* social reality" (Hawes, 1976, p. 352; cf. Gronn, 1983). These two essays, taken together, suggest that communication constitutes the social reality that is, in and of itself, an organization. This conclusion, combined with the proposition that organizations are conceived as cultures (which appears consistent with Hawes's characterization of social reality) lends support to the claim that communication constitutes organizational culture.

While Philipsen (1975, 1976) is not specifically examining organizations, his ethnography of communication and cultural analysis of communication make an argument for viewing communication as constitutive of collectives' cultures that parallels the fourth corollary. Philipsen's (1975) examination of speaking in "Teamsterville" emphasizes speech as a cultural form and how it constitutes culture. Carbaugh (1985), extending Philipsen's ethnographic approach, defines organizational culture as "a shared system of symbols and meanings, performed in speech, that constitutes and reveals a sense of work life; it is a particular way of speaking and meaning, a way of sense-making, that recurs in the oral activities surrounding common tasks" (p. 37). In a study of a television station Carbaugh (1988b) applies the cultural communication perspective, demonstrating how terms in members' talk construct the symbolic reality of the organization.

SYMBOLIC CONVERGENCE THEORY

Approaching organizations from symbolic analyses of groups, Bormann (1975, 1980, 1982, 1983, 1988, 1990; Bormann, Howell, Nichols, & Shapiro, 1982) has developed symbolic convergence theory, a broad theory that encompasses the notion that communication constitutes the social reality of collectivities. From the 1960s Bormann was moving toward this perspective from his work on small-group communication. The development of fantasy theme analysis and symbolic convergence theory was built upon a speech communication tradition that saw groups as developing through their interaction (Bormann, 1969) and symbolic forms as central to the development of dynamic shared group realities (Bormann, 1972, 1980, 1983, 1990). Symbolic convergence theory, in spite of its name, does not imply that groups or organizations are without conflict, competition, or ambiguity. Bormann, Pratt, and Putnam's (1978) analysis of male response to female leadership and Sharf's (1978) analysis of group leadership both demonstrate that symbolic convergence theory contributes to understanding division in leadership emergence. The movement toward viewing social collectivities as emerging through communication provides a strong theoretical basis for viewing organizations as developing cultures through communication (e.g., Bormann, 1988). Bormann's approach can be interpreted as a symbolic interactionistic viewpoint (Bantz,

1972), and, as such, it provides additional support to the OCC perspective.

STRUCTURATION AND CRITICAL THEORY

Other communication researchers have approached organizational culture from a different direction, principally that of structuration and critical theory (Conrad, 1983; Conrad & Ryan, 1985; Deetz, 1982, 1992; Deetz & Kersten, 1983; Deetz & Mumby, 1990; Mumby, 1987; Poole, 1985; Poole & McPhee, 1983). According to Poole (1985), "structuration refers to the production and reproduction of social systems via the application of generative roles and resources" (p. 101). The use of this perspective, based primarily on Giddens' work (1979, 1984), in organizational communication tends to characterize communication as a generative mechanism in the production and reproduction of social systems. As such, the notion of the communicative process contributing to and being affected by the existent, yet changing, patterns parallels the OCC view that communication constitutes organizational communication culture. OCC emphasizes, however, that not only can communication produce (create) and reproduce (maintain), but it can also transform organizational meanings and organizational expectations.

The critical approach to communication (Adoni, Cohen, & Mane, 1984; Deetz, 1982, 1988, 1992; Deetz & Kersten, 1983; Deetz & Mumby, 1990) has drawn on the Frankfurt school (e.g., Adorno & Horkheimer, 1944/1979; Habermas, 1971). In organizational communication the critical approach has been characterized as having a goal of social change (Putnam, 1983) to establish "free and open communication situations in which organizational, societal, and individual interests can be mutually accomplished" (Deetz & Kersten, 1983, p. 148). This social change is effected through understanding, critique, and education (Deetz, 1982). The critical theorists assume that repressive patterns (often labeled ideology) are inherent in deep social structures and that communication activity often conceals those repressive patterns. The critical organizational researcher then makes her or his goal to expose the underlying structures hidden beneath the surface of communicative activity (e.g., Mumby, 1987). For critical theorists who make structure unchangeable through communication the OCC perspective is not consistent; for critical theorists who empower human communication the OCC perspective can be consistent.

Underlying the argument that communication constitutes organizational culture is symbolic interactionism (although structurationists and critical theorists may be uncomfortable with such an association [see Blumer, 1969, pp. 53–54]). Symbolic interactionism provides a conceptual foundation of the centrality of communication in the creation of collectivities. To paraphrase and modify Duncan (1967): It is in communication that organizations emerge and continue to exist. Viewing organizing as a communicative process allows one to characterize communication as definitional.

The label organizational communication culture signals the centrality of communicative processes in constituting the culture that is an organization. Throughout I will refer to organizational communication culture, or OCC, rather than organizational culture to mark this commitment to communication as constitutive of the culture that is an organization.

CHAPTER THREE

Messages

It is an axiom that organizations cannot exist without communication. And communication, of course, cannot occur in the absence of messages.

—C. Stohl and W. C. Redding

Messages are central to understanding an organizational communication culture because messages are the tangible traces of the communicative process. While communication involves more than the use of messages (e.g., the creation of meanings), messages provide the publicly available data for the analyst. Since messages are available to organizational members as they create, maintain, and transform organizational meanings and expectations, messages are the route to understanding OCC. This chapter (1) presents an argument for the significance of messages in interpreting OCCs, (2) details the characteristics of messages, and (3) specifies and differentiates message types.

Interpreting from Messages

Since symbols are the only available data for studying meaning (Duncan, 1967) and messages, by definition, display symbols, it follows that messages are the available data for identifying meanings. Messages publicly present and re-present the symbols necessary for assaying meanings (Geertz, 1973, p. 12). Messages are, therefore, the data base for analyzing OCCs for they provide access to organizational meanings and organizational expectations.

Locating messages as the critical data base for research has a long tradition in organizational communication research exemplified in the work of numerous writers (e.g., Bormann, 1972, 1980, 1983; Hawes, 1973, 1974, 1976; Stohl & Redding, 1987; Tompkins & Cheney, 1983; Trujillo, 1983). The methodology of

OCC relies upon publicly available data because of the central position of messages in communication and the need to conduct the analysis of OCC from data available to the analyst.

It is important to note, however, that messages include those created with the researcher; thus, an organizational member's interpretations made in response to a researcher's inquiry are legitimate data for OCC inquiry (the importance of interpretations is discussed below and in Putnam & Pacanowsky, 1983). The researcher is engaged in intepreting organizational members' interpretations. The systematic gathering of messages for OCC analysis is presented in chapters 4 and 5. The use of messages as foundational for these interpretations does, however, provide constraints on the interpretive process.

Messages Characterized

Organizational communication messages are social phenomena created by others, for others, and with others. Messages are social phenomena because they are constituted in direct interaction with others or project their use by others (e.g., as I write this I project someone reading it). *Communicative interaction,* the creation of messages with others, involves the direct interaction of two or more individuals who simultaneously create, exchange, and use messages. The creation of more permanent messages by or for others, the making of *documents,* involves the projected interaction of a person or group with another person or group. The creator of messages frequently imagines the audience for those messages and how the audience will use the messages. For example, television and film producer Garry Marshall ("Happy Days," "Laverne and Shirley," *Pretty Woman*) imagined his television audience busy playing, cooking, talking, and occasionally watching (Apple & Williams, 1979). Documents created by others may be used by organizational members, thereby turning a document into a *documentary interaction.* Following the concept of media use (Katz et al., 1974), this view suggests that organizational members choose to read written material, watch videotapes, and listen to cassette tapes, thus using documents created by others (Bantz & Simpson, 1990). In so doing, the members engage in a documentary interaction with those who created the message. The notion of documentary interaction is thus a symbolic interchange with the document's creator (G. P. Stone, personal communication, 1972).

There are numerous examples of more permanent messages created by others, for others, and with others within organizational life. Messages are created by nonmembers for organizational members (e.g., an Internal Revenue Service memo announcing that all employees must file a new W-4 form); messages are created by nonmembers under the supervision of members for members and nonmembers (e.g., annual reports, the corporate headquarters building); messages are created by members for other members (e.g., procedures manuals and training videos created by training and development departments for all employees); messages are created by members for nonmembers (e.g., public relations creates news releases); and messages are created among members (e.g., audio recordings of everyday face-to-face interactions such as meetings).

Messages are the available "traces" of communication. Whether transient, emerging in communicative interaction and publicly existing for only moments, or being created as documents and persisting for centuries (e.g., the Dead Sea Scrolls, St. Peter's Cathedral in Rome), messages are available to organizational members. By characterizing messages as available within an organization, messages become a dynamic, available, and creatable resource for organizations. Organizational members live within a message environment, which they both use and create.

As a university member, I live within an organization that provides numerous documentary messages available to me: college bulletins, a student newspaper, an administration newspaper, departmental memos, college memos, university memos, and newspaper reports of public statements by members of the Board of Regents, administrators, and faculty. These are documentary messages that I may or may not come into direct contact with (do I even pick up the student newspaper?), messages that I may or may not process (do I read the memos in my mailbox?). Similar questions can be raised about how I use messages created with others. Do I come into contact with communicative interaction messages by joining in on office conversations? Do I listen to the messages exchanged in conversations in which I participate?

With both documentary messages and communicative interaction messages organizational life presents us with a complex multidimensional mosaic of messages (after Becker, 1968, 1983). Individuals travel through time and space and are exposed to a broad range of messages in the information environment. Each day as I enter my departmental office there is a panoply of messages that I can use—conversations between students and secretaries, memos in my mailbox, signs posted on the bulletin board, plus all the new paperwork on my desk. The mosaic of messages is made up of tens, hundreds, thousands of messages of varying degrees of availability, clarity, and value.

Further, the messages available to a person include those that she or he creates or participates in creating. Thus, a college catalog may include a course description that I drafted and which a colleague edited before it was published and became another part of my message environment. Or I may issue a memo on departmental requirements and distribute it to my colleagues. Those messages are not only part of the message mosaic for other members of the organization; they are also part of the mosaic for me. My relationship with those messages differs from those I have with messages I don't create (because in creating them I am doubly involved in using messages—simultaneously creating and consuming). The messages become part of the organization's time-space mosaic of messages. At another time and place I may encounter those messages and perhaps not even recognize that I contributed them. Organizational members' use of messages can include those created by themselves for others, those created by others for them, and those created with others. While the message mosaic offers organizational members a vast array of messages, for them to become significant in organizational life the members must *use* those messages.

Message Types

COMMUNICATIVE INTERACTION

The organizational messages created with others arise out of communicative interaction, which involves talk among organizational members as well as the nonverbal aspects of that exchange. Communicative interaction is best seen dramatistically and is related to the concept of performance.

Talk

The importance of everyday talk to organizational life had frequently been overlooked until the 1970s, when Hawes (1974) and others (e.g., Johnson, 1977) stressed the importance of talk to organizing. This view was built on the argument for studying the methods of everyday life (i.e., ethnomethodology, Garfinkel, 1967) and, to a lesser extent, on the careful examination of everyday language and its functions (e.g., speech act theory, Austin, 1962; Searle, 1969). In addition, the emergence of discourse and conversational analysis in the past 20 years has reinforced the importance of carefully studying the actual talk that goes on in organizations (see Jacobs, 1988; Jacobs & Jackson, 1983; Jefferson, 1972; Sacks, 1972; Wieder, 1988; Zimmerman, 1988).

The significance of talk to social life was amply demonstrated by Philipsen's analysis of talk in an urban neighborhood (1975). Philipsen and his associates have continued this work elucidating the relationship between talk and culture (see Carbaugh, 1985, 1988b; Katriel, 1986; Katriel & Philipsen, 1981; Philipsen, 1975, 1976; Ting-Toomey, 1985). By emphasizing the interdependency of talk and culture these scholars support the contention that talk is central to organizational life—whether it's "work talk," "task talk," or "talk talk" (see, e.g., Pacanowsky & O'Donnell-Trujillo, 1982, 1983).

The understanding of communication in organizations depends upon analyzing the talk of organizations. Thus, Example 3.1 from Caddow's (1986) police study or Example 3.2 from Coughlin's (1981) study of a meat wholesaler can each be analyzed for its contribution to understanding the organization. Even though the talk may be nearly incomprehensible to an outsider (Ex. 3.2) or may involve "sick" humor (Ex. 3.1), it is a vital part of the organization.

Example 3.1
Suburban Police Department

Officer 1: So how's detectives?
Detective 1: It's 8 to 5 with weekends and holidays off. It's alright.
Officer 2: How are you?
Officer 3: Not too good. It's time to go home. I've had enough this day.
Officer 4: I saw one of your buddies.

Detective 2: I still have some left?
  Officer 4: She's a hooker. She had needlemarks and collapsed
       veins, blue veins.
Detective 2: Oh, one of those friends. So, anyway, how do you like
       being back?
  Officer 4: I love it.

(Caddow, 1986)

Example 3.2
Wholesale Meat Supplier

Rick: Say, Dick? I'm checking on Simeks for rib ends.
Dick: I'll drop those combos. Now he wants bone ins?
Rick: No, rib ends.
Dick: Fresh?
Rick: I'll ask him. Do you think he'll take them Friday?
Dick: Well . . . [*walked out of the room, sounding displeased with the
       question*].
Rick: I quoted him 75 based on our truck, 1000#. They'll call back if
       the customer wants them.
Dick: I gave one combo out. I don't want to be short.
Rick: I'll call Gail. We don't want the truck to be short.

(Coughlin, 1981)

Nonverbal

In most of the examples used thus far the emphasis has been on
talk per se—the verbal articulation of linguistic forms. The work
of the discourse analysts (e.g., Beach, 1985, 1989; Jacobs & Jackson, 1983) has clearly supported the need and vitality of such
analyses. The dramatistic view of communicative interaction,
however, suggests that analyzing only the verbal component of
communicative interaction may limit our understanding of communication inasmuch as the drama of communication is accomplished nonverbally as well as verbally (see Goffman, 1959,
intro.). The need for studying nonverbal aspects of the communicative act has been noted for more than 30 years (e.g., Hall,
1959, 1966), and numerous studies have been reported (for reviews, see Burgoon & Jones, 1976; DeVito & Hecht, 1990;
Knapp, 1978; Mehrabian, 1971).

    There are numerous ways of defining these nonverbal as-
pects. Several sources provide a full introduction to nonverbal

communication (e.g., Knapp, 1978), but for our purposes, discussion of four key aspects of nonverbal communication (paralinguistics, kinesics, proxemics, and haptics) will suffice. Paralinguistics include nonlinguistic verbal elements of talk such as filled pauses ("um"), tone ("you *what?*"), and accent ("I'm from Ohia"). Kinesics center on the physical motion of the speaker as she or he communicates, including hand gestures, pacing, body language (see Birdwhistell, 1972). Proxemics refers to the speaker's use of space and includes the classic example of cultural difference in speaking distance (e.g., North Americans typically keep an 18-inch "bubble" around them while speaking to adults with whom they are not intimately involved, while Latin Americans prefer to speak to others at a closer distance [see Hall, 1959]). Haptics is the use of touch in communicative acts, including touching the other with one's hands and also physical contact such as being with others in close quarters (e.g., on airplanes or buses) or in greetings (e.g., giving hello hugs). These nonverbal elements are potentially significant aspects of the messages in organizational communication. To illustrate take the following imaginary scene: "The new MBA [master of business administration] interviews for a job with the CEO":

Example 3.3
MBA Interviews with CEO

Walking into the CEO's office, Sharon Smith is introduced to the CEO by the CEO's secretary. The CEO walks from behind her desk pointing to the three chairs gathered around a coffee table and says, "We'll be more comfortable here." The two sit down, and the CEO makes direct eye contact and firmly says, "Tell me about your finance project." The candidate replys haltingly, "It will be done in May." The CEO, maintaining direct eye contact, leans forward, waves off the answer with a sideways hand gesture, and says, "No, not when will it be done, what are you doing, what are you learning?" ending with an upward inflection on *learning*. The candidate smiles, leans forward, and pours out an extensive description of the project.

The subtle and obvious aspects of nonverbal behavior in the communicative interaction are important for understanding the interaction. The interplay of the CEO's authoritative vocal tone and direct eye contact connect with the candidate's weak response to suggest the different roles the CEO and the candidate play in this meeting. The CEO's dismissive gesture in response to the candidate's initial reply and her curiosity, as expressed in her subsequent question, are linked with an enthusiastic description of the finance project. The interlocking of these two people's interaction demonstrates that the messages exchanged in this interview are constituted not only by the linguistic but also by the extralinguistic nonverbal behaviors.

Dramatism

The concept of communicative interaction is dramatistic. In the dramatistic metaphor social interaction is seen as having the character of drama—with action interpretable through roles, staging, plot lines, and performance. This view of social interaction is founded on the work of Mead (1934), supported the early development of symbolic convergence theory (e.g., Bantz, 1975b; Bormann, 1972, 1973), and is central to the work of Burke (1969a, 1969b), Burke's followers (Duncan, 1967; Tompkins, Fisher, Infante, & Tompkins, 1975), and Goffman (1959, 1974; cf. Pacanowsky & O'Donnell-Trujillo, 1983). The dramatistic notion offers the opportunity to expand messages beyond the narrow constraints inherent in talk, or *discourse* (i.e., limited to language use).

Performance

The notion of communicative interaction is related to the concept of performance (Conquergood, 1983; Fine & Speer, 1977; Turner, 1980), which Pacanowsky and O'Donnell-Trujillo (1983) have demonstrated is useful in understanding organizational communication. In the context of performance communicative acts are conceived of as "presentations," with others, within specific social contexts. In a performance the "actors" within a communicative setting are mutually constructing their actions—that is, they are performing.

  The term *communicative interaction* is chosen rather than *performance* because it suggests the characteristics of performance critical for understanding organizational communication culture (that communication is interactional and contextual) but does not carry with it some of the perhaps problematic implications of *performance*. For example, while performance may imply only face-to-face interaction, communicative interaction does not; while performances may be seen only as improvisational, communicative interaction can be both scripted and improvisational (cf. Pacanowsky & O'Donnell-Trujillo, 1983).

Resource and constraint

Organizational communication interactions constitute messages as individuals interact, creating and using these messages. Their interactions must be located within the cultural context they create and which they are constrained by (cf. Pacanowsky and O'Donnell-Trujillo, 1983, pp. 131–134). Viewing communication as interactional is consistent with the view that characterizes communication as a mutual process involving more than one individual. This emphasizes that communicative interactions are *collaborations*, even when one individual may talk far more than the other, or others (e.g., at a board of directors meeting). The interaction involves participants creating messages (e.g., "Desert Hospital, may I help you?") as well as participants using mesages, where usage is typically indicated by the messages they create in response to a message (e.g., "Is this the emergency room?"). Communicative interactions are collaborative constructions of ongoing lines of actions (Blumer, 1969, chap. 1). Unrecorded speech without others present is not interactional and therefore is not communicative interaction.

Communicative interactions are also constrained by their cultural context (there may, in fact, be genres of informal communicative interaction, as there are of formal public address [see Campbell & Jamieson, n.d.; Jamieson & Campbell, 1988]). The messages created in communicative interactions are influenced by the organization's cultural tradition. We are unlikely to hear a Ku Klux Klan endorsement in the homily of a Roman Catholic mass, but physicians are not surprised when they are asked for their opinion during a hospital board meeting.

Variability

The dynamic nature of the verbal and nonverbal dimensions of communicative interactions, as well as the synergy inevitable in the combination of the two, means the messages that communicative interactions yield are quite fluid and transient. Furthermore, by definition communicative interactions involve more than one person, which stimulates greater variability in message creation. These factors combine to suggest that, while communicative interactions range from the highly repetitive and routinized (such as customer-cashier interactions [see Hawes, 1973]) to the unique (a novice corporate employment recruiter interviewing a schizophrenic accountant), they are open to variability introduced by any of the participants. Communicative interactions, then, may produce highly uniform messages, apparently random messages, or any variation in between.

DOCUMENTS

This section details documents as messages by (1) presenting Johnson's definition of documents (1977) then illustrating documents and communicative interactions; (2) differentiating documents and communicative interactions based on their informativeness, personal richness, and potential for being edited; and (3) considering the persistent nature of documents, which makes them more "standardized" messages than communicative interactions.

Documents defined and illustrated

Johnson (1977, chap. 3) argues that documents are messages that are more enduring than communicative interactions (which Johnson labels "displays"). The defining characteristic of documents is their *temporal permanence;* documents last longer than messages from communicative interactions. Thus, documents have a "permanent" structure, where permanence is temporally relative. Characterizing documents in this manner permits organizational communication analysts to consider a wide range of documented messages: letters, memos, annual reports, procedure manuals, buildings, and the arrangement of space within buildings, to name a few. The notes on "Health Care Inc.'s" work environment (Ex. 3.4) suggest how both interior decoration (wall decorations, lighting, and carpet) and the use of space (e.g., no paper clutter, family pictures) are relatively enduring messages available to members of the organization.

Example 3.4
The Health Care Inc. Environment

Pictures on wall are water color scenes of
  Minneapolis
Lights are not fluorescent; warm lighting, lamps on
  desks
Carpet gold with brown stripes, emphasizes
  warmness
Very clean, no paper clutter
Each individual office is different, not same gold/
  brown color scheme.
Secretaries and receptionist have pictures of their
  children and by their children hanging by their
  desks, on computers and so on.
Hanging plants
Administrators have larger plants in their office.
Their offices are reflections of their personalities.
                                        (Schroeder, 1985)

The contrast between documents and communicative interactions is apparent in the following examples: conversations are communicative interactions, and memos are documents; speeches are communicative interactions, and videotapes are documents; waving hello is a communicative interaction, and a building is a document; singing the company song is a communicative interaction, and wall decorations are documents; a telephone call is a communicative interaction, and a database is a document. Communicative interactions are characterized by their transient nature, while documents tend to persist.

By broadly defining documents to encompass buildings as well as memos the full range of an organization's messages are included. Buildings and space have clear communicative as well as practical dimensions. From the progressive symbolism of San Francisco's Transamerica pyramid through the stylish yet private (no visible "front entrance") Federal Reserve Bank of Minneapolis to the open invitation of fast food franchises, organizational buildings are documentary messages created for both organizational members and customers.

Documents: Informativeness, personal richness, editing

Johnson (1977, chap. 3) further distinguishes communicative interactions and documents by arguing that documents are less informative, less personally rich, but more subject to editing than communicative interactions. Because communicative interactions have verbal and nonverbal channels available and because those acts "place" more information in those channels, communicative interactions have the potential to provide more information per se and also more information about the communicators (i.e., to be more personally rich) than do documents (see, e.g., Hawes, 1976). A speaker provides more nonverbal information than a writer, and this "leakage" of information presumably gives us a fuller understanding of the speaker (whether this information is accurate is another question, since evidence indicates that people are not particularly reliable at identifying deception [see Miller & Burgoon, 1982]).

On the other hand, documents give the creator a greater ability to edit and control the message than do communicative interactions. The "real-time," ongoing nature of communicative interactions makes them irreversible and nonrepeatable (Barnlund, 1962), so it is extremely difficult to edit our messages after they are expressed (with, e.g., "I didn't mean to say that— forget it") since others have already heard or seen the message. Documents, unlike communicative interactions, are designed for editing. Whether it is a memo that goes directly from my lips to the stenographer to the typist or an annual report that is drafted and revised ten times, it is possible to edit the document before it is publicly distributed. Even after publication the document can be "withdrawn for editing." Documents can be "remodeled" over time, whether they are a loose-leaf procedures manual that is revised by changing pages or a school building where the "open" classrooms are made into "traditional" classrooms by putting up walls and adding doors.

Persistence and standardization

The temporal persistence that characterizes documents facilitates the standardization of messages in organizations. While individuals can always differ in their interpretations of messages, the persistence of documents across time makes it more likely that there will be similarity in collective interpretations. In this way documents contrast with communicative interactions, which are much more variable in substance. So, while communicative interactions may have either maximum or minimum variability, documents constrain the variability of the message exchange toward the minimum variability end of the continuum. Communicative interactions, by virtue of their interactive nature, may easily become variable in their structure (a cashier asks me "Cash or charge?" and I say, "Neither," so the next step will be different from that of the majority of prior customers); documents, on the other hand, are programmed and are therefore less interactional. Thus, the words of an annual report do not change as one is reading them, while the cashier's words may change from one customer to the next. Even with new technology, such as using an automated bank teller, the programmed nature of the interaction means that the sequencing of interaction is not variable outside of the program. (As artificial intelligence develops computer systems that learn and perhaps become as frustratingly "human" as humans—i.e., unpredictable, inconsistent—then this distinction between communicative and documentary interaction will need to be refined.)

The persistence of a document makes it able to be more standardized than the messages within communicative interactions. A videotape of a speech, for example, would be a document, since it is more persistent than the speech itself. Thus, the videotape offers the potential for uniformity of a message as part of communication. The refrigerator sign noted by Blecha (1982, Example 3.5) is a message that persists and is standardized in its wit as well as its concern:

Example 3.5
Nonprofit Organization That Sponsors Workshops

Refrigerator in the corner of office has sign:
   As a favor to the innocent persons who occupy nearby areas, please keep a close eye on any food you may place in the refrigerator. It has been the case lately that some things have not been eaten promptly and therefore have turned a strange shade of green, and, to put it politely—it stinks! Your cooperation in this matter would make certain people very happy. Thank you, thank you, thank you.

(Blecha, 1982)

The persistence and uniformity of documents is one of the principal reasons that they are often emphasized in certain organizational contexts. Johnson (1977, chap. 7) presents Weber's (1947) view that organizations frequently create written documents precisely for the purpose of providing uniform guidance to organizational members for handling situations. Thus, government agencies write documents that specify their practices, such as purchasing procedures. The procedures spell out, in great detail, the competitive bidding process (e.g., minimum bids, required deposits, deadlines). The detail is designed to "prevent misunderstanding" and "eliminate" unfairness. The hope is that, by making a more permanent message describing bidding practices, both the vendors' and the agency's behavior and communication will utilize those standardized messages. Subsequent communicative interactions may refer to those documents: "You said in the request for a proposal that the bids were due on January 15th; you cannot reject ours because it came in at 4:55 P.M. on the 15th."

"Yes, we can. The RFP [request for proposal] said by the end of business on the 15th!"

"You closed at 4:00 P.M. that day because of a bomb threat, not because it was the close of business! We'll sue!"

The persistence and uniformity of documents will be an important characteristic to consider when assaying messages to infer organizational communication culture. That is, because documents last, they have the potential to span time and space (thus, they can be used by organizational members at different places simultaneously and across time). When this potential is realized such messages have a powerful role in the construction of meanings and expectations in an organization. Military organizations, for example, extensively document their leadership hierarchy through training manuals, insignias, and codes of military law. The multiplicity of documents contributes to the persistence of hierarchy within the constructed meanings and expectations of members of the military.

THE INTERRELATIONSHIP OF COMMUNICATIVE INTERACTIONS AND DOCUMENTS

The messages of communicative interactions and documentary interaction are interrelated in at least two ways. First, communicative interactants may make use of documentary messages. Thus, in the example of a vendor-agency bidding dispute the vendor uses an organizational document within the interaction as evidence. Hawes (1976) analyzes how land-use planners use a written document in their talk. He suggests that speakers (1) personalize documents, (2) demonstrate a more complex logic than that present in the document itself, and (3) use the documents in quite different ways than those indicated by the document's written intentions. Hawes demonstrates the value of considering the interrelationship of documents with talk and the benefits of comparing the two.

Second, documentary messages may refer to communicative interactions, as in the memo that opens: "As was discussed in our meeting of 10 July." There is, in fact, a whole class of documents whose purpose is to record communicative interactions: the minutes of meetings, transcripts of trials, videotapes of bank teller transactions. These documents transform transient interactions into persistent records. The significance of this transformation is illustrated by the formal requirement under *Robert's Rules of Order* that each meeting's agenda include approval of the documentary record of the prior meeting (i.e., the minutes). The importance of this function of documenting communicative interactions makes the question of who takes minutes and writes them an important organizational issue. The process of recording communicative interactions is also illustrated by the significance attached to courtroom transcription, in which strict accuracy is at a premium. The requirement that courtroom communicative interaction be documented (a written transcript made) before a substantive appeal can be filed demonstrates the significance of this transformation and also two possible advantages of documents—persistence and portability (not all documents, however, are easily portable—e.g., buildings).

Conclusion

Attending to and gathering messages provides the basis for interpreting organizational communication culture. Communicative interactions provide a panoply of data as members gossip, give orders, interact with clients and customers, coordinate with other units, and solve problems. By virtue of their persistence documents are sources of data that can provide access to messages that would otherwise be difficult to obtain by virtue of time and space (e.g., minutes of meetings held years before, see

Ball, 1988, 1990). By generating a full store of records of communicative interactions and documents one will have the basis for
analyzing and inferring, as one seeks to understand an organization.

Chapters 4 and 5 detail the process of gathering messages as
an organizational observer. Readers who are familiar with field
research techniques may wish to move rapidly through these
two chapters and focus their attention on the analysis of messages, beginning in chapter 6.

CHAPTER FOUR

Getting Started: Preliminary Choices in Gathering Organizational Communication Messages

David motions for me to buckle up and heads the cruiser toward Interstate 13, where he thinks our culprit will head trying to get out of town. We make the interstate and are soon hitting speeds close to a hundred with lights flashing and siren ringing.

David once told me that good cops look relaxed when the tension is on, while bad cops always show the strain. Well, David doesn't look exactly like he's on a Sunday drive, but compared to me he's cool, with one steady hand on the wheel and the other flitting across the instrument panel attending to the lights, siren, and radio. My knuckles are pale from gripping the shotgun jiggling in its cradle before me and hanging on to the handhold of the door. I can barely manage the appearance of even limited self-control. Blood is throbbing in my ears. My powers of speech have vanished. I am scared.

—J. Van Maanen

Van Maanen's tale of the "Union City" police department paints an impressionist picture of both police work and fieldwork (1988, pp. 109–115). The stunning energy of a chase, the fear of being out of control, and the deflation of losing the suspect parallel the challenge, pleasure, and frustration of fieldwork.

In order to understand an organizational communication culture we must go into the field and gather messages. That task, like Van Maanen's, is simultaneously a very difficult and a very rewarding one. Its difficulty can only be suggested here in the variety of choices and discipline necessary to do good fieldwork; its reward can also only be suggested, since the challenge, excitement, intrigue, and near vertical learning curve of fieldwork occurs *in the field*. While some readers will use the OCC method to help them understand an organization from messages acquired solely through their participation in the organization, other readers will systematically gather messages through fieldwork. Chapters 4 and 5 are devoted to the process of doing fieldwork, that is, how to gather messages for OCC analysis and inference.

The task of gathering messages can be divided into two phases. The first involves a set of preliminary choices that need to be made, which guide the project. These choices are preliminary both in the sense that they occur at the beginning of the project and that they are tentative and will be reconsidered as data gathering proceeds. The second phase is the heart of the project, the stages in communication fieldwork. (These chapters only touch the range of methodological issues involved in gathering organizational communication data. Those concerns are considered in a substantial related literature in participant observation [e.g., Loflund, 1971; Loflund & Loflund, 1984; McCall & Simmons, 1969], qualitative methodology [e.g., Filstead, 1970; Lincoln & Guba, 1985], grounded theory [Browning, 1978; Glaser, 1965; Glaser & Strauss, 1967], and ethnography [e.g., Agar, 1980; Hymes, 1974; Sanjek, 1990; Spradley, 1979; Van Maanen, 1983, 1988]).

Messages are the data necessary to understand the OCC; gathering those messages is the focus of chapters 4 and 5. This chapter considers the preliminary questions a researcher faces: (1) what the boundaries of the OCC are, (2) what role to adopt, and (3) what the researcher's "attitude" toward the OCC is. Chapter 5 describes the techniques for gathering data by detailing a 10-stage process: (1) selecting an organization, (2) deciding on team or solo research, (3) gaining entrance, (4) building balanced rapport, (5) identifying messages, (6) creating a journal, (7) "writing through" the journal, (8) coordinating data gathering, (9) exiting in phases, and (10) repeating stages as necessary.

Three major issues need to be discussed when considering the gathering of messages: (1) defining the limits of the organizational communication culture investigation, (2) the researcher's role in relation to the organizational communication culture, and (3) the researcher's "attitude."

Limiting the OCC Investigation

The field-worker needs to consider options and make choices that narrow the scope of a project. The choices involve both conceptual and practical considerations. The conceptual issues are whether the OCC is homogeneous and whether it has apparent boundaries. The practical issue is that investigators must establish limits by circumscribing their project so it can be done thoroughly and so the project can proceed on a reasonable schedule.

OCC PARAMETERS: HOMOGENEITY AND BOUNDARIES

One of the most difficult issues in following an approach that characterizes organizations as communicative cultures is defining the parameters of the culture. There are at least two major parameters that need to be considered: the boundedness of the culture and its homogeneity. When the metaphor of culture is used in anthropology frequently the "culture" is physically bounded (e.g., the Shetland isles, a Samoan village), thus providing a visible boundary of what is to be studied. Similarly, when studying a small organization limited to a single unit in a single location the physical parameters may provide adequate markers of the OCC. Frequently, however, in organizational studies, no clear physical boundaries can be applied because organizations may be spread across several continents yet their members work intensively together (this has become more common with the use of computers and telecommunications technology). Hence, the limits of the OCC investigation must not simply be geographic but also based on some other aspect of the organization. A conceptually sound approach is to limit the investigation according to specific characteristics of the OCC.

The question of homogeneity asks the degree of similarity or diversity (heterogeneity) within organizational cultures. As an organizational characteristic, this property has been described by Deal and Kennedy (1982) as the contrast of strong and weak cultures. A strong culture specifies how most members usually perform (Deal & Kennedy, p. 15). A strong culture will provide a homogeneous set of values, beliefs, and attitudes (e.g., Proctor & Gamble, see Deal & Kennedy, 1982, chap. 2). A weak culture is far more diverse, diffuse, and loose. This argument can be seen to parallel the concept of total institutions (Goffman, 1961), in which the culture is extremely structured and consistent throughout. The fictional organized crime organization in *The Godfather* (Puzo, 1969), for example, is a culture that tightly weaves together ethnicity, religion, and social values to create a complete code of conduct. Such highly homogeneous organizations make it possible to understand much of the OCC from a study of a "slice" of the organization. The consistency of the culture through the organization means one can infer the whole from a limited portion (this is the principle underlying the sampling of only a portion of human blood and generalizing to the entire stock).

While there are organizations that illustrate such a strong organizational culture and a tendency toward homogeneity through the organization, many organizations are far less tightly woven and far less homogeneous. This heterogeneity presents a problem in gathering messages and performing an analysis. Heterogeneity is especially salient when viewing organizational culture as constituted in communication since diversity of communicative life yields diversity of organizational communication culture. Such a diverse OCC may be seen as nonuniform, like a painting by Jackson Pollack, with a multiplicity of colors dripped across the canvas, leaving streaks of color and texture which contrast not only with each other but also with the white canvas on which they rest. Organizational communication cultures, then, may vary from extreme homogeneity to extreme heterogeneity. They may be as internally consistent and uniform as a medieval narrow palette painting, as rich and intense as the work of Van Gogh at Arles, or as striking and inconsistent as a painting by Jackson Pollack. Some studies may discover a unidimensional culture (such as Benedict's Dionysian or Apollonian cultures, 1934), but more often studies find OCCs to be complex and contradictory images mixing color, light, line, and even medium.

Given the possibility of such diversity, limiting the research project is a judgment call that may need to be reassessed as the project proceeds. If I begin examining a television station and discover such differences among departments that I am unable to grasp the OCC, I may need to narrow my study to a department or some portion of the organization that makes sense (e.g., because news departments quite frequently are distinct from other units of television stations they are logical units to study, see Bantz, 1985). The degree of heterogeneity within an organization may affect the limits one must choose, which will, in turn, shape the ongoing project.

PRACTICAL BOUNDARIES

Researchers will need to consider a number of practical limits to their projects and establish reasonable practical boundaries that are consistent with the relevant conceptual issues. The most common practical limits are of two broad types: researcher resources and conditions established by the organization.

Researcher resources

The most precious resource for most researchers is their time, followed by their coresearchers' time, supplies, and money. The finite limits to these resources entail making choices in any research project. For the OCC project the implications of time limitations are significant. Substantial time is needed to gather messages, analyze those messages, and make inferences about the OCC. Since an increased scope of the organization (particularly one high in heterogeneity) means an increased time commitment, investigators will frequently need to restrict their study. Thus, students using the OCC method have often limited themselves to a single unit of an organization and focused on understanding its OCC. Such a practical decision requires clearly identifying the limits of the OCC as a single unit. With increasing resources the researcher expands her or his options but, ultimately, must make those practical decisions. For most researchers, for example, it would be impractical to investigate the OCC of a multinational conglomerate that includes dozens of companies operating on several continents in hundreds of cities. The creative researcher, however, may be able to enlist sufficient volunteers to participate in gathering data so that such a wide-reaching project is possible. (As this example suggests, one advantage of team research is that it expands the study's boundaries by increasing the "person power.")

Conditions established by the organization

Frequently, researchers find that the organization they are studying seeks to constrain the scope of the study. These limitations may include the duration of the study, access to people, access to messages, reporting results, or provision of some quid pro quo. Like the resource constraints, these conditions are part of the research process. Investigators can and should negotiate with organizations concerning such conditions (as is done with other elements of the study). The critical aspect of such conditions is that their negotiation be considered a part of the data-gathering process. That is, messages about limitations are messages and are likely to be useful in developing an understanding of the organization. If we are told we should not talk with the manager of the marketing department, then we may ask why and negotiate. The negotiations then become data, but such messages are made in response to the researcher and are not independent; they therefore carry the implications of that lack of independence. Also the consequences of such conditions on the project and its viability need to be weighed. If conditions are so stringent that it is unlikely that an adequate pool of messages can be generated, it is risky to proceed unless there is reason to believe the conditions are subject to renegotiation.

Finally, by narrowing the field of analysis one might find oneself working within a distinct subculture of the organization, and therefore, claims of representing the entire organization must be tempered. It is quite evident that many organizations are umbrella cultures for diverse groups that may share more culturally with similar subcultures in other organizations than with other groups within their own organization. This is especially apparent with units dominated by strong occupational cultures, such as engineering, medicine, music, and academics (see, e.g., Becker, 1951; Becker, Geer, Hughes, & Strauss, 1961). The diversity within an OCC is, for both practical and conceptual reasons, a continuing concern in understanding organizations.

The Continuum of Researcher's Roles

While participant observation is the technique of choice for organizational culture researchers, it is not the only technique appropriate for data gathering (Bantz, 1983). Researchers may, for a variety of reasons, choose to study an organization that they cannot directly observe. Thus, Gold's (1958) continuum of researcher's roles, which ranges from complete observer to complete participant, needs to be expanded.

GOLD'S ROLES

Gold (1958), extending Junker, suggests that the participant-observer's role can vary from *complete observer* through *observer as participant*, and *participant as observer*, to *complete participant*. This continuum of involvement suggests that the researcher's role varies by (1) the degree to which the researcher participates in the social life of the organization and (2) the degree of mutual awareness among all participants that the researcher is conducting a study. Thus, in studies with complete participation the researcher is fully involved in the field life and is not identified as a researcher. In participant-as-observer the researcher is involved in field life, but at least an informant knows the researcher's role. In observer-as-participant the researcher is clearly known and identified but takes part in the social exchange of field life. When the researcher is a complete observer she or he is unknown to the participants and takes little or no part in the field life.

AN EXTENSION

A methodology that requires the researcher either observe or participate precludes the study of organizations with restricted access (e.g., organizations with secrets), organizations that refuse access, and organizations outside the present (e.g., the Nixon White House). Before precluding such organizations from study I recommend assessing the adequacy of the message pool available for study. The availability of numerous memoirs, official and personal documents, and audiotape recordings of meetings, for example, may represent a sufficiently large message pool that an organizational communication culture study of the Nixon White House is possible. The question, then, is not the ability to directly observe or participate but, rather, the availability of messages. In fact, in organizations that limit the researcher's physical access a participant-observer could find her- or himself unable to gather sufficient messages, while a nonparticipant with access to documents could obtain an adequate pool.

The most likely approach to gathering messages is to gain access to documents that are maintained in and of the organization. The use of historical documents is traditional in communication studies of public addresses (see, e.g., Hochmuth's study of Lincoln's first inaugural address, 1954). In addition, that method has been useful in attempting to understand organizational and group activity, such as Ball's continuing study of decision making in the Kennedy and Johnson administrations (1988, 1990). Other sources of data for such analyses include organizational outputs and memoirs (see Bantz, 1983). Historiographers provide a useful guide to the careful consideration of such documents in terms of the point of view of the document's creators and retainers, the document's authenticity, and related issues (see Bormann, 1965, chap. 9).

Studying organizational communication culture without any direct observation or participation places severe constraints on the researcher's ability to gather messages. As long as the researcher consistently considers the implications of those limitations, it would be presumptuous to preclude such analyses and, consequently, certain types of organizations from study.

The availability of messages that can be gathered without participant observation opens the possibility for *nonparticipation* to be a legitimate role for the researcher. Gold's continuum is extended, then, to include the roles of nonparticipant, complete observer, observer as participant, participant as observer, and complete participant.

FOUR ASPECTS OF A RESEARCHER'S ROLES

The researcher's role can be characterized by considering four aspects of her or his degree of involvement with the OCC: (1) the degree of *sociality* between researcher and organizational members, (2) the *perspective distance* of the researcher relative to the organizational members and their messages, (3) the degree of *access* to organizational messages, and (4) the degree of *independence* of the message's creation from the researcher.

The question of sociality turns on the extent to which the researcher and the organizational members develop interpersonal relationships and the type of those relationships during the course of the project. The researcher's relationship with members may be a highly uncertain, relatively unformed, stranger-stranger relationship (see Berger & Calabrese, 1975; Gudykunst & Kim, 1984, for the implications of this). The researcher's relationship with members could develop into a very complex and rich friendship-type relationship. Between these stark contrasts there are numerous shadings of relationships (task: i.e., cordial but formal; task-friendship: i.e., work oriented but personally supportive) and relational development (see Miller & Steinberg, 1975). Differing research roles will be based on differing levels of sociality—from low (stranger-stranger) to high (friendship). While it is difficult to characterize the overall pattern of sociality (because there is variability in relationships from member to member), sociality here reflects the general pattern in researcher-member relationships.

The question of the researcher's perspective distance is related to the question of sociality. In developing a social relationship with the members the magnitude of the differences between the researcher's and members' perspectives is critical. If researchers are to identify certain aspects of the organizational culture, they will need to be something of cultural strangers (Agar, 1980), yet to understand the OCC they will need to come to know the organization from the perspective of its members. This is a paradox in that *strangers can see the organization but only members can know it.* Thus, I need to assess my role as a researcher vis-à-vis the organizational members throughout a project. If I begin a project as a stranger and end as a member, my role is quite different than if I begin as a stranger and end as a stranger. The researcher's involvement is, therefore, characterized by the variation in the difference between the researcher's perspective and the organizational members' perspectives. Given that this distance will change during the course of most projects, it needs to be considered throughout. (There is a vast literature in anthropology related to these issues, see Wagner, 1975.)

The degree of access to organizational messages is an important aspect in considering the researcher's role using the OCC method. Access will vary with the openness of the organization (e.g., open vs. secretive) and the corollary degree of access granted to (or obtained by) the researcher. This question is vital, since messages are central to OCC analyses. Thus, being a complete participant may give a person access to some depth of messages in an area of an organization, but not to any breadth. Using the case of the Nixon White House again, it is likely that a nonparticipant researcher using the tapes would have more access than any researcher granted permission to study the organization. This is likely because researchers would likely have been blocked from some meetings that were recorded. Access will vary on whether one can gather messages from communicative interactions directly, gather documentary messages, and gain reports of communicative interactions that occurred when the researcher was not present. Each researcher will need to consider not simply the amount of access but also its type—that is, it may be limited but very deep, broad but shallow.

The fourth aspect to be considered is the independence of the organizational messages' production. Given that the researcher examines messages to develop an understanding of OCC, it is important that the researcher be aware of the extent to which the messages gathered are "dependent on" the researcher. As researchers become part of the social interaction, they become part of the message construction. As such, messages are influenced by researchers. This may be because old messages are hidden, because new messages are modified, or because new messages are created specifically for the researcher (cf. Douglas, 1976, chap. 4). Consideration of the potential influence of the researcher on message creation is an important aspect of examining the researcher's role.

Researchers, whether singly or in teams, can occupy five different roles when gathering organizational communication messages.

NONPARTICIPANT

Because the nonparticipant role is difficult to justify and the most likely to fail, it is rarely used. The general approach depends on documents as the message pool, and its usefulness depends on the richness of the documentary message pool. In assessing the nonparticipant's role in terms of the four key aspects it is apparent that sociality is a moot question, since there is little or no researcher participation in the organization. At the beginning of a nonparticipant study the perspective distance will reflect the researcher's a priori position with respect to the members. If I did, for example, a nonparticipant study of a television news department (of which I know a good deal), my perspective would be closer to the organization than it would be when beginning a study of a sheet metal firm (of which I know nothing). As a study progresses, any change in the researcher's perspective will reflect the researcher's work with the documentary evidence. While such changes can be substantial (I suspect that M. Hochmuth *knew* Lincoln well by the time she completed her study of Lincoln's second inaugural address, 1954), the lack of communicative interaction limits the depth of change. Concerning the question of access, nonparticipant researchers are more likely than participants to be severely limited in their access to a variety of messages (especially those created in communicative interactions). Finally, nonparticipant researchers have little worry that the messages they gather are independent of them. There are organizations that do consider how researchers will judge them (remember that Richard Nixon's rationale for recording Oval Office conversations was to provide a historical record), but, in general, documents are saved for audiences other than researchers (e.g., lawyers and judges).

The nonparticipant researcher's most serious test is the adequacy of the message pool available, followed by the difficulty in reducing the perspective distance between the researcher and members so as to be able to infer from those messages meanings which are consistent with those inferred by members. On the other hand, the nonparticipant researcher has little concern for the difficulties of developing sociality and managing its consequences nor little reservation that the messages analyzed were produced in response to the researcher.

COMPLETE OBSERVER

The complete observer has minimal contact with the members of the organization, perhaps studying organizational life from a station outside of the activity (e.g., viewing an outdoor restaurant from outside the restaurant). Such a complete observation is accomplished by researchers positioning themselves to witness communicative interactions without participating in those interactions. There are, for example, a limited number of organizational opportunities—such as retail shops or restaurants—which allow for observation from outside the organizational space. Shopping malls, for example, are strong possibilities, for stores often have large expanses of glass, and there are "outdoor" restaurants. In addition, the researcher may unobtrusively gather documentary messages, such as advertisements from newspapers and menus from signs.

Complete observers, like the nonparticipant, find sociality an irrelevant question for their research. The complete observer's perspective distance, like that of the nonparticipant, depends on an a priori relationship with the organization, although the actual observation of communicative interactions tends to reduce perspective distance since they provide more rich displays of the individuals involved. The complete observer's degree of access to messages is likely to be quite limited. The setting will determine whether the researcher can clearly hear the verbal elements of communication as well as see the nonverbal ones. In the absence of a substantial documentary message pool the absence of a strong verbal data base would doom an OCC study. Thus, the viability of the complete observer's role rests on gaining access to an adequate verbal message pool. While not impossible, this is certainly difficult. Finally, the complete observer, like the nonparticipant, need not spend much time considering whether the messages created are independent of the research. If the organizational members are sufficiently aware of the observer to modify their messages, then the researcher has moved from being a complete observer to participating in organizational life.

OBSERVER-AS-PARTICIPANT

The label observer-as-participant signals that the observer plays some role in the communicative life of the organization. At this point on the continuum participation involves not participating in the task life of the organization (except to the extent that not to do so would violate interactional norms—e.g., not to help a person who fell while working would be considered impolite in most groups) but, rather, participating in the routine communicative interactions of everyday life. Thus, the observer-as-participant may engage in everyday conversation, may ask organizational members questions for clarification, and engage in similar communicative activities.

The researcher's participation introduces sociality as an aspect of the study, for by definition the observer-as-participant involves her- or himself in building social relationships with organizational members. That relationship is typically one of casual acquaintance, but the development of interpersonal relationships situates the researcher within the organization's life and initiates a more active process that can affect perspective distance. Through social interaction the researcher *can* shorten the distance between her or his perspective and the members' perspectives. While the role of observer as participant makes perspective distance more dynamic, the restricted type of participation limits the intensity of that dynamic. Taking the role of the observer as participant provides the researcher with additional access to organizational messages by allowing messages to be created (e.g., answers to questions) and by permitting a "closer" view of organizational activity (e.g., I can sit in the restaurant, be a customer, and observe and gather messages).

The observer-as-participant may have substantial access to gathering documents, whether by collecting existent documentary messages or by recording physical documentation. The observer-as-participant will have more access to communicative interactions than the complete observer. Thus, participation provides greater opportunity to gather messages for analysis. As participation increases, however, the role of the researcher in the communicative processes of the organization increases. Consequently, the creation of messages is less independent of the researcher. When taking the observer-as-participant role this effect is minimal. Any participation opens the possibility, however, that members will create messages in both communicative interactions and documents under the influence of the researcher (e.g., a researcher is told "the way things are" by a member who is trying to get on the record "the way things should be").

PARTICIPANT-AS-OBSERVER

In this role the investigator is known to be an observer, but actively participates in weaving the fabric of organizational life. The researcher is likely taking on work in the organization, although quite routine work—helping with mail, answering telephones, carrying equipment. At least some of the members are aware of the researcher's role as observer.

The participant-as-observer role is marked by a developmental pattern not greatly unlike that of new members to an organization—that is, new members experience entry and assimilation in a complex process as they move from being organizational strangers to becoming members (Jablin, 1987; Louis, 1980). As a result, consideration of the four aspects of involvement must include an examination of the time spent and the "stage" of involvement.

As the researcher moves from being an identified stranger ("researcher," "newcomer") to substantial participation in organizational life, the degree of involvement sociality will increase. Because the role requires much fuller participation than those previously discussed, the development of a relationship with the organization will proceed substantially further. Correspondingly, the type of relationships that develop (e.g., coworker, friendship) will engender a higher degree of sociality. As relationships develop and sociality increases, the perspective distance between the participant-observer and the members will likely decrease. The participant will be able to understand the members' views more clearly when doing what the members do. The need for organizational play becomes apparent, for example, when one does a highly repetitive and mentally undemanding task along with members.

The increased participation provides access to a wide variety of communicative acts—formal, informal, public, private, on-site, off-site. The degree of access to documents will depend on both the access granted to members and that granted to researchers. In most situations this role will permit observing, collecting, and recording an array of documentary messages. The advantage of participation is that the researcher can create access by building relationships with other members. The increased access created through participation means that the messages accessed are less independent of the researcher. From a memo announcing the researcher's presence (to meet the researcher's ethical obligation to inform participants) through conversations over coffee, the universe of messages within the organization is constructed with the researcher playing a part. The gathering of messages is facilitated by participation, yet the researcher must be aware that at the same time those messages are also more dependent upon one's involvement.

In considering the participant-as-observer role keep in mind that the effect of the "known researcher" will change across time. Organizational members may "forget" or minimize the researcher role as time passes and relationships develop with the researcher. There is, however, some debate about the likelihood that such minimization will occur (Douglas, 1976, chap. 3). Although field-workers have occasionally been included to a remarkable extent in members' lives, once a participant-observer is labeled a researcher members have the option of invoking the "observer" label at any point in time. Thus, the effect of being identified as an observer is quite dynamic, and, therefore, how the "researcher" identity influences the project should always remain an open question.

COMPLETE PARTICIPANT

When adopting the role of the complete participant the researcher enters the organization as a new member and takes on the responsibilities of membership. If the organization is a work organization, this means taking a job and doing the job; if it is a social organization, this means participating fully in the social "tasks" of the organization (e.g., for a community softball team playing ball is the task). As a complete participant, the researcher is not identified as a researcher but, rather, as a *member*. Anonymity and the deep and broad participation by the researcher (relative to the other research roles) clearly influence all four aspects of the researcher's role: sociality, perspective distance, access, and message independence.

Donald Roy's study "Banana Time" (1959–1960) is a classic illustration of the complete participant role. For the study Roy worked for several months in a manufacturing firm and recorded the activity. His experience provides a valuable description of how sociality, perspective distance, access, and message independence related to his involvement. As Roy worked with the group, he developed a relationship with them, and they integrated him into their group, not only as a task member, but also as a peer, invited to join in their joke making. Roy developed a substantial degree of sociality with the group that combined with doing the same tasks to substantially narrow the perspective distance. As a complete participant doing extremely boring and repetitive tasks, Roy could better "know" how important the group's diversions were. Roy labels these occasions "times" (banana time, coffee time, lunchtime, quitting time). The times serve as diversions from the mundane but "necessary" tasks.

After the initial adjustment period Roy's approach appeared to provide unlimited access to the communicative interactions of his coworker group. At the end of the day Roy would record notes on events. Working in an isolated room meant that his access to communicative interactions outside the group was very limited. He had some access to organizational documents; he had copies of organizational documents given to him as an employee and would be able to get access to certain other organizational documents (e.g., his own notes on physical layout, material off the bulletin boards). But his access was constrained by the organization's perception of where it was legitimate for an employee to be; an identified researcher might have gotten access to some documents and communicative acts that Roy would not have been permitted to see because he was an employee.

Complete participants know that many of the messages they gather are not independent of their involvement for the participants, as a people, are integral to the communicative processes. The distinction between this role and the known observer roles is that here the messages being produced are dependent on the researcher *as a person* but independent of the researcher *as a researcher*. For the complete participant assaying one's influences on the message pool depends on how consistent the researcher is with the other organizational members. Thus, the question is: How different are messages created for you from those created for other organizational members? rather than: Are these messages being created to impress me as a researcher or to hide something from me as a researcher? In other words, it does not matter if messages are being created to impress, as long as "impressing" is a common reason that members create messages within the organization.

Certain aspects of each researcher role demonstrate that no role is ideal but that it is necessary to consider the implications of each role. In addition to these aspects, the ethical issues of each role should be weighed. For OCC research, as for any other, it is necessary to weigh the benefits of the study against the risks—in particular, risks beyond those that the organizational members would experience in everyday life and risks of embarrassment, ridicule, or legal liability. The reader unfamiliar with these issues is urged to review the guidelines for the ethical conduct of research (e.g., APA, 1973).

The Researcher's Attitude

Finally, and also important, before beginning to gather data OCC analysts need to consider their personal positions relative to the organization—that is, the *researcher's attitude*. The notion of attitude encompasses here the fundamental characterization of the researcher's perspective on and relationship with the organization. The dimensions of attitude are likely to include: respect-disdain, maintain-change, support-overthrow, dependence-independence. These dimensions reflect but expand Burrell and Morgan's (1979, chap. 2) distinction between the sociology of regulation and the sociology of radical change and

Putnam's (1982, 1983) distinction between naturalistic and critical research.

Burrell and Morgan (1979) distinguish between two approaches to organizations. They characterize the *sociology of regulation* as concerned with such ideas as consensus, order, integration, cohesion, and the status quo. In contrast, they present the *sociology of radical change* as focusing on such ideas as structural conflict, domination, and emancipation. Making the assumption that an organization should be characterized in terms of regulation or change will contribute substantially to the researcher's attitude. If I am committed to supporting the organization, assuring cohesion, and maintaining order, my attitude will be constrained on such dimensions as maintain-change or support-overthrow. If I am committed to radically altering the organization because it is oppressive, then my attitude will be constrained on those same dimensions, but at the opposite ends of the scales.

Putnam (1982, 1983), building on Burrell and Morgan (1979), distinguishes between critical and naturalistic interpretive research in organizational communication. The critical approach necessitates an attempt by the researcher to identify the disparate viewpoints within organizations and to reveal that disparity and its corollary repressiveness to those less powerful within the organization. This presumption is based on a neo-Marxian perspective that places the responsibility for liberating those who are oppressed on the researcher (see Deetz & Kersten, 1983). This perspective will influence the attitude of the researcher and, consequently, what data are gathered and what interpretation is given to the data.

Naturalistic research is characterized as an attempt to reflect the activity of organizing with as little "interference" as possible (see Bantz, 1983; Lincoln & Guba, 1985; Putnam, 1982). This approach is sometimes simplified to imply that the researcher does not take a theoretical/philosophical perspective into the setting and that the researcher does not have an opinion about what she or he finds. Given the well-made argument (O'Keefe, 1975) that a tabula rasa approach is impossible, such a stereotype is misleading. In fact, the naturalistic perspective can be better characterized as founded on Blumer's (1969) argument that "the task of the research scholar who is studying any sphere of social life is to ascertain what form of interaction is in play instead of imposing on that sphere some preset form of interaction"

(p. 54). Blumer argues that social life is unlikely to be consistently a matter of conflict, game, or cooperation; rather, it is likely to move among those forms at different times. Thus, the naturalistic researcher must be open to whatever "models" of interaction are efficacious to explain the interaction.

The researcher's attitude will be a complex of interrelated dimensions, including maintain-change, dependence-independence, even love-hate. The researcher's attitude cannot be simply characterized as regulation-radical change or critical-naturalistic (although those distinctions are important). One's attitude toward an organization and its study is likely to be multidimensional and potentially nonuniform. Thus, a researcher may wish to radically change an organization yet may be dependent upon it and have some respect for it.

Throughout a project, but especially when beginning, a self-assessment of the researcher's attitude is important, for it will inevitably shape the work. By being self-reflexive the researcher can become aware of how her or his personal attitude shapes a project—from making fundamental assumptions through data gathering to interpretation.

Conclusion

Gathering messages for understanding an organization requires working through some preliminary choices about the limits of the organizational communication culture investigation, the researcher's role, and the researcher's attitude. While the researcher makes these choices at the beginning of the project, they are only tentative and will be reconsidered during the investigation. Little in fieldwork is final, and certainly these choices are not. Once these preliminary choices are made researchers can devote their energy to the joy and frustration of actually gathering data, which is the focus of the next chapter.

CHAPTER FIVE

Gathering Messages

Your overall goal is to collect the *richest possible data*. Rich data mean, ideally, a wide and diverse range of information collected over a relatively prolonged period of time.

—J. Lofland and L. H. Lofland

Having considered the researcher's role, the boundaries for the study, and the researcher's attitude, the foundation is laid for detailing specific techniques for gathering data in an OCC study. This discussion is designed to encourage the reader to consider many possible ways of gathering the messages necessary to understand an organizational communication culture.

In order to develop a broad and deep pool of messages to analyze the researcher needs to select from a wide variety of available techniques. These include participant observation fieldwork (which is discussed in some detail below), use of memoirs, organizational output, and gathering organizational documents. This section builds on the work of Douglas (1976), Lofland (1971), and others (see Bruyn, 1966; Filstead, 1970; McCall & Simmons, 1969). With the major exception of the ethnography of communication (see Philipsen & Carbaugh, 1986), there is little literature available on doing communication fieldwork. In developing this section I have extended Pacanowsky's (n.d.) brief guide to organizational culture fieldwork to include a procedure for identifying, gathering, and recording messages. That procedure consists of 10 steps:

1. Selecting an organization
2. Deciding on a team or solo approach
3. Gaining entrance
4. Building balanced rapport
5. Identifying messages
6. Creating a journal
7. Writing through the journal
8. Coordinating data gathering

9. Exiting in phases
10. Repeating steps as necessary

SELECTING AN ORGANIZATION

The question of which organization to study is one of the least formulaic in the research process. Researchers who are interested in particular theoretical viewpoints may be drawn to a particular type of organization which they feel best exemplifies the theory (hence, I was drawn to news organizations as excellent examples of Weick's, 1969, theory of organizing as equivocality reduction). Researchers may specialize in a certain type of organization (e.g., hospitals, high-technology research facilities) for a variety of reasons, ranging from personal affinity through social responsibility. Researchers may be a part of communicative networks that facilitate their access to some organization or type of organization (I know some health care consultants who will serve as entrée for me to hospitals). Researchers also may be asked by a particular organization to study it for any number of reasons. Thus, serendipity often plays a part in selection process.

Whether I select an organization or set of organizations for theoretical, methodological, personal, or convenience reasons it is essential that I identify those reasons (e.g., I should know whether I'm studying a hospital because it is accessible through friends or because I feel it is socially responsible), for those reasons are part of the perspective and attitude guiding my approach to the project. Not only will those reasons help frame the project initially, but they may also change or develop in the course of the project (e.g., I may start out studying news organizations because they illustrate Weick's, 1969, theory but continue to do so because they are socially important). This development will both reflect the research process and influence its progress. Discovering that I am increasingly drawn to the social importance of health care, for example, may indicate that my observations are moving toward aspects of the hospital that emphasize patient care or that I am becoming part of the social reality of that section of the staff that emphasizes social responsibility (e.g., volunteers, nurses).

The rationale for selecting an organization needs to be a conscious choice and should be monitored as an indicator of the researcher's development from the first days in the field through her or his departure (see Geer, 1964). Monitoring does not imply that one must or will prevent change and development but, rather, that changes, pressures, and feelings in the researcher need to be part of the understanding that frames the research process.

TEAM OR SOLO?

A theoretical, methodological, and practical question in gathering messages for analysis is whether the researcher should operate singly or as part of a team. While the "Lone Ranger" mode has been widely used in participant observation research, the team approach has much to recommend its use.

Inasmuch as social relationships between researcher and organizational members will vary in their development, much as any other interpersonal relationship, the use of a single researcher will limit this development to the researcher's interpersonal range. That is, the type of relationship that can develop will be restricted by the researcher's interpersonal style and ability. By utilizing a team the researchers can, where appropriate, create a mix of social, demographic, and interpersonal styles. Douglas (1976), a principal proponent of team research, assembled a team that included male and female, young adult and "settled adult," property owner and "beach folk," in order to have easier access to a nude beach (Douglas & Rasmussen, 1977). The team of Bantz, McCorkle, and Baade (1980) varied in age, gender, knowledge of journalism, knowledge of organizational theory, and interpersonal style. Such a mix facilitated the development of separate foci for observation, a range of interpersonal contacts, and differing degrees of ease of entry in their study of a news organization.

The team approach, then, provides a diversity of information relationships that are likely to generate a fuller view of an organization. The drawback to the approach, particularly for organizational studies, is that some organizations may be unwilling to permit more than one researcher into the setting, for fear of disrupting the work pattern. By limiting the number of researchers simultaneously in the setting, this concern can be allayed, but it is not easy to eliminate. The team technique also necessitates recruiting a number of skilled researchers and coordinating their work, both time-consuming activities.

GAINING ENTRANCE

A researcher's success in gaining entrance to an organization is difficult to predict. The number of persons who simply march into an organization and ask for—and receive—permission continues to astonish me. At the same time other people will spend weeks trying to find an organization willing to accept them (one student finally turned the "refusals" into a study, since she was unable to gain entry within her time limits).

What constitutes entry? If I am going into an organization as an unidentified complete participant, then gaining entrance is defined in terms of how I "join" the organization. If I am going to be an identified participant-observer, procedures for the ethical treatment of research participants requires that I get their permission. This requirement may be met by getting permission from the organization's (or division's) supervisor, who then provides the organizational members with a standard project description (identifying the researchers and their purpose, assuring confidentiality and anonymity) and informing them of their right to ask the researchers to leave a setting at any time. Such a procedure adequately informs the individuals of the project but must be handled carefully to ensure that subordinates genuinely feel they have a choice. The explicit or implicit power of those in positions of authority makes it important that the subordinates be clearly informed of their right to ask the researcher to leave.

There are a number of guides to entering an organization (e.g., Kahn & Mann, 1952) that identify the core issues. Central, yet extremely difficult to accomplish, is a sense of the organizational setting and norms before one enters; this helps direct one to the appropriate individuals. How to know the structure and norms before entering is problematic. Kahn and Mann (1952) recommend that researchers use a multilevel approach, targeting the person with the most authority within the organization and working downward—by asking for permission to ask the next person down for permission—thus, avoiding offending the top officer while not putting subordinates in the position of having been ordered to cooperate. The difficulty of operationalizing this notion is evident in the uncertainty of knowing who is the appropriate top leader for a particular setting. At the IBM facility in Boulder, Colorado, for example, is the relevant superior the CEO in New York, the regional vice president, or the plant manager in Boulder? To answer such a question the more one knows about IBM the better. Thus, the approach should be established in advance by obtaining key information, perhaps contacting friends who have been employees, consultants, or researchers associated with IBM. They may be able to help suggest the optimal pattern of entrance. If the target organization is small or unknown, however, getting reliable information about the organization prior to contact may be difficult.

Gaining entrance as an organizational researcher raises a problematic question: What if the organization asks for or you feel it is necessary to provide a quid pro quo. There seems to be little consensus in communication research on this question. Given that communication researchers are frequently asked to serve as consultants to organizations, an additional problem often arises. Often researchers want to provide a copy of their report to the organization, or the organization will request it; more problematic, however, is that some organizations will ask the researchers to provide "consultant-like" information on the organization. Some even go so far as to request the researcher to make consulting-style recommendations for changes in the organization. The risks here are that researchers may: (1) find their study dramatically influenced by such a request (limiting or shaping the information gathered), (2) be asked to provide consulting services they are not competent to provide, (3) be asked to provide such services in a situation in which they feel it is inappropriate (e.g., without proper follow-up), (4) be asked to provide feedback that could harm those studied, and (5) be ethically opposed to such consulting activity. While feedback is typically characterized as a reasonable quid pro quo, these risks suggest that a researcher should carefully consider a request to provide feedback to the organization.

The problems of entrance can be summarized as covering at least five questions: (1) Should the researcher be identified or unidentified? (2) Who is the appropriate target for an entrance request? (3) Do you need to make a formal and/or informal request for entrance? (university human subjects committees may require formal approval from the organization); and (4) What are the nature of and limits to any agreement with the organization to provide a quid pro quo? Finally, organizations will ask: (5) What are the time limits of the study? These questions need to be resolved before seeking entry into an organization.

BUILDING BALANCED RAPPORT

From the time one enters an organization and continuing through a study, one of the researcher's principal problems is developing rapport with organizational members. The problem can be framed in terms of the researcher's role—complete participants, for example, develop different rapport than complete observers. The nature of the role and the purpose of the project will require differing styles. Rapport must be conceived of as a continuum from "under-rapport" through "optimal rapport" to "over-rapport" (cf. Miller, 1952). The anchor points of the continuum are going to be negotiated from the perspective of the role taken. What constitutes under-rapport for a participant-observer, for example, may be optimal for a complete observer.

Four indicators can form a pattern to suggest the degree of rapport (over-, under-, intermediate). The four indicators involve (1) the ability to distinguish the members' perspectives from the researcher's; (2) the ability to recognize, identify, or participate in social niceties (e.g., shaking hands appropriately, drinking the right drinks); (3) ability to recognize, identify, or follow work practices (e.g., carrying out specific tasks, knowing when to work hard and when to loaf); and (4) ability to recognize, identify, or follow social communication practices (e.g., using appropriate jargon, tone, rate, and accent).

Researchers can use the four indicators to determine if their rapport is appropriate for the different participant observation roles. Thus, complete participants who cannot distinguish their perspective from the members', who can participate in but cannot identify social niceties, work practices, or social communication, have developed such a high degree of rapport that they are no longer able to "see" what they are participating in; they are experiencing over-rapport. On the other hand, complete participants who can very easily distinguish perspectives, do not participate in social niceties, do not follow work practices, and do not follow social communication patterns share little with the members, which means they have under-rapport with them.

Ironically, for a complete observer a parallel pattern holds. Over-rapport is signaled by difficulty in distinguishing perspectives and the inability to recognize social niceties, work practices, and social communication patterns. Under-rapport is associated with an ability to easily distinguish a range of perspectives and the inability to identify social niceties, work practices, and social communication patterns.

The two middle continuum roles, participant-as-observer and observer-as-participant, share common characteristics of both under-rapport and over-rapport and are distinguished only in terms of the question of whether the researcher recognizes or can describe work practices. In both roles the pattern of over-rapport involves an inability to distinguish perspectives and the inability to identify social niceties and social communication patterns. The participant-as-observer who shows over-rapport finds it difficult to describe to others work practices in which they are taking part because in time they take the practices for granted. The observer-as-participant with over-rapport finds it difficult to recognize work practices even when they are pointed out. The pattern for under-rapport is similar. For both roles the observer can easily distinguish perspectives, does not participate in social niceties, and does not follow social communication practices. Under-rapport is signaled when: (a) the observer-as-participant cannot describe to others observed work practices and (b) the participant-as-observer cannot recognize the work practices of *other* members.

These identifiers of the anchor points for each role suggest the dynamic nature of rapport. Rapport is best thought of as a process of working out the different relations with members while keeping sufficient distance relative to the role adopted. The researcher's paradox is similar to that of the dramatist who must successfully balance empathy and aesthetic distance. The researcher working in the participant role, like the audience for drama, needs to understand the events observed, but needs sufficient distance to be able to see the events in a context. Too much empathy, or over-rapport, leads to an inability to observe, while too much distance, or under-rapport, inhibits knowing the "inside" of the organization. As suggested in the discussion of perspective distance, one must ask: How can I be close enough to *know* and far enough to *see?*

IDENTIFYING MESSAGES

The researcher's principal methodological task is to gather a sufficient pool of messages that is necessary for a quality analysis of the organizational communication culture. This section suggests strategies for identifying messages and considers the difficult criterion of assessing sufficiency. Subsequent sections consider how one gathers and records messages.

Identifying messages requires being aware of and sensitive to the plethora of messages within organizations. Identifying task talk as messages within an organization is easily taken for granted when studying organizational communication. Less likely to be assumed, but equally important, nontask talk messages are necessary for study. The deprecatory terms applied to nontask talk (chit-chat, gossip, BS) tend to reinforce a bias toward task communication in which it is seen as essential and all other communication is unimportant. Avoid such a bias. Management writers (e.g., Peters & Waterman, 1982), those in communication research (e.g., Bormann, 1975), and organizational communication scholars (e.g., Hawes, 1974, 1976; Pacanowsky & O'Donnell-Trujillo, 1982) point out that nontask communication is critical in the life of groups and organizations. Without considering the nontask talk it would be impossible to compare task and nontask talk for similarities and differences; the researcher could not characterize the full range of communication within the organization.

As discussed in chapter 3, in addition to talk, the exchange of verbal messages, nonverbal elements of communication (paralinguistic, proxemics, kinesics, and haptics) are critical elements in *communicative acts* and need to be considered. The level of sophistication in identifying nonverbal elements of communicative acts will vary with the specific skills of the researcher (e.g., training in phonetic or nonverbal transcription would permit very different identification and recording of messages than that done by someone without such training). Whatever one's specific skills, the researcher needs to identify the nonverbal as well as verbal elements of communicative acts.

In addition to communicative acts, the researcher needs to identify the documentary messages of the organization. The search for documents should include the obvious—bulletin boards, memos (getting on the regular mail distribution list), the human resource department's brochures, and even the trash cans (which may provide indicators of what is not worth saving). When you have identified who the gatekeepers are in the organization (i.e., those people who decide what information is distributed in the organization), see if they will provide you with documents, including both those they select for distribution and those they reject. Gatekeepers may be willing to discuss how they make selection decisions and how they learned to make those decisions. Such information is valuable for understanding the patterns of message selection and editing in the organization. In information-processing organizations, such as news organizations, gatekeepers play a critical role in the overall flow of messages as well as the production of the product (see Bantz et al., 1980; White, 1950).

While researchers may have difficulty gaining access to some documentary messages, most researchers will often be overwhelmed with the volume they are able to see. There is a wide range of possible documentary messages, and how likely it is that you will be granted access varies. The financial records of a corporation, for example, may be very valuable, and, though a researcher is unlikely to see the organization's tax returns, its annual report may be available. Access to most personnel records is typically restricted for legal reasons, yet directories, seniority lists, lists of public employee salaries and corporate officers' salaries, and similar material are likely to be available. Internal media provide an enormous and rich possible source. While some types of memoranda are likely to be closely held, others will be publicly displayed or distributed. There are numerous examples of public documents such as training tapes, brochures, and reports for which access may be easy. New technologies may influence the availability of documents; for example, gathering messages becomes much easier when one has access to files containing electronic mail messages produced within the organization. Gathering messages may be made more difficult even in this case, however, if access to electronic mail files are defined as more private than print mail and hence less accessible to the researcher. External media material is usually available, but time is needed to find news releases, recruiting brochures, and public reports. Finally, the degree of access to physical structures will vary greatly among organizations. The facades of most buildings are usually quite accessible, but security areas are generally restricted. In cases of restricted access the help of an informant or the use of memoirs may be helpful (e.g., DeLorean's detailed description of the fourteenth-floor executive offices at General Motors, Wright, 1979, chap. 2). Further, physical structures need to be carefully recorded by drawings or photographs, which tend to be intrusive, and this puts an additional constraint on gathering such messages.

CREATING A JOURNAL

The fieldwork journal is at the core of the OCC analysis. The journal is a record of the researcher's impressions, observations, and organizational messages. The journal is created by writing up the notes one generates in the field then working through the journal repeatedly, reviewing, refining, and expanding the notes. To fill out the message pool one adds to the journal whatever documentary messages can be obtained, including transcriptions or indexes of audio- or videotapes collected, and other items such as organizational totems (e.g., company coffee mugs or plaques). The focus in this step is on generating field notes and includes the initial writing up of the journal. (Pacanowsky's [n.d.] unpublished assignment guide, *The Organizational Culture Fieldwork Journal*, stimulated my thinking in this area [see also Sanjek, 1990]).

Field-workers must make notes on their observations. Sometimes these notes may be made openly and continuously while observing. If open note taking would be disruptive or inappropriate, then the observer might take notes intermittently—at times when she or he cannot be observed (e.g., when people leave the room), in a private setting (while bathroom stalls are often suggested, a car will do), or at a later time (as soon as possible after leaving the setting). Whichever technique is used, the researcher must have a practical and efficient notebook. In most cases this means choosing one of moderate size (e.g., a 5" × 9" stenographer's pad) so that it is comfortable to hold. It means choosing one that has firmly attached pages (e.g., a steno pad is preferred over legal pads or loose-leaf paper). It mean avoiding large pads because they are awkward, more noticeable, and do not fit in files well.

The tape recorder alternative

Pacanowsky (n.d.) strongly encourages researchers to use audio- or videotape to record interactions. This recommendation is particularly valuable when the researcher wishes to make a detailed analysis of the members' talk (e.g., Scheibel, 1986) and is useful in other circumstances as well. There are three caveats that need to accompany such a recommendation. First, recording will be especially disruptive or threatening to some individuals. Obvious examples include organizational members who regularly engage in talk about behavior that is legally or ethically proscribed; it is doubtful, for example, that employees in a massage parlor would give an observer permission to record conversations (see Warren & Rasmussen, 1977). Less obviously, experience has shown that people in certain occupations may be either hypersensitive or insensitive to being recorded. McCorkle (1987) found, for example, that journalists seemed distracted by note taking and that audio recording only worked when interviewing in a social setting (a restaurant) and after permission to do so had been given. The researcher must be attuned to how participants feel about being tape-recorded.

Second, the use of recorders, particularly in interviews, can induce note-taking laziness. The researcher may feel less compelled to take complete notes, knowing that the equipment is recording (this, of course, is exactly when the batteries run out). In addition to risking losing the record on technology (never a good idea), less attentive interviewers may fail to stock their short-term memories with the details that help them recreate events when working on their journal and develop that sense of understanding that is essential to such projects (e.g., by noting nonverbal details).

Third, while researchers are often obsessed with gathering more data, audio and video recordings have the potential to overwhelm the researcher with data. To adequately index 100 hours of audiotapes to locate specific examples is a laborious task; transcribing 100 hours of tape is a monumental task (the rule of thumb on the time it takes to transcribe tapes is from 5 to 10 hours per hour of tape). The recording researcher needs to be very thoughtful about the purpose to which the recordings will be put and also very organized from the outset, labeling tapes and indexing them as the project moves along. Otherwise, the time spent deciding how best to use the tapes will be substantially greater than the time spent gathering them.

Taking notes

While the specifics of what one records may vary by project, in general, a field-worker is going to try to record the communicative acts she or he observes. This means attempting to record everything possible in a setting—an impossible task, of course. But by trying to record the maximum amount, one is far more likely to be thorough than by only recording certain details. This means recording task conversations including nonverbal elements, nontask conversations, employee-employee talk, employee-customer talk, and so on. When taking notes on the scene write as fast as possible. If unable to record in the presence of the members, determine how long you can observe before it is necessary to record some of the observations. This time will vary dramatically by individual. The late author Truman Capote was rumored to be able to leave a cocktail party and recreate conversations verbatim; most of us, however, have dramatic limitations and must identify them and discover ways to circumvent them. As a person, for example, who visualizes in memory ("I can picture it on the page"), it is important for me to take notes regularly but to do so in a way that helps me visualize the event and the setting; visualization helps me to describe events in writing. In developing a note-taking system experiment and find out what works for you. In general, frequent recording, with special attention on recording items that help stimulate memory (visuals, sounds, smells) will yield more thorough notes.

In gathering these messages individuals often ask: "What am I looking for?" This question raises the important issue of how specific one should be when initiating a study. Given the perspective that argues you are attempting to describe an organization's communication culture, it is imperative to avoid premature conceptual closure. Being responsive to the organization is not only my theoretical stance, for example, it is essential to minimize the tendency to define in advance what concepts, issues, or variables should be observed and recorded. The imperative to record messages is vital to this effort. By focusing on recording organizational messages the researcher may be able to minimize the likelihood that a priori conceptual frameworks will prematurely restrict what data are seen as relevant. (Note, however, it is a conceptual perspective that leads to my emphasis on messages.) Such an effort is consistent with Blumer's (1969) point, quoted earlier, that researchers must be open to the complexity of social life. To avoid premature closure observers need to begin data gathering by focusing on the members' communication, *not* on the method per se. By focusing on members' communication the observers' notes are richer, more complete, and less targeted to the specifics of the method.

Notation schemes

In taking notes it is helpful to develop a clear and logical notation system. Using codes for names, for example—B for superior/boss—save time. Events that recur frequently can be coded, and variations on the pattern can be indicated (e.g., the repetitive phrase "Valley Pioneer, may I help you?" could be coded as an "SPA," standard phone answer, while "Valley Pioneer, what do you want?" could be coded as a nonstandard phone answer [NSPA], with the specific deviation noted). A map of the physical setting and code locations assists the recording process. The particular system should emerge from the project, but it is critical to document the system as it develops and keep multiple copies of the documentation—in two years you are unlikely to remember what each code represents.

To facilitate developing a notation system and writing later, generate a list of members' names (usually assign them codes so that, in the research setting, someone looking at your notes cannot be sure to whom you are referring). By generating a list of frequent activities you can develop codes for them as well as begin to identify differences in the relative frequency of activities.

Getting ready to write

Be sure to record not only verbal messages but also the nonverbal aspects of the messages. Include nonverbal aspects of the setting—including often overlooked but potentially salient aspects such as temperature, humidity, smells, lighting, background noise. These aspects help create a fuller understanding of the setting and contribute to recall.

When leaving the setting, even for a short period, take that opportunity to expand your earlier notes—adding phrases you couldn't get down quickly enough, aspects you now remember, and so forth. If you are leaving for more than a short period (e.g., more than an hour), consider word-processing the notes you've completed already.

When you leave the setting for the day get to a typewriter or word processor as soon as possible. Do not talk about your observations with others, for that "dumping" of your memory might exhaust material stored during your observation. Do not add more information to your already strained memory (i.e., don't read, avoid serious conversations), because you might "force out" important information.

Writing notes

The process of transcribing your field notes into a journal involves typing up the notes taken in the setting, adding additional information as it comes to mind, adding brief commentaries as appropriate, and generally trying to record everything you can. Ordinarily, saying "do everything" is specious, but, given the difficulty for most humans of accurately recording from memory, the challenge is functional. Do not allow yourself to become bogged down trying to remember a particular event nor looking for some relevant citation in a reference. If you feel a block, make a note and keep writing. Being disciplined in transcribing notes and developing them will produce a more complete journal for analysis. In typing the journal it is valuable to indicate the "source" of the comment. That is, if you are transcribing verbatim quotations recorded on-site, indicate this by the pattern of typing (see Table 5.1). If you are recording a comment for analysis, indicate that; if it is something you remembered later, indicate that. By doing so, you will better be able to assess the types of information you have available when you do your analysis.

The form of one's notes generally should be guided by simple rules—leave space for comments, number pages, distinguish between dialogue and your comments, and so on. For those analysts who might use a computer analytic system such as Ethnograph® (Qualis Research Associates, 1987), you need to follow the system's requirements; for example, Ethnograph requires that you use only 40 columns of the page, which permits space for comments in the remaining columns. Whether you use a specially designed computer program or a basic word-processing program, the computer is ideal for keeping your journal, since it permits easy insertion of comments and reformating of pages for various analyses. Obviously, the danger with computers is that data can be lost, so you should keep multiple backup records of the information. *Do not trust disks or computers.* Make multiple disk copies, and store them in multiple locations. Consider keeping a copy on a main-frame computer if you have access to one; this way it is easy to upload your journal and have it

Table 5.1
Example of a Field Note Notation

January 5, 1992 Page 01/05/92/03	*Always date and page number*
[AC is off. Uncomfortably hot.] [Lynn covering phones for Laura.]	*Brackets indicate researcher's* *comments.*
Lynn: Good afternoon, CheapTix. That's today at four? Johnson, D? Thank you for calling. [Lynn hangs up and sighs.] *Lynn:* Damn them! *Jan:* I don't know who they are, but damn 'em! *Lynn:* Another no-show! *Jan:* Another commission gone!	*Verbatim transcription indicated by* *speaker's name, followed by colon and* *standard type.*
(This was the first reference to the effect of cancellations on income. See page 01/09/92/10 for details of commissions.)	*Parentheses mark notes added later.* *These help make connections among* *events.*

accessible if necessary. You also can print the lengthy journal cheaply and rapidly on high-speed computer printers.

"WRITING THROUGH" THE JOURNAL

The journal writing process, as described above, is iterative. You take notes on the scene, add notes immediately after leaving the scene, transcribe the notes, add new comments and additional observations, then write through the notes again. The writing-through process for a fieldwork journal is a variation on revising a manuscript by retyping the manuscript again. Rather than re-typing what has been done before, the researcher reads through the comments and narration a second and third time, adding new comments about the observation. These comments may be additional bits of information—for example, you may have over-looked recording the identity of a visitor to the organization, you may now remember that the heat was off that day and the office was cold, or you may remember that an event occurred out of the ordinary sequence. These addenda are written into the journal with indications that they were added at a later date.

The comments will also include theoretical and methodological insights stimulated by or reflected in the journal. As you work through the journal, you will note observations that reflect methodological problems or answers to methodological questions. Noting them as they appear is essential to developing a text for your subsequent work. Similarly, theoretical insights may occur or observations may appear as excellent examples for theoretical questions. Taking note of these connections will stimulate subsequent working-through of the journal.

When one does research with a team the working-through process can become more complex. Up to the point of collecting the different researchers' journals together, the working-through process continues as indicated above. The working-through may include team meetings, which should be documented in the journal and used as part of the working-through. At some point in the data gathering the different journals of each team member may be joined—either simply assembled or actually interwoven so that observations appear chronologically. When this collection occurs each team member can work through the entire set of journals. While not as convenient, it will be more useful if there is a single set of all the additional comments of the team members (i.e., a master journal). If time or distance preclude maintaining such a master journal, then members can add their comments in their copy of the combined journal, and those comments can later be collated into a master journal. (Obviously, working with a word processor can make this entire process much easier; one can create a file of comments indexed by date and page of the journal so they can be easily added to the master journal.) Whichever technique is used, it is worth a reminder that there should not be only one copy of the individual journals or the combined journal.

COORDINATING DATA GATHERING

Coordinating data gathering suggests that the researcher balances the breadth and depth of the message pool in a manner consistent with the developing analysis and the theoretical perspective. In its simplest form this suggests that the researcher needs to review the journal and the analytic notes periodically to identify gaps in the data—that is, messages that have been overlooked or underrepresented. This assessment can guide the gathering of additional messages and also become part of the journal record, indicating where anaylsis problems may develop.

Using the organizational communication culture method necessitates reviewing the notes both for an assessment of the data's completeness and its sufficiency for OCC analysis. Researchers coordinating their data gathering within the OCC method will need to consider whether there are adequate messages to identify vocabulary, themes, architecture, and temporality as well as the symbolic forms of metaphor, stories, and fantasies.

Glaser and Strauss (1967; Glaser, 1965) offer a systematic approach to coordinating data gathering, which they label the constant comparative method. The method involves developing theory from data (a grounded theory, cf. Merton, 1957, pp. 9–10) and intertwining the further development of theory with subsequent data gathering. Glaser and Strauss (1967) argue that the analytic process begins before data gathering is complete. This permits "theoretical sampling" (pp. 45–77), in which the researcher seeks instances to illustrate or test the evolving theory generated in the analysis. To avoid simply finding what one expects intentional sampling needs to be done carefully. Similarly, reviewing one's journal and identifying settings, events, and specific messages that are underrepresented there can be useful.

Browning (1978) developed a grounded theory of organizational communication based on team observations and interviews of a regional planning organization. Working with field reports (as summary papers on each observation and interview, they were similar to but not identical with the fieldwork journal), Browning identified mutually exclusive communicative "incidents," which he analyzed in terms of their "dimensions." These dimensions were then used to develop descriptive labels, or categories, for each dimension. The labels, which were not mutually exclusive, were used to categorize the incidents. From this stage Browning developed relationship patterns among the incidents leading to cluster relationships among the variables represented by the categories. By following Glaser and Strauss's (1967) approach Browning, or any analyst using their approach, will work from the data to develop a theory.

EXITING IN PHASES

The most difficult question in seeking entry into an organization is: "How long will you need to be here?" There is no "real" answer to the question. To confound matters it is a question that is typically important to those in the organization (organizational time is an important concept in many organizational realities). Even after working on a project it is difficult to know when you are "done" (since completion is a misnomer in such a process). At the onset of an investigation the answer is unknowable. (The need for a practical "working" answer has led me to combine my best guess [say, nine months] and what is practical for them [say, three months] and ask for a reasonable time—six months. I also hope that later we will have become so sufficiently taken-for-granted in the setting that no one will notice that we have been observing for nine months.)

When the researchers begin to feel they have the necessary data for doing their complete analysis then it is time to plan how to leave the organization. While a project may have a very specific exit date associated with it—a written agreement between the researcher and the organization or a return plane ticket—a phased-exit alternative can be useful. A phased exit is a plan for a systematic withdrawal from the setting, much like a strategic retreat (i.e., you don't just turn tail and run but, rather, back out, incrementally gathering data as you go).

The phased notion suggests that researchers may lower their profiles systematically. If there is a team, for example, one researcher may withdraw from the setting completely while others are reducing their frequency of observation. There may be a reduction in the number of times a week observation takes place or in the length of each observation (depending on the need for theoretical sampling or on what type of observation is still providing the most valuable data). Phased exit also suggests leaving with the door still open to permit brief follow-ups to check out the analysis as it proceeds or to gather additional messages when needed.

The phased exit should involve informing your organizational contacts that you are "drawing down" your involvement. It should make clear that this is being done not because you have completed your work or because you are no longer interested but, instead, because you are at a new step in the project. With such an exit line it will be clear why you are interested in returning for short follow-ups and discussions with the organization's members.

"DO-LOOPING": REPEATING STEPS AS NECESSARY

In discussing the OCC method, the concept of iteration is invoked numerous times, for the understanding of OCC is not simply accomplished, but is created through sequential reexamination of the organization, the journal, the analysis, and the report. The final step in data gathering is to repeat whatever steps are necessary. Using the jargon of computer programming, this final step invokes the possibility of a "do-loop," in which the process goes back to an earlier point and continues forward again. The do-loop is invoked when the examination of the journal or preliminary analyses suggest incompleteness, inaccuracy, lack of clarity, or simply puzzlement. When this occurs the analyst returns to an earlier step—identifying more messages, gathering them, writing through again, and so forth. The dynamic nature of organizing and of research requires such do-looping.

Conclusion

As these last two chapters suggest, gathering organizational communication messages is part of the analysis and inference of the OCC method. Having gathered a pool of organizational messages, including the verbal and nonverbal elements of communicative acts and documentary messages, having done so through observation and interviewing, having developed a fieldwork journal from those observations and interviews, having appended sets of documents to that journal, having worked through the journal at least once, and perhaps having done theoretical sampling and analysis, you would be well down the road to interpreting an organizational communication culture. The description presented here and in the following chapters suggests that data gathering precedes any analysis. In fact, the analysis of messages and symbolic forms, as well as the inference of organizational meanings and organizational expectations, will begin before the phased exit from the setting. Again, the researcher must take care to avoid the risk of making premature theoretical conclusions, but neither should the researcher wait for all the data before beginning an interpretation.

The next two chapters detail the process of analyzing messages and their symbolic forms. Chapters 8 and 9 then focus on the inferences that can be made about organizational expectations and organizational meanings.

CHAPTER SIX

Analyzing Messages: Vocabulary, Themes, Temporality, and Architecture

> Begrimed yet bedazzling, the yeoman leaned even closer to Veronica.
> "You bring news of our Southeast outlets?" she asked, averting her gaze.
> "A 3.7% growth in market share, Milady," he replied devilishly.
> Defiant flames danced in her proud eyes. "And what of the Midwest region, rogue?!" she challenged.
> In a voice like glowing embers, he whispered . . .
> "A net increase of 6.23% after factoring the unit price discount ratio!"
> Now THAT's a sales report!
> —B. Hammond, from the comic strip "Duffy"

The stark contrast between the "romance novel" style sales report and a typical organizational report makes Hammond's parody effective. We have not seen organizational reports written with that vocabulary, in that form, nor with that flow. Analysis of organizational messages is essential to understanding not only what is happening in an organization but also the fundamental character of the organization. By analyzing messages carefully, then moving to analysis of the symbolic forms in the messages, the interpreter of organizations can grasp the foundation of an organizational communication culture and begin to infer the shape of the culture. This chapter focuses on the analysis of the basic elements of a message: vocabulary, themes, temporality, and architecture.

Message Analysis

The analysis of messages has a long tradition in communication fields—from *The Rhetoric* of Aristotle (1954), which has provided a valuable guide to the use of proof and arrangement, through twentieth-century studies of the order of argument. The OCC method cannot encompass the range or depth of possible analyses of messages and symbolic forms. Instead, it should stimulate and guide the analysis of messages, thereby moving the interpreter toward an integrated understanding of the organizational communication culture.

The interpreter of an organization will have a plethora of messages available for analysis. The interpreter will have systematically gathered messages by recording communicative interactions and accumulating documents. Interpreters will have collected messages to the extent that they record their experiences in the organization. The interpreter will have a record of messages to work from, a field work journal, which will include notes, reflections, observations, and a collection of documents.

The analysis of messages begins with data gathering, note taking, and journal writing. Researchers will be "analyzing" and "interpreting" in their journals as they review the journals. The analysis of messages will be done in an iterative fashion, as the interpreter identifies aspects of messages, gathers more data, reconsiders earlier interpretations, identifies and reidentifies aspects of messages, and so on.

The analysis of messages centers on identifying and interpreting four elements in messages—vocabulary, themes, temporality, and architecture. Analysis of the patterns in construction can provide the basis for subsequent interpretation of organizational meanings and organizational expectations. This chapter details each of the four elements, suggesting how the investigator can identify and interpret each element. It then outlines strategies for "managing" the analytic task—record keeping and cross-checking.

One of the difficult aspects of message analysis will be to treat the messages gathered as semi-objectified data—that is, to distance oneself from the messages sufficiently to be able to "see" the elements of the messages. It is not easy, for example, for people working in a planning agency to understand that "plan" is an invention and, therefore, a problematic concept, since they take plans for granted (L. C. Hawes, personal communication, 1974). If you have been a full participant in the organization, you need to distance yourself from the project sufficiently to identify the critical message elements. One of the advantages of systematically analyzing messages at this point in the research process is that it can facilitate distancing by encouraging the researcher to consider all four elements and their components.

Vocabulary

The organizational socialization literature (see Jablin, 1987; Louis, 1980) suggests that knowing the language of an organization is indicative of and necessary for full membership in the organization. Similarly, participant observation researchers often are told that the ability to use language appropriately demonstrates the acquisition of organizational membership knowledge. For the workers in the medical products firm studied by Haugen (Ex. 6.1) to do their work—and for Haugan to understand it—they needed to learn what *three sixty tens, Federal, old code*, and *sixty ten mode number* meant. Given the centrality of vocabulary to message exchange, it is the first element in the analysis of messages.

Example 6.1
Technical Vocabulary in a Medical Products Firm

[*Jenny leaves and Sandee enters, again in a hurry.*]
Sandee: Do we have three sixty tens on those two forties now?
  Dave: Yes, and we ship them Federal.
Sandee: So how do I record them?
  Dave: Use the old code under the sixty ten mode number.
Sandee: Thanks.

(Haugen, 1985)

VOCABULARY AS BASIC

Vocabulary is a basic language skill that develops from childhood throughout our lives. No matter how we learn words and their uses (e.g., memorization, seeing their use), it is a lifelong process that extends into our organizational lives. In order to function people need to have a sense of how words are used by competent communicators in their world or organization. Organizations and occupations develop word usage that helps them accomplish their work (see Hummel, 1977, chap. 4). The range of such terminology is illustrated in *Newsweek*'s "Buzzwords" column, which lists a half-dozen or so terms from various organizations and occupations (see Ex. 6.2).

Example 6.2
Vocabulary of Hotels, Postal Service, and Amtrack

> *Primate:* A demanding or disruptive guest.
> *Bertha:* A guest who orders copious amounts of food from room service.
> *Ron and Nancy:* A husband who is agreeable to everything and a wife who is impossible to please.
> ("Buzzwords," 1990a)

> *Gorillas:* Nighttime mail-sack movers at postal stations.
> *Pat the can:* Picking up from collection boxes.
> *Marriage mail:* A two-part mailing, consisting of a postcard and an advertisement delivered together.
> ("Buzzwords," 1989)

> *Foamer:* A basic rail fan, i.e., one who "foams at the mouth" when he talks or thinks about trains.
> *Amshack:* Small modern station built to a standard design.
> *Stabbed (verb):* To make a train late because of factors other than the crew or faulty equipment. Usage: "The dispatcher in Harrisburg stabbed train 14."
> ("Buzzwords," 1990b)

Vocabulary is central to the construction and use of messages, since words are the building blocks of verbal messages. Whether communication is characterized as mutual social construction (as in the OCC perspective) or as information transfer, understanding vocabulary's development, nature, and use is essential. From the social construction perspective understanding the similarities and variations in vocabulary is vital to understanding how organizational members coordinate their activities through messages. From the view of communication as information transfer understanding the common interpretation and use of vocabulary permits an understanding of how communication influences members. The student of organizational communication needs to identify and analyze organizational vocabulary.

IDENTIFYING THE VOCABULARY

Identification of the organizational vocabulary begins early in the research process. If researchers assume more of a participative role, they must learn the vocabulary to function within the organization. Vocabulary learning should not be taken for granted. Communication researchers need to be particularly attentive to words and phrases that may be: (1) new and strange (e.g., *EMT* for "emergency medical technician"), (2) old and strange because they are used in a new way (e.g., *radio*, referring to a two-way radio rather than the one-way radio in most automobiles), or (3) old and familiar but worthy of note (e.g., *patients, accidents*). Being careful to record all three of these types is essential to identifying vocabulary. In addition, the careful recording of communicative acts and collection of organizational documents will provide a substantial record of the pool of messages. This will require some distancing, particularly for the researcher who has gathered data as a participant.

New and strange

Identifying the "new and strange" vocabulary is the easiest for the analyst, as "strangeness" makes the words stand out (they become the visible figure on the message background). The individual studying a high-technology company without a background in such technology is likely to immediately notice a vast array of unfamiliar terms: *GIGO* (garbage in, garbage out), *stacks* (computer memory stack), *CAD* (computer-aided design), *vector processor* (computer that handles numbers by using vectors), or *giga-flops* (millions of operations). As these examples suggest, acronyms are common in organizational life and may be valuable indicators of frequently used terms, as evidenced in military organizations (NORAD, AWACS, CID, AFB) and medical organizations (DRG, MRI, RN, MD). While some new and strange language may be as straightforward as an acronym (DRG) for designated rate group, other usages may be problematic. Some of the language may be offensive (e.g., Grenz, 1989, reports that paramedics refer to serious burn cases as "crispy critters"); some may be so difficult to understand that help is required (e.g., studying a scientific lab and hearing researchers refer to "six-dimensional space"); some may be shortened words such as *za* for "pizza" (Rombough, 1991).

Old and strange

The case of old and strange vocabulary is particularly interesting and potentially frustrating because the meaning may seem clear when it is not. When I changed universities a few years ago, for example, I called up the new university's computer center for instructions on bringing a computer tape to their (IBM) facility. I was told that on an IBM computer, a "block" could be as large as x, so I recorded by data on the tape with a block half that size (.5 x). Unfortunately, blocks on CDC computers, which I was familiar with, and on IBM computers refer to different things. The term was familiar, but it referred to something significantly different.

The difficulty one has identifying the old and strange vocabulary will vary substantially. For individuals who have found that their taken-for-granted understanding of old terms is not consistent with some of the understandings in the observed organization, the old and strange will be easier to recognize (e.g., I now know that *block* means something different on IBM and CDC machines). For those observers who have not seen instances of inconsistency between their understanding and the members' understandings, seeing the old and strange within the organizational pattern may be difficult. It is not impossible, however, if the analyst utilizes at least one of two approaches.

First, the analyst needs to compare the use of and response to vocabulary in a variety of settings, as recorded in the journal. This comparative process, valuable for identifying all three types of vocabulary, is especially useful for the old and strange. Noting the subtlety of variations in language use may cast a shadow over the familiarity assumption. That shadow may spur reconsideration of the analyst's understanding of a given term.

Second, the analyst can review her or his interpretation of the vocabulary with members of the organization. After hearing the analyst's understanding of a term the members may highlight alternative interpretations of terms the analyst believes are old and familiar. In that way old and familiar vocabulary may need to be considered as old and strange. The researcher's ability to utilize this technique will vary with the researcher's role (e.g., complete observer vs. participant-as-observer), ethical considerations such as her or his potential to influence the setting, and whatever agreements were made to provide feedback to the members.

Old and familiar

The taken-for-grantedness of old and familiar terms makes identifying such vocabulary use problematic in two ways. One, it is simply difficult to recognize and take seriously some vocabulary use (e.g., would I note that physicians are called "Dr. X" by nurses, while physicians refer to nurses by their first names, when "everyone knows that"?). Two, identifying familiar vocabulary could lead to reducto ad absurdum (e.g., studying miniscule elements such as *and, the,* and *are*). The difficulty underlying both of these concerns is where to "draw the line" — how to assess what is worthy of note within the organizational communication culture and what is consistent with the larger language culture. The answer here seems to rest on the reference point of the researcher's study. If the researcher seeks to detail a U.S. corporate headquarters OCC as part of a comparison with a Japanese corporate headquarters OCC, then attention to much of the taken-for-granted language of each organization is necessary, inasmuch as OCC rests on the larger (national/ethnic) communication culture. A researcher working with a more narrowly circumscribed analysis would need to attend to old and familiar vocabulary to the extent that it is endemic in the organization (e.g., the use of *we* by managerial leaders). The prevalence and rootedness of vocabulary use in the organization can be assessed by repeated reviews of the message pool during analysis (another benefit of continuing journal writing through the analysis process).

As the identification proceeds, the analyst needs to record the denotative vocabulary use within the organization (e.g., "the computer" refers to an electronic machine) as well as the connotative use within the organization (e.g., "a Cray facility" not only indicates a computer center having a Cray supercomputer, but it also connotes a serious scientific computer center). The tone of many of *Newsweek's* "Buzzwords" (Ex. 6.2) illustrates that organizational terms not only identify but also characterize (e.g., using *primate* to describe a disruptive guest). Because the denotative and connotative use may vary from time to time and setting to setting, it is important to conceive of vocabulary as *in use.* One does this by noting who is participating in a particular communicative act, when and where that act occurs, and the effect associated with the term.

The recording of denotative and connotative use is based on the analyst's identification of specific indicators of use (e.g., someone says, "When we say 'asap' around here we mean drop what you are doing and do it right now"), inferring use from behavior (e.g., in all instances when a person was told "do it asap" they dropped their current projects and completed the asap request), or inferring use from other communicative acts or documents (e.g., someone says, "Please leave—I have an asap project to do").

When recording the connotative use of vocabulary the analyst will frequently use nonverbal indicators of the value associated with the terms. Thus, when engineers at Data General referred to a machine as a "kludge," they were reported to have said it with disgust (Kidder, 1981, p. 45). The term *kludge* identified (denoted) a specific design and implied (connoted) that the design's inefficiency and lack of elegance were distasteful to the engineering group. Adequately recording nonverbal information in communicative acts will be critical to a thorough analysis of the vocabulary's connotative use.

VOCABULARY EXEMPLIFIED

Kidder's (1981) description of a computer development team at Data General Corporation provides a rich illustration of the variety of vocabulary used within an organization. As a manufacturer of computer hardware, Data General's language is laced with technical terms such as *chip, logical address space, mode bit, 32-bit supermini, hexaddress, redix, mantissa, swapbites, core dump, overflow, rings, PAL, BASIC, ROM, DEC, CPU,* and so on. Vocabulary use also reflects the division of tasks with terms such as *Hardy Boys* (for the hardware design group) and *Microkids* (for the software design group). It provides a good example of connotative language, as their use of *IBM* implies a positive standard against which competition is judged.

METHODOLOGICAL IMPLICATIONS

Vocabulary study—identifying and recording vocabulary use— is an ongoing and iterative process. It begins with the researcher entering the organization and needing to make sense of the organization's vocabulary. It continues through the journal writing process, as the researcher records messages and notes problems in interpretation. It becomes essential as message analysis requires thorough and repetitive review of the message pool. Finally, the vocabulary study of the organization continues when examining themes, architecture, and temporality, for each of these elements both builds upon and shapes the analyst's understanding of vocabulary.

Identification of the terms means developing a recording system. An excellent way to achieve this is to develop an index card system (or computer data base) of the words, including where they appear in the journal (by date and page number) and how the words are interpreted in the organizational messages. By recording instances in which the words appear the analyst will be able to return to the text and and locate a word's usage within its context and also be able to note when such usage occurs, thereby pointing to the temporal dimension of vocabulary (e.g., seasonal language use such as *year-end, fiscal year, holiday*, or *new budget*). The indexing approach also permits easy alphabetizing of the terms for subsequent reference and makes preparing an organizational "glossary" simple.

Themes

Theme is a venerable concept in message analysis. It has been central to the analysis of literature (e.g., thematic development in *Hamlet*) and rhetoric (e.g., themes in presidential addresses). While themes have been defined as frequently occurring topics in organizational communication (Johnson, 1977, p. 122), frequency is only one aspect of the definition of themes in organizations.

CRITERIA FOR THEMES

There are two criteria that define themes. First, a topic exhibits a frequency of occurrence greater than one; a single instance of any topic is not thematic. Second, a theme represents at minimum a simplex of ideas and at maximum a multiple complex of ideas. Combined, these criteria suggest that the multiple occurrence of interconnected ideas constitutes themes. Example 6.3, from Haugen's (1985) study of a medical products firm, illustrates a potential theme, labeled by the participants "3:30 zoom." The topic appears more than once, and even these two brief excerpts suggest it connects time of day and increased

Example 6.3
Two Afternoons in a Medical Products Firm

[*3:30 Jenny rushes in as I notice the computer room is very loud and busy. Jenny hands a stack of orders to Dave.*]
Jenny: 3:30 zoom, huh!
Dave: Looks that way [*small chuckle*].

[*3:05 I notice the computer room has become loud, Jenny walks quickly in. She places many computerized order forms for Dave on his desk.*]
Jenny: The 3:30 zoom is starting early today.
Dave: Let's hope it ends quicker.
Jenny: That would be nice [*both chuckle*].

(Haugen, 1985)

workload. Haugen's analysis reveals that the topic is thematic since in other talk it also connects with supervisory demands and equipment performance.

Another example of a theme in messages is the periodic occurrence of managers' budget planning. The problems in planning in uncertain environments (e.g., "Is the recession ending?") is thematic in most such discussions. It easily meets the frequency criterion, although note that the periodicity of budget planning discussions (e.g., annual or quarterly) illustrates that frequency need not refer to hourly, daily, or even weekly communication. Budget planning discussions typically meet the second criterion because they often consider budget planning within a complex of related topics — politics, evaluation systems, economics, divisional status, and so forth. The interconnectedness of budget among topics and time make budget planning a general theme within many organizations.

IDENTIFICATION OF THEMES

The analyst identifies themes by noting multiple occurrences of topics, then noting whether these themes are related to other ideas or topics in the message pool. The identification of repeated topics will begin as the researcher works through the journal, where the reappearance of topics will be noted and commented upon. Identification will continue as the analyst examines the message pool for vocabulary and its use, inasmuch as vocabulary frequently points toward themes (e.g.,

ROI—"return on investment"—is an indicator of a productivity theme in many businesses). When focusing specifically on themes the analyst will include the themes identified in the earlier passes through the journal and search the message pool for additional instances of thematic development.

THEMES EXEMPLIFIED

While gathering data in a team observational project, we became aware that the television news organization we were studying (Bantz et al., 1980) exhibited "conflict" as a theme. Members frequently talked about conflict within the organization, often tying it with other issues such as pay, performance, and corporate ownership. Members also frequently detailed the conflict they "discovered" in doing the work of preparing news stories, typically connecting it with past events, personalities, and economic arrangements. Finally, members also regularly created organizational products (e.g., newscasts, news stories) that built upon a conflict model—presenting two or more sides disagreeing about an issue—then embedded both those conflicts and the model itself within a view of society and social responsibility. The pervasiveness of conflict as a theme in television news organizations suggests that conflict may be a characteristic of their organizational cultures (see Bantz, 1985).

METHODOLOGICAL IMPLICATIONS

Like vocabulary, theme analysis is facilitated by careful record keeping of themes as they are identified. The card index, or data base, approach again permits locating and cross-referencing themes (which is very helpful for looking at the interrelationship of themes) as well as marking their ebb and flow (which will contribute to temporality analysis).

As themes are identified, the analyst interprets the theme within the message pool. At the beginning such interpretation is likely to be very sketchy and tentative, with much of the interpretation being suggestive, not definitive. As the project progresses, particularly as the remaining elements of message analysis are completed and analysis of symbolic forms is done, the thematic interpretations may be reconsidered and developed.

Temporality

"If, according to Harold Wilson, 'a week is a long time in politics,' then 10 years is a mere moment in intelligence [service] terms" (West, 1983, p. 181).

The role of time in the communication process has been discussed principally in terms of the nature of the process itself (Berlo, 1960; Monge, Farace, Eisenberg, Miller, & White, 1984; Smith, 1972) and the developmental nature of communication (Berger & Calabrese, 1975; Miller & Steinberg, 1975). Monge and his associates (1984) have emphasized the need for longitudinal studies of organizational communication, and their work illustrates how the temporal dimension can be assessed in such studies. Recent essays outline the importance of temporality in understanding culture (Maines, 1989), social theory (Lewis & Weigert, 1981; Maines, 1987), language (Zerubavel, 1987), and interaction (Denzin, 1987).

Temporality is a critical aspect to be analyzed when examining messages in order to describe an organizational communication culture. The analysis of messages provides an important opportunity to assay the temporal dimension of the organization. This section describes the process of identifying temporality within and between messages, then examines temporality in more detail, and considers the methodological implications. Identifying temporality within messages will focus on the pace and duration of the messages.

WITHIN MESSAGES

Message duration is an important aspect of communicative temporality. Zerubavel (1987) suggests that duration is a symbolic code; therefore, people may associate the amount of time allowed for an event with its significance. Cuban prime minister Fidel Castro's famous multihour speeches not only are of a different temporal order than a 15-second television spot, but also may be of a different symbolic order. The analyst needs to be able to characterize message duration in "objective" measures of the clock, which makes it vital that she or he record temporal markers during observations. Then the OCC analyst will be able to assess whether or not objective duration has symbolic significance in the organization.

In addition to the objective duration, it is valuable if the researcher can assess the members' interpretations of message duration. An event's interpretive duration is the experience of time rather than the clock measure of time (Flaherty, 1987, labels this the "experience of duration"). As anyone who has heard speeches knows too well, a speech of 30 minutes on the clock could be 5 minutes in interpretive duration or 90 minutes in interpretive duration.

Pace and rhythm are another aspect of the temporal dimension of messages. With communicative acts pace can be assessed by speaking rate in number of words per minute. A message lasting 30 seconds is quite different if 100 words are spoken in that time than if only 20 words are spoken. The pace will often interact with the rhythm of speaking so that some messages are more "lyrical" and others more "staccato." Fast-food restaurants during a rush provide an excellent example of the staccato message, as orders are called out in a brief code at a rapid pace. The pace and rhythm of documents, particularly written and audio-video documents, can be assayed through word counts, visual cutting rate (i.e., the number of image changes per minute), and meter (as in poetry). Martin Luther King, Jr.'s classic "I Have a Dream" speech, now turned into a cultural document via film, illustrates temporality within a message, as King develops a rhythm in his delivery of individual sentences, shaped into stanzas by the refrain "I have a dream."

BETWEEN MESSAGES

The number of messages that are constructed and used within a time period can indicate the message *rate* in a communicative exchange or of the production of documents. The message rate may be fixed by genre—the rate of annual report letters by corporation presidents, for example, is one per year. More frequently, message rates will vary. Different organizations may have general patterns of message rates, and different organizational settings and times of the year may affect message rates.

Organizations provide numerous examples of temporally patterned messages. Organizational calendars lead to end-of-the-fiscal-year reports, daily sales reports, weekly sale summaries, monthly profit and loss statements, quarterly performance reviews, annual bonuses. With the advent of new technology organizations may find changes in between-message temporality.

Grocery store chains, for example, can, thanks to computer-based optical scanners, obtain daily or even hourly inventory reports instead of weekly or monthly reports. One distinct indicator that the temporal patterning of messages may be extended across time is the construction and remodeling of buildings. Some organizations may erect new buildings rapidly as new messages or frequently remodel buildings to modify messages, while others occupy buildings unchanged for years (e.g., contrast the changing styles and rapid building of McDonald's restaurants with structures in the Vatican).

Message rates will vary by setting within an organization as well. I suspect message rates decrease among grain traders as they leave the floor of the Minneapolis Grain Exchange for their offices. Instead of exchanging dozens of messages per minute, they may review their day with supervisors at a rate of 10 messages per minute. (Readers who saw the film *Trading Places*, with Eddie Murphy and Dan Ackroyd, may remember such rate changes.) While this example may be overly dramatic, setting is likely to influence message rate within many organizations.

Finally, message rates in many organizations may vary across time. I suspect that the rate of message exchange in Phoenix retail stores fluctuates greatly between December or January highs, with the influx of tourists, and August lows, when even the "locals" look for cooler climes. Temporal variation is sometimes simply related to the number of organizational members on hand (many organizations have great variations in hiring related to seasons). Sometimes these variations are related to getting certain seasonal tasks accomplished (e.g., balancing the books by the end of the fiscal year, restocking shelves by morning, getting all the old passengers off and the new passengers on the airplane in 20 minutes).

TEMPORALITY EXEMPLIFIED

Temporality has been identified as a critical characteristic of executive life. Mintzberg (1973) found that the executives he observed averaged 12-minute unscheduled meetings, 68-minute scheduled meetings, 6-minute telephone calls, and 26 pieces of mail each day. In a study of mutual fund portfolio managers Power-Ross (1984) found a much more rapid communicative pace. She found that the managers received an average of 103 pieces of mail a day from which they saved 15.7 pieces and spent an average of 4.25 minutes per item reading. They participated in scheduled meetings averaging 34.7 minutes and unscheduled meetings averaging 36 minutes. Their average telephone call lasted 4.3 minutes. Power-Ross found fund managers talking rapidly, reading and scanning quickly, and meeting nearly constantly as they managed million-dollar portfolios and made decisions to move in and out of the stock market (which itself is a moving target). The temporality of such an organizational life is quite different than that in a large manufacturing concern, such as one that makes automobiles, where product development may take years (e.g., Wright, 1979).

Even more dramatically than the case of automobile manufacturing, intelligence services operate on extended time frames. The quotation at the beginning of the section on temporality, from *The Circus: MI5 Operations, 1945–1972* (West, 1983), suggests that intelligence services operate on a radically different temporal basis than politicians, mutual fund managers, workers in emergency rooms, or high technology manufacturers. West casually reports that an intensive debriefing of a defector extended over nine months (p. 147). He reports that, when trying to catch a double agent, "watchers took up their positions in the spring of 1960 and continued their operation for more than a year" (p. 67). These are "short-term operations" in the counterintelligence efforts to identify agents who may have been recruited in the 1930s and had been active for 30 years.

METHODOLOGICAL IMPLICATIONS

To identify the pacing of messages it will help greatly if the observer notes the timing of communicative acts and when documents were issued. This includes the simplistic task of indicating the beginning and end of communicative acts. In addition, the observer's perceptual sense of time is an important aspect, which should be recorded in the journal.

Systematically seeking temporal patterns from the journal and documents will involve comparing times between messages and times indicating the duration of messages. It will involve examining the messages for "quantity" relative to the duration of the message; it will involve looking for commentary on both the duration and pacing of messages (e.g., the researcher may have noted difficulty in recording a message because the speaker talked too fast). The researcher should also be sensitive toward messages about temporality (e.g., "It's been so busy!" or "3:30 zoom"). Such messages will both highlight parts of the message pool that need detailed temporality analysis and help explain how temporality is interpreted by the members.

With documents temporality analysis is often facilitated because the organization dates most documents. Also, the physicality of documents makes measuring their duration easier (e.g., examining the frequency of documents, see Hanson, 1987). When the documents in question are buildings their temporality can often be assessed through clear dating (checking cornerstones and building permits). Even the type of structure may suggest the temporal dimension of the organization. Those that build massive, solid buildings may evidence expectations of greater permanence (e.g., Germany's Third Reich, see Speer, 1971). In contrast, having watched the boom-and-bust cycle of schools, my neighborhood elementary school district still builds brick schools but includes space that can be converted to classrooms for a few years at low cost and also utilizes "temporary" modular buildings.

Temporality analysis carefully examines how time relates to messages, both within and between them. The study of temporality should begin early in the data gathering and continue through it. As the researcher begins to identify temporal patterns, it is valuable to check these patterns with members of the organization, get their feedback, then reconsider the pattern.

Architecture

The analysis of message architecture includes the arrangement of topics, syllogistic form, physical arrangement of space, form of written documents, and related aspects of message structure, architecture, and form. The analysis of message structure has consumed a good bit of attention in communication research, as a review of research on attitude change indicates (Zimbardo & Ebbessen, 1969). The tradition of examining message arrangement is long in critical studies of literature and rhetoric (e.g., Brockriede & Scott, 1970, chap. 2). While message form is less an object of research in organizational communication, writers have made numerous recommendations on this topic (e.g., Conrad, 1985, chap. 9). The analysis of physical architecture is an ancient tradition that currently includes a variety of approaches to people's understandings of buildings and space (e.g., Norberg-Schulz, 1980, Rapoport, 1982; Scheflen, 1976; Sundstrom, 1986).

In the OCC method the architectural elements of messages make an important contribution to understanding temporality and themes. They are also vital in inferring patterns of organizational meanings and expectations. While the techniques for analyzing messages may be used for a variety of media, for explanatory ease here we will illustrate the identification of architecture by examining three media: communicative acts, written documents, and the physical arrangement of space. In doing so, architecture will be examined and the related methodological issues presented.

COMMUNICATIVE ACTS

Attention to the arrangement of communicative acts will begin early in a project as the observer attends to and records numerous messages. The careful recording of communicative acts is essential to their detailed analysis. From the instant the acts are observed researchers will begin to note their structures, and with attention to details their architectural arrangements can be considered. Analyzing the arrangement of communicative acts can include looking at relationships within and between messages. The structural analysis of communicative *interaction* has been studied by discourse analysts such as Jefferson's (1972) research on side sequences, Beach's (1985) study of courtroom transcripts, Alberts' (1988) investigation of couples' complaints, and Nofsinger's (1975) work on "getting the floor" as well as much analysis by behavioral studies of dyadic (Sykes & Brent, 1983) and group interaction (Ellis & Fisher, 1975; Fisher & Hawes, 1971). While it is beyond the purview of this chapter to detail the techniques of discourse, conversation, or interaction analysis, the researcher who finds such techniques potentially valuable should consult other sources (e.g., Ellis, 1991; Ellis & Donohue, 1986; Nofsinger, 1991). Here we limit our focus to preliminary types of structural analysis that may contribute to the understanding of messages within the context of an OCC study.

The architecture of communicative acts can include consideration of the *intensity structure* and *substantive lines of development*. The intensity structure of communicative acts refers to how the verbal and nonverbal elements create a pattern of emotional force. A message from the boss, as seen in the following fabricated example, illustrates consistently high intensity:

> *Boss:* Come on, you lily-livered creeps, show some guts—tell me to my face which of you gentlemen (*sarcastically*) opened your mouth to the auditors about the cost overruns down here?

Contrast this with a message that moves from supplication through making threats to supplication again. The structural analysis then needs to note the pattern of intensity within the message.

The intensity pattern can be inverted so that the dropping of one's voice signals important information. Thus, Word (1992) notes that psychiatric nurses lower their voices when talking about problematic patients. Attention to the shifts in the intensity structure contributes to understanding the architecture of communicative interaction.

Consideration of the substantive lines of development within messages includes argumentative analysis (applicable to both communicative acts and written documents, see Ehninger and Brockriede, 1978). The question here concerns what arguments are made and how they are arranged. The argument could be a simple syllogistic arrangement of claims such as:

> *Subordinate:* In the past two years all the Accountant IIs have been sent to the Sunny Farm School to learn the Neo-Modal Auditing System. Now that I have been promoted to Accountant II, I am requesting support to attend the Sunny Farm School next month.

This fabricated message illustrates a classic deductive syllogism (e.g., All men are mortal; Socrates is a man; therefore, Socrates is mortal) by arguing: All Accountant IIs go to Sunny Farm; I am an Accountant II; therefore, I should go to Sunny Farm. A similar strategy, suggested by Bettman and Weitz (1983) in a study of corporate annual reports, is to analyze the patterns of causal reasoning. Identifying the structure of arguments, including the type of causal reasoning used, provides a basis for understand-

Example 6.4
Paramedics' On-Scene Communication

P1 (to EMT): How many patients do we have?
    EMT: Two. This is the worst (*pointing*). Bilateral amputations
            to the arms. The second patient is in the ditch over
            there complaining of back and shoulder pain. He's alert
            and oriented. This was a hit and run.
P1 (to P2): I need MAST pants, backboard. I'll set up the airway
            (*begins treatment of patient in silence*).
P1 (to EMT): Hold C-spine. (*P1 continues treatment while P2 tends other
            patient. AirEvac lands.*)
P1 (to RN): This is a head to toe survey. First of all, all we know is
            this is a hit-and-run. There are two patients, this is the
            worst. Patient 1 has a road rash, amputation. . . .
                                    (Grenz, 1989, pp. 16–17)

ing what is plausible or implausible, persuasive or unpersuasive, appropriate or inappropriate in an organization. The communicative interaction between paramedics, patients, and others at an accident scene illustrates the architecture that emerges between messages (Ex. 6.4). The first paramedic (P1) asks the on-scene firefighter (emergency medical technician, EMT) to provide orientation then makes a request of his partner (P2), followed by instructions to the firefighter (EMT), followed by a review with the Air-Evac nurse (RN). In Grenz's data (1989) paramedics frequently followed a similar interaction structure, moving between orientation, orders, and action. Similarly, Grenz describes their interaction as they are driving to an emergency call in a manner that resembles a conversation between a pilot and navigator.

While the architecture of communicative interaction is dynamic, attending to the patterns of message structure such as intensity and substantive lines of development will contribute to understanding messages. Examining other possible architectural characteristics such as "talk turns" (Sacks, Schegloff, & Jefferson, 1974), interruptions (Tanen, 1990), simultaneous talk, and silence (Basso, 1970; Bauman, 1983; Braithwaite, 1990) may be valuable in a particular study. The specific architectural features examined will emerge from a close reading of the journal. When observing the salon "Hair and Nail," for example, D.

Brown (1991) noticed a "deliberate" verbal architecture for "never does anyone enter without receiving a 'hi,' or leave without receiving a 'bye' accompanied by the usual name or nickname from those within eyeshot. Regardless of what they were doing, each of the employees took a moment to do this" (p. 7). Attention to the architectural features of interactions will contribute to identifying organizational expectations (e.g., the style of communication at Hair and Nail) and organizational meanings (e.g., "friendliness").

WRITTEN DOCUMENTS

The more formal the organization, the more prevalent are written documents. Thus, large formal organizations often seem to be buried in written documents: procedure manuals, memos, reports, training manuals. Identifying the arrangement of written documents begins in earnest as the researcher reviews messages systematically for structure within them. The architecture of written documents will include their physical qualities, arrangement of the text on the page, and the lines of development in the text.

Physical qualities

The physical qualities of the messages may be useful in assessing the message in the organization. Consider the weight and quality of the paper on which a memo appears. We note, without surprise, that the CEO's memo is on 20-pound, watermarked bond. If, instead, we observe a CEO's handwritten note on recycled computer paper, we should certainly consider the significance of the choice of this paper (e.g., it could mean "we are frugal" or "we are environmentally responsible"). Similarly, whether the text is handwritten, typed, computer printed, or professionally printed may be relevant to an assessment of the message. Contrast, for example, an official annual report, with its pictures, special articles, tables, and legally approved data, to a casual memo scribbled to a coworker. The mode of putting information on the page may be a message, for example, that indicates formality or informality.

Arrangement of text

Awareness of a standardized form for written documents is

valuable both for considering its potential importance as a consistent part of the message pool and in assessing violations of the standardized form. If an organization has a standard memo form (including To:, From:, Re:, Date:, single-spaced paragraphs with a line in between) or a restaurant ticket lists appetizers at the top, meals in the middle, desserts at the bottom, and drinks on the back, it needs to be noted as part of the message architecture. This kind of standard form can then be contrasted with a document whose text is scribbled across a scrap of paper. Therefore noting the frequency, subject, writer, and target for standard and nonstandard notes is valuable, so that patterns can be identified and deviations from those patterns can be noted (e.g., does the CEO only send handwritten notes to potential superstars?).

Lines of development in text

More significant and more difficult is analyzing the form of argumentative development in organizational messages. Contrast the typical data-oriented sales report with the romance-novel style in the Duffy comic strip quoted at the opening of this chapter. The lines of development in a text may be quite straightforward or very complex.

The standard lawyer's letter illustrates the straightforward approach by stating the problem, indicating the remedy sought, making a specific threat, and setting a deadline for response. Thus, when an insurance company canceled a policy just issued to me, my attorney father wrote the company with a description of its acts (specifics and dates), why the acts were inappropriate (that the grounds cited were in error and the manner of notification was improper), what the insurance company must do (immediately admit their error), and what he would do if they did not (file a protest with the insurance commissioner). Another simple example of architectural arrangement in documents is arrangement of topics in a fixed order (e.g., I've tried always to refer to vocabulary, themes, temporality, and architecture in that order).

Other forms are much more artistic and complex, such as a speech by President Truman that Brockriede and Scott (1970, chap. 2) characterized as matching a musical form known as contrapuntal. Organizations even specify the lines of development when they request information, for they may ask for specific data, in a specific order, supported with specific arguments. Thus, the chief financial officer (CFO) may require that requests for store-remodeling funds state current sales, projected costs, projected increased sales, and provide a rationale for why the remodeling will lead to the specific sales increase. The CFO may even rule out specific arguments (e.g., that improvement in appearance is an acceptable goal).

When considering all three of these arrangements—physical qualities, arrangement on the page, and lines of development within the text—it is valuable to consider them in conjunction with temporal analysis. Analyzing temporality and architecture together can be useful in better understanding the OCC. Variations across time will frequently highlight message architecture as the appropriate forms change (e.g., new stationery, new logos, different headings) and the lines of argument change (e.g., economy is out, quality is in).

PHYSICAL ARRANGEMENT OF SPACE

From the beginning of any observation of, or participation in, an organization the exterior and interior of buildings—the physical arrangement of space—will be important. Space influences our impressions of organizations, our participation in them, and our understanding of their cultures (cf. Hattenhauer, 1984). Contrast, for example, the openness, large glass windows, bright colors, large signs, and ample parking of a typical convenience store (e.g., Circle K, 7-11, AM/PM) with the limited windows and doors, subtle colors, discreet sign, and inadequate parking typical of an exclusive jewelry store (e.g., Tiffany's). Recording the physical arrangement of space will proceed from the outset of a project, including the detailing of the physical environment of the organization via a map or floorplan, descriptions of physical space (color, arrangement, "feel"), and perhaps photographs and drawings. The notation will include not only the "framing" of space via walls, but also the objects within space and their arrangement. Thus, it is important to draw a floor plan showing walls as well as desks, files, word processors, and other equipment in an office.

For most OCC studies developing a reasonable description of the spatial arrangements will suffice. The researcher's goal is not to exhaustively consider all the possible interpretations of physical architecture, but to assay how physical arrangements of space function as messages in the organization. Thus, as a basis, the researcher needs to describe the spatial arrangements, to consider how spatial arrangements may relate to other aspects of architecture, themes, vocabulary, and temporality, and to consider whether members utilize spatial arrangements as organizational messages—and, if so, to examine those interpretations.

Description

The initial recording of the spatial arrangements constitutes the researcher's base description. In addition, the researcher may record additional information at different times then compare the descriptions (this is especially useful in organizations that change frequently). Through a careful review of the journal, in order to prepare a summary description of the spatial arrangements in the organization (including any changes across time), the researcher will provide a description of the dynamic nature of physical architecture. Shaver and Shaver (1992), for example, describe how a U.S. Indian Health Service clinic waiting room changed across several years, with each change distancing the patient more from the staff (e.g., an open counter gained a glass window; the window got covered with paper to prevent patients from seeing staff while they were working; the window system was replaced with a telephone booth arrangement in which patients pick up a phone and wait, listening to a busy signal until a receptionist answers).

Space and other message elements

In gathering data and developing a summary description the researcher should consider the relationship of space to vocabulary, themes, temporality, and other aspects of message architecture. In an organization with a high-frequency exchange of messages the analyst should consider the possibility that spatial arrangements may facilitate that temporal pattern (e.g., the trading pit at a commodity exchange). Space is frequently a theme in organizations (who ever has enough space?), which may direct the analyst to assessing how the spatial arrangement itself may relate to specific themes. Architectural analysis will need to consider the interrelationship of forms. Where, for example, are bulletin boards relative to pedestrian travel (do we post Equal Employment Opportunity posters in a building that no one ever enters or in a high-traffic area?)? Examining the interrelationship of space with other elements will signal when space is constituted as a foreground message in the organization, rather than being simply the plane on which messages are created and used.

Space and members' constructions/interpretations

It is easy for the researcher to suspect that for many individuals the arrangement of physical space, although part of their psychological stimulus field, is not part or at least not central to their communicative life. Focusing on organizational communication culture, before devoting a major effort to identify how members interpret spatial arrangements, the analyst needs to consider to what extent members utilize those arrangements as message forms. Such an assessment may necessarily be quite crude, but possible techniques include noting whether members overtly communicate about space and how it affects them ("This is such a dark room"), whether changes in spatial arrangements have occurred recently (creating new buildings, giving new office assignments), examining historical documents for discussions of space and its changes, and asking informants about whether spatial arrangements are an important part of the communicative world of the organization. If by the use of these techniques it appears that spatial arrangements are important to members' interpretations in the OCC, then additional work needs to be done to understand those interpretations (cf. Corman, 1990).

While the most logical approach is simply to ask members for their interpretations, this technique has the drawback of making members aware of the ground on which they constantly act and may induce more interpretations than the members would ever generate on their own. Thus, as a starter, reviewing the more indirect sources of information about members' interpretations (e.g., documents, conversations) can provide the researcher with the material needed to begin a synthesis of patterns of interpretations. After becoming familiar with those interpretations using informants to check the researcher's conclusions may be helpful.

Inasmuch as one could devote an extreme amount of time to analyzing the architecture of messages, the researcher needs to consider the other elements of message analysis and set limits to

the scope and depth of architectural analysis. This may mean selecting particularly salient messages in the organization—
whether salience is measured by their frequency or some other
gauge of importance (such as who constructed them). The
choice should, of course, be made in line with the goals of the
study.

Interrelationship of Elements of Message Analysis

As the discussion of spatial elements indicates, the four elements of message analysis are interrelated and synergistic. Our
analysis of each element will be enhanced by what we find
when we examine the other elements. In addition, as one develops the analysis of each of the four elements, it is valuable to
consider specifically their interrelationship. By doing so, one
may find the interconnectedness of architecture and temporality
(e.g., curt orders are given frequently); vocabulary and themes
(e.g., the boss is nicknamed "Vampire," and people talk of the
boss as a vampire); and vocabulary, themes, and temporality
(e.g., in emergency rooms "seconds are lives! I need it STAT!").

Example 6.5
Teachers in a Public School

> *T3:* Yup. This is where we all come to bitch and moan about
> everything under the sun . . . especially Dr. Zero.
> *Scotty:* God, it was a great day until you mentioned him. Now it's
> shot.
> *T3:* Sorry Scotty. Ha, ha.
> *Scotty:* In all seriousness there isn't a teacher in this building who
> respects that man.
> *Observer:* Why?
> *Scotty:* Well, after you've been lied to, cheated on, treated like a
> child, you tend to lose respect.
>
> (Richard, 1983)

The richness of interrelationships among the message elements makes their careful examination rewarding. Example 6.5
illustrates in one interaction among teachers in a high school
how a label ("Dr. Zero") interconnects with a theme (respect)

and through observer questioning is connected to another theme (being deceived). Vocabulary and themes are frequently connected in strongly connotative terms. Thus, Haugen (1985) found frequent disparaging references to the medical supply company as a "zoo." Blue (1991) observed room-service staff discussing whether a food server tricked a guest to gain a tip in addition to the one automatically added to the bill. The question "Did you trap the pigeon?" brought together a connotative meaning for the guest (*pigeon*) with a connotative meaning for garnering the second tip (*trap*), suggesting the theme of gathering additional income and the interrelationship of vocabulary and theme.

CHAPTER SEVEN

Analyzing Symbolic Forms: Metaphors, Stories, and Fantasy Themes

Many old stories are being thrown out, and new stories, which are sure to shape our perceptions for decades to come, are undoubtedly being written.

—"Talk of the Town"

Collective communicative life is made rich and coherent through the symbolic forms of metaphors, stories, and fantasy themes. There are the national and international stories that are being written and rewritten in the events of European unification, East European transformation, and the end of the cold war ("Talk of the Town," 1990). There are the rich and powerful metaphors in organizations as people talk about people, performance, the past, and the future (Koch & Deetz, 1981; Krizek, 1990; Pepper, 1987). Revealing fantasy themes emerge in small groups as members dramatize events in other times and places (Bormann, 1990; Bormann et al., 1978). When examining organizational messages for vocabulary, themes, temporality, and architecture the interpreter finds stories, metaphors, and fantasy themes.

Scheibel (1990) proposes the analysis of metaphors, stories, and fantasy themes as "the symbolic triad" of organizational life. Using the musical metaphor of a triad, he suggests that metaphors, stories, and fantasy themes arise together and interact with one another. Analyzing these symbolic forms is a critical step in understanding organizational communication cultures. Each of these symbolic forms has a substantial literature and has been applied in organizational studies. Accordingly, this chapter cannot even begin to suggest in detail all of the relevant literature, but will present each symbolic form in turn, outlining the concept, how it can be analyzed, and its role in contributing to an organizational communication culture.

Again, each of these symbolic forms appears in messages and can be built on and related to the elements of message analysis—vocabulary, themes, temporality, and architecture. To analyze these forms one must first accomplish the difficult task of identifying them in messages, then study them with appropriate techniques, according to the conceptualization of the symbolic form one adopts. This process will begin early in a project as one notices metaphors, stories, or fantasy themes during observation and records them in a journal. Identification of symbolic forms continues through the analysis of messages for vocabulary, themes, temporality, and architecture since they play an important role in symbolic forms. The exploration of symbolic forms depends upon careful consideration of the conception of each symbolic form, followed by detailed analysis.

Inasmuch as an analysis of one symbolic form, say metaphors, could constitute an entire project by itself, you might ask why an analysis of symbolic forms is included in the OCC method? The answer rests on the twin beliefs that (1) symbolic forms are extremely rich sources of knowledge for interpreting organizational communication cultures, and (2) the method must offer a wide range of possibilities for the interpreter to use in understanding an organization. Without several possible ways to explain the organization the interpretation will be severely limited. The organizational interpreter may find each of these three forms—metaphor, stories, and fantasy themes—in a given organization. She or he is likely, however, to emphasize those forms that are central to the specific organization and the analyst's theoretical views and methodological skills. In one organization metaphors may provide greater insight; in another stories may be a richer source; in a third organization fantasy themes may be most valuable; and in a fourth it may be the intersection of metaphor, stories, and fantasy themes that is most revealing.

Metaphor Analysis

Metaphors have long concerned literary, rhetorical, and philosophical scholars (Aristotle, 1954; Lakoff & Johnson, 1980; Ogden & Richards, 1923; Osborn, 1967). Metaphors have been valuable in the analysis of organizations (Koch & Deetz, 1981;

Krizek, 1990; Moore & Beck, 1984; Pepper, 1987; Sackmann, 1989; Smith & Eisenberg, 1987). Pepper's (1987) thorough review of organizational metaphor research and basic conceptions of metaphor provides the basis for my discussion.

Lakoff and Johnson (1980) argue that "the essence of metaphor is understanding and experiencing one kind of thing in terms of another" (p. 5). Metaphors consist of two elements, here called *focus* and *frame*, which are illustrated in the following sentence: "Fred is a turkey." In this straightforward metaphor *Fred* is the focus, and *turkey* is the frame. The metaphor offers an alternative "understanding and experiencing" of the focus "in terms of" the frame. A baseball coach, for example, might describe a player in this way: "He's got all the tools in the tool box" (Krizek, 1990, p. 46). Here the focus is on *He*, and the frame is *tools*. The relationship here is that players *are* made up of tools (e.g., speed, throwing, and hitting ability); thus, this coach's metaphor characterizes baseball players mechanistically (Krizek, 1990, chap. 4).

As a symbolic form in organizational communication, metaphors can provide insight into the social construction of numerous aspects of the organization—its members (e.g., having tools), its work, and its play. With their symbolic richness metaphors also provide useful data for inferring organizational expectations and meanings. An analysis of metaphors, at the simplest level, requires (1) identifying metaphors, (2) interpreting the metaphors, and (3) identifying the relevant organizational elements in the relationships embodied in the metaphors (after Pepper, 1987).

IDENTIFYING METAPHORS

The best route to identifying metaphors is to become aware of their pervasiveness then work through their interpretation. Lakoff and Johnson (1980) sensitized people to the prevalence of metaphors in everyday interaction. Table 7.1 exemplifies frequent types of metaphors presented by Lakoff and Johnson: conceptual, orientational, ontological, personification, and metonymy. Conceptual metaphors present fundamental relationships between two concepts. Orientational metaphors relate directionality (e.g., up-down) with another concept (e.g., strong-weak). Ontological metaphors relate the nature of existence with another concept. Personification is a specific type of

Table 7.1

Examples of Lakoff and Johnson Types of Metaphors

Conceptual Metaphors:	
Argument is war.	"Your position is indefensible."
Time is money.	"I can't spend my time in this manner."
Orientational Metaphors:	
High status is up; low status is down.	"We're on top now."
Up is good; down is bad.	"Our prospects are looking up."
Rational is up; emotional is down.	"This conversation has fallen to a new low."
Ontological Metaphors:	
The mind is a machine.	"His mind is like a computer."
Groups are containers.	"I work in an organization."
Personification	"The weather wiped him out."
Metonymy:	
The institution stands for the people responsible	"SYNDXX robbed me."
A place stands for the institution	"The president's office called."

Source: Adapted from Lakoff and Johnson, 1980, chaps. 1–8.

ontological metaphor that attributes human qualities to nonhumans or inanimate objects, thus, connecting the two. Metonymy is to take one thing and use something related to it to represent the whole.

In an organizational interpretation the identification of metaphors is based on a close examination of the OCC journal, noting metaphors in messages. There are potentially hundreds of metaphors in the messages gathered. Taking the time to identify the metaphors will give the analyst a sense of their prevalence and a general impression of the types of metaphors used. Both tasks are useful for subsequent analysis.

INTERPRETING METAPHORS

Additional metaphor analysis should be conducted when the analyst is convinced that (1) the analysis will contribute to better understanding the OCC and (2) the amount of time is justified by the potential benefit. To estimate the amount of time consider that Pepper (1987) spent more than 100 hours analyzing over 900 metaphors generated in writing by members of an organization. The time to consider such an analysis is when a researcher finds that the identified metaphors suggest new understandings that have not been found either in the message analysis or in the analysis of other symbolic forms. Krizek (1990) began his study of baseball rookie camp expecting that stories would be the critical symbolic form, yet his analysis led him to discover that metaphors were vital to understanding the symbolic reality of the camps. If the metaphors appear heuristic, then the time spent examining them will be well spent. Finally, if the analyst does not analyze the metaphors, proceeding along through the other steps in the OCC method but feeling that questions remain, then it is worth reconsidering metaphor analysis.

Example 7.1
Copy Machine Conversation in a High-Tech Manufacturing Firm

X: Well, the company has to be loyal to its long-term employees.
N: I wouldn't want to make the decision of who stayed and who had to go.
S: Well, I wouldn't want to either, but I think they should be a little more consistent with the troops.

(Coupe, 1986, p. 6)

To illustrate the decision to analyze the metaphors consider the exchange in Example 7.1. Speaker X personifies the organization by attributing a human (or animal) characteristic, loyalty, to an inanimate collectivity. Speaker S invokes a military metaphor, referring to organizational members as "troops." In this particular organization the significance of layoffs made the personification of the organization a potentially important metaphor and one worthy of further exploration. The representation of an organization in human characteristics can be an important indicator of the organizational communication culture, as it articulates expectations about appropriate rights and responsibilities and contributes to the construction of the "organization" as meaning.

The first step in a detailed analysis and interpretation of metaphors is to identify their foci and frames. In Example 7.1 this requires noting the explicit occurrence of *company* as the focus and *loyal* as the frame in X's statement. Further, there are two possible metaphors in S's statement. First, given that the interaction focuses on employees, the reference to "the troops" implies that "employees are troops," where *employees* are the focus and *troops* are the frame. Second, the reference to "they" as representing the company and its managers creates a focus that connects with the implied frame (*army*), suggesting that "the company is an army." In both cases the speaker invokes a familiar military metaphor.

Once the focus and frame are identified and a preliminary intepretation of the metaphor drawn, the organizational interpreter can begin to record and catalog the types of metaphors in an organization, noting not only which metaphors occur frequently, but also which are powerful. Thus, the metaphor of firings as a "holocaust" at the collection agency (see Ex. 1.2) or another that depicts X as a traitor may be powerful, even if they only appear a few times. By considering the frequency and force of metaphors the organizational interpreter will view the symbolic landscape of an organizational communication culture.

Story Analysis

Example 7.2
Interning at IBM

I was selected as a student intern at IBM. Before starting I asked them if I needed to dress in what I had heard was the IBM manner: a white shirt with dark suit, dark tie, dark socks, and dark shoes. They said, since you are a student, all we would expect is that you dress well. However, I decided to always wear the white shirt and dark jacket, dark slacks, dark socks, and dark shoes. This worked until the day after I moved apartments. I woke up to find no clean white shirt, only a light blue short-sleeve shirt. So I wore it. At lunch I went out to the IBM credit union and was standing in line. My supervisor's boss came up behind me, pointed out that my tie had blown over my shoulder in the wind, looked at my clothes, and said: "Going bowling?"

(Anonymous, 1983)

"War stories," such as the one in Example 7.2, are common among organizational veterans. They are often told to newcomers to warn them about the limits on behavior. To understand their power one must examine the tale carefully and locate it within the symbolic reality of the organization. Thus, understanding that the IBM uniform (symbolized by the white dress shirt) is formal, businesslike, and at minimum middle class and that colored shirts are informal and bowling is often associated with the working class helps the researcher locate the story's contribution to inferring IBM's organizational communication culture.

Story, or narrative, analysis has a long tradition in anthropological studies of oral tradition (Turner, 1980) and in oral interpretation / performance studies (Conquergood, 1983). Fisher (1984, 1985, 1987) has been the most effective recent exponent of the perspective for the analysis of rhetoric. Recently, the technique has been applied to organizational studies (M. H. Brown, 1985, 1990; M. H. Brown & McMillan, 1991; Browning, 1989; Cooper, 1989; Martin, Feldman, Hatch, & Sitkin, 1983; Schwartzman, 1983; Wilkins, 1983).

While story analysis may be justified simply on the grounds that organizational members frequently tell stories, it does, in fact, have strong theoretical foundations. The story analysis can be anchored in a number of theoretical perspectives. Here I follow Conquergood (1983) and situate the approach in the performance perspective developed in both oral interpretation and anthropology. This perspective characterizes performance as "making, not faking" the experience of life (Conquergood, 1983, p. 27). The performance perspective characterizes communication as involving reflexive mechanisms, which Turner calls "cultural performances," and these mechanisms include stories, histories, films, and dramas. Turner (1980) links "reality" and performance. Performance focuses and clarifies reality.

Storytelling, in the performance perspective, is central to the construction of social reality. Pacanowsky and O'Donnell-Trujillo (1983) argue that organizational communication constitutes culture through *rituals*—personal, task, social, and organizational rituals. They suggest that the boredom of everyday work leads members to use communication as *passion*, including storytelling (personal stories, collegial stories, corporate stories) and passionate repartee. Pacanowsky and O'Donnell-Trujillo note that communication is part of *sociality* as individuals engage in pleasantries, sociabilities, and privacies. They propose that organizational communication must also be seen as *politics* including the showing of personal strength, the cementing of allies, and bargaining. Finally, Pacanowsky and O'Donnell-Trujillo argue that organizational communication is enculturation: learning (and teaching) the roles, initiation, and learning (and teaching) the ropes.

Building on Turner (1980) and Pacanowsky and O'Donnell-Trujillo (1983), I frame stories as cultural performances that reflexively construct the life experiences of the storytellers. Stories can indeed reflect passion, as Pacanowsky and O'Donnell-Trujillo suggest, and they also contribute to other aspects of organizational life. The substance of the stories often evidences politics (Martin, 1982). Stories have served as a socializing medium for as long as there has been oral history; hence, organizational storytelling is very often a medium of enculturation (M. H. Brown, 1981; Krizek, 1990; Louis, 1980). It seems that stories may be essential to sociality; we share private aspects of the organization through stories (Schwartzman, 1983). Storytelling becomes part of the rituals of organizational life (e.g., at every orientation new employees are told the story of a new employee's purse having been stolen from her desk to warn them to be careful with their things). Stories are multifaceted cultural performances that are characterized by the active participation of the members of the organization as they construct stories together.

IDENTIFYING STORIES

Of the three symbolic forms, stories are usually the easiest to identify. We all do storytelling; we recognize storytelling; we participate in storytelling. The organizational interpreter, looking for stories in organizational messages, reviews the journal, noting places where members presented narratives of "real" people acting in either another time or place or else "imaginary" people acting in any time or place. There are stories of self as well as stories of others. There are stories of what we would be doing right here and now if we weren't doing what we are doing (thus, creating an imaginary character acting in the same time and place). There are stories that appear to be in common among organizations (Martin et al., 1983), and there are near mythic stories (Mumby, 1987, analyzes one from IBM).

While there will inevitably be fewer stories than metaphors, the organizational interpreter still must consider and choose which stories are likely to contribute to an understanding of the organization. Stories of one's personal exploits on the weekends, for example, may not be central to organizational meanings and expectations. Yet in some organizations social behavior may be extremely important, especially when that behavior is tied to task responsibilities (see, e.g., Bormann et al.'s, 1982, story of the hard-driving sales representatives who outdrank their customers; and Ex. 7.6.)

THE ANALYSIS OF STORIES

There are a number of possible approaches to the analysis of stories (M. H. Brown, 1985, 1990; Martin, 1982; Schwartzman, 1983), including the fantasy theme analysis approach, which emphasizes examining the dramatizations for heroes and villains, plot lines, and persona (see Bormann, 1972; and the final section of this chapter). Here I will provide a guide to analysis by showing how stories can be interpreted as demonstrating rituals, passion, sociality, politics, and enculturation (Pacanowsky & O'Donnell-Trujillo, 1983) and how, thus interpreted, stories can contribute to understanding an organization's meanings and expectations. As the discussion will make clear, these types of stories are interrelated, since stories as rituals may be enculturation stories and stories of passion may well be stories of politics.

Stories as/of rituals

The identified stories can be descriptive of rituals or be ritualistic themselves. Stories that describe rituals or their violation can be important in understanding the symbolic character of the ritual and how it is part of the organizational meanings and expectations. In Vonnegut's *Player Piano* (1967), for example, the story is told about a young man who violated an important annual ritual (the Oaks) by yelling and how, after that faux pas, his career was stopped. The story makes explicit the appropriate behavior at this ritual (i.e., competition is OK, but it is solemn competition) and thus contributes to understanding the norms of the organization (see chap. 8). By examining stories one can identify the nature of the ritual, even when the story is one of the breakdown of the ritual, because disruption too reveals the ritual pattern (cf. Garfinkel, 1967).

The identified stories can themselves be rituals or part of rituals. A ritual storytelling may be constitutive of organizational life. Organizations frequently have ritualistic ceremonies that mark the beginning or end of some project or time period (Deal & Kennedy, 1982, chaps. 4, 5). The organizational interpreter will often find stories told as part of those rituals (e.g., stories of past successes). Examining those stories for the heroes and villains, values and outcomes, will assist in better understanding the culture.

Passion

Pacanowsky and O'Donnell-Trujillo (1983) describe storytelling as a mode for injecting passion into organizational experience, particularly for those workers engaged in very dull and routine tasks. Raising the emotional level of activities occurs not only by performing the activities, but also by retelling them. Storytelling constitutes the critical element in the cultural performances of organizational passion. The analyst should consider how stories contribute to an organization's level of passion and whether the stories are personal, collegial, or corporate. The level of passion can be a valuable indicator of an organization's meanings and expectations.

Stories that increase passion are rife in heavily routinized organizations. Thus, factory workers, such as the clicker room workers studied by Roy (1959–1960), or the bakery workers, with whom I worked for five months after graduating from college, frequently tell dramatic stories. The bakery workers told stories, for example, of "how we got the bread out even though . . ." (e.g., the oven was down for three hours). The interpreter can assess which organizational members are presented positively in these stories, what raises the passion of the members, and why members act as they do. Through this assessment the interpreter has a basis for inferring organizational expectations about "good work" (norms) and the reasons for working (motives), as discussed in chapter 8.

In addition to stories that increase passion, some storytelling is also used to reduce passion—to cool out the members after peaks of intensity. I remember vividly, for example, a story told to me by a funeral director of how he "always" got auto accident ambulance calls when dressed in his best funeral suit, with morbid details of trying to do the work of an ambulance operator in

Example 7.3
Emergency Medical Personnel in the Telephone Room

Arnold: This is what happened. Kurt was handling this call and the
   guy [the homeowner] did shoot him [the burglar] and Kurt
   asked him [the homeowner] if the guy [the burglar] was still
   breathing. The guy [homeowner] said he didn't know and
   was acting all cocky that he had shot someone until all of a
   sudden the guy [burglar] who was shot got up and started
   walking out of the house. That is where Cool Hand Luke
   took over. Kurt was totally yelling at the guy [homeowner],
   "Don't shoot him again! Just leave the house, he isn't going
   to get that far—don't shoot him, don't shoot him." Kurt was
   totally screaming. It was so damn funny.
Kurt: I wasn't yelling.
Arnold: You are right. You were screaming.
Kurt: Whatever Arnold.
Arnold: Whatever Kurt.
Greg: Good god there are some crazy fuckers out there tonight.
Arnold: Tonight?! What about every night?
Kurt: I know that guy totally shot him in the chest, like how far
   was the guy really going to get?

(LaPointe, 1991, pp. 7–8)

one's best suit. The story seemed to be one of passion reduction,
injecting a humorous turn into an unpleasant task ("gallows humor"). Similarly, the cathartic recounting of close-calls by members of sports teams and, I assume, by airline crews can clearly
be seen as passion reduction yet can contribute to the OCC.

  Stories and the communicative interactions in which they are
told may be complicated combinations of passion and other
types of stories. Example 7.3 illustrates gallows humor following
a very serious telephone call for an ambulance, yet the story is
told partly to tease "Kurt" for losing his composure. The ca-
tharsis is blunted by the teasing, so the story contributes to sociality as well as passion.

Sociality

Sociabilities are "joking . . . gossiping, 'bitching,' and 'talking
shop' " (Pacanowsky & O'Donnell-Trujillo, 1983, p. 141). Stories
can enact or describe organizational sociality. Stories are frequently told in terms of interactions that fit the characterization

of sociabilities. The stories can be a put-on (e.g., "Lynn tried to down-load an elephant to a PC [personal computer]"), reveal inside information (e.g., "Did you hear the story about how they got married in a surprise wedding?"), serve as a vehicle for complaining (e.g., "Michael was reprimanded for forgetting his time card!"), or simply be a shop story (e.g., "I asked my supervisor last year, then . . . ").

Stories may be used as part of the private sociabilities in confessing, supporting, consoling, and criticizing (Pacanowsky & O'Donnell-Trujillo, 1983). Roy (1959–1960) reports a series of thematic stories that illustrate sociability. Roy's coworkers in the "clicker room" elaborated on such stories as "Danelly's farm," based on Danelly (i.e., Roy) owning two acres, or "George's daughter's marriage." These stories appeared and reappeared across days and were part of the workers' sharing of their private lives.

The substance of stories is valuable in assaying organizational sociality. Storytelling can contribute to the patterns of organizational meanings and expectations by exemplifying wisdom and foolishness, success and failure, and humor and seriousness within the social life of the organization. I was told a story, for example, about Frank Rarig, a founder of what is now the Speech Communication Association, responding to a phatic greeting ("How are you doing?") with an extended exposition on his health and business. Unfortunately for the person who asked the question, the two were standing outside in the depths of Minnesota's winter. The substance of such a story, in conjunction with other such examples and the analysis of messages, can contribute to inferring the meanings and expectations of the OCC. (Is the story told representative of the organization or representative of Rarig? Are there stories about other organizational members showing disdain for phatic communication? Is the story related to temporal factors and the development of expectations about the use of time?)

Politics

Like rituals and sociality, politics are both enacted by storytelling and described in stories. Stories contribute to all three of the political performances Pacanowsky & O'Donnell-Trujillo (1983) discuss: showing personal strength, cementing allies, and bargaining.

The ancient tradition of epic storytelling suggests that the performance of stories may demonstrate one's personal strength.

Quite often, the stories may illustrate the power of an individual in the organization, as in stories of superhuman efforts by organizational leaders (e.g., corporate leader H. Ross Perot's efforts to extricate his staff from Iran extended to launching his own military-style rescue mission, Follett, 1983). Further, the limitations of personal strength can be dramatized, as in an organizational story told to me in Example 7.4:

Example 7.4
Limitations of Personal Strength

Two young faculty went to visit the department chair to encourage him to terminate a probationary secretary. The two faculty explained their conviction that the secretary was incompetent and that retaining her would produce great grief. The chairperson took some umbrage at these young folks telling him his task, and when the young faculty persisted in their request he snapped: "Don't you know how much power I have?" Upon hearing this, one of the young faculty members jumped up, pointed at the other faculty member, and said to the chair: "So, turn him into a hippopotamus!"

This story enacts the limits of power. As such, it can contribute to understanding the dynamics among professors and administrators in this organization. Further, the repetitive recounting of the story may influence the ongoing development of the OCC. In this case the story was told years later by one of the "young faculty members," now himself the department chair. By virtue of the current chair doing the telling, the story not only told of the professors' irreverence for power in the past, but enacted that irreverence in the present.

The performance of stories for cementing allies may dramatize an individual's value to the organizational culture and the need to support the individual's sponsor in the organization. In this way the story may dramatize the use of quid pro quo in building organizational alliances. Such stories might present the meteoric rise of a young executive's career as being built on the pattern of favors traded (e.g., stories of the executive's "logrolling" by exchanging favors with others). Such a story would contribute differently to an understanding of an OCC than a story of alliances built on high performance and respect.

Finally, stories will frequently contribute to an understanding of the politics used in bargaining. Organizations are replete with stories of bargaining interactions within the organization and with other organizations. The answer to the question "Why is Jan only paid that much?" may well be a story dramatizing salary negotiations between "Jan" and the organization. How the story is used—as an example of appropriate bargaining or of stupidity in action—as well as the substance of the story will influence the story's contribution to the OCC. In other words the telling of the story may help constitute an aspect of the OCC— such as a concern for salary, fairness, or equity—as well as illustrate bargaining strategies within the organization.

Enculturation

Enculturation is the broadest type of performance on Pacanowsky and O'Donnell-Trujillo's (1983) heuristic list, for the other performances (ritual, sociality, and politics) are all part of enculturation. Storytelling is an important part of organizational enculturation, or socialization (Krizek, 1990, chap. 5). Pacanowsky and O'Donnell-Trujillo emphasize two types of enculturation: learning (and teaching) roles and learning (and teaching) the ropes. Enculturational performances, then, are performances wherein new organizational members are taught what, how, and why activities should be done (learning the roles) as well as the way things are *really* done (learning the ropes).

Example 7.5
Coach at a Professional Baseball Rookie Training Camp

I wish you guys could have been here last year. Some of you might have been. You didn't hear J. W. or D. S. complainin' about this bunting stuff. I'll tell ya, J. W. in particular made himself a good bunter. Probably has seven or eight maybe ten bunt singles this year—each one worth a couple thousand extra bucks on his salary next time his contract's due. He wasn't no good bunter when he got here, but he sure as hell left as one. He'd get out there even before seven and turn on the machine and take maybe fifty or sixty extra pitches and bunt them all over—down the first base line, down the third base line, all over. He made himself a good bunter. Ya see where he's at now.

(Krizek, 1990, p. 71)

The analyst can determine the role of stories in learning roles and ropes by considering the performative context and the substance of the story. "Trainers," for example, frequently use stories to make job requirements clear. Krizek (1990) observed a minor league bunting coach tell the story presented in Example 7.5 after hearing the players complaining about how hard they worked. The story exemplifies the appropriate behavior for a rookie, the type of effort expected for success, and the possible outcome if the listeners work as hard as J. W. Similarly, in a study of a computer consulting company (Ex. 7.6) a veteran consultant tells a brief story to teach a newcomer how to find potential contracts (Breidenstein-Cutspec, n.d.).

Example 7.6
Computer Consulting Veteran

You can find potential business everywhere! Once I went to a Model 330 conference and they had a hot tub in the hotel. I sat in the tub to relax and in comes this woman wearing a paper bathing suit. I started up a conversation about it and then we switched to business talk. Within an hour I wound up with a big contract! Never give up and never underestimate the potential of any situation.
(Breidenstein-Cutspec, n.d., p. 17)

Stories that contribute to learning the ropes will frequently involve learning about politics. Thus, telling a newcomer to the department the hippopotamus story with great glee about stumping the department chair enacts the way power and politics "really" function around there. It is quite different than a story told to me of a CEO who threatened to fire a vice president because the vice president disagreed with the CEO during a meeting (Ex. 7.7). In both cases the stories provide an indication of what the different roles of superior and subordinate mean in each organization. Either story helps a newcomer learn how to behave and what to expect of a superior.

Finally, there may be stories, substantively about enculturation, that tell of successes and failures by newcomers. Such stories can, of course, be considered in terms of their performance and their content. Their story lines can cast valuable light on how enculturation is viewed within the organization. In a study of television station production personnel (e.g., camera operators), Ewart (1985) found the employees telling stories of newcomers (sometimes

Example 7.7
Story Told by the "Food Company" Vice President

The meeting of the Food Company's top managers was to discuss a proposal for a new product. During the meeting the CEO clearly supported the proposal. After some discussion he turned to the second in command (a vice president) and asked for his opinion. "Number Two" gave it—directly suggesting that entering this market was a mistake. The proposal received preliminary approval, the meeting concluded, and the CEO called Number Two into his office. The CEO was furious with Number Two's failure to support him. He yelled at Number Two and threatened to fire him. Number Two responded, "Don't ask for my opinion when you don't want it. If you want me on board just tell me in advance. I understand you're the boss—so just let me know."

themselves) who joined their station and were treated to a "sink-or-swim" style of organizational socialization. The newcomers were not trained, were not told specific requirements of their job, then were sharply criticized (often publicly) for failures to perform to station standards. Also in the enculturation genre news service reporters tell stories of their first experiences of "diving in": taking the "hot seat" at one of the computer terminals and getting their first brief story on the wire in two to three minutes (Cooper, 1989, chap. 2). Analyzing such stories can provide important information about the organization's expectations of newcomers and the meanings surrounding work, performance, and members.

In summary, as we have seen in this section, the analyst can identify stories in the message pool and interpret them by considering how stories of ritual, passion, sociality, politics, and enculturation contribute to the development and maintenance of an organizational communication culture. Stories are rich and valuable sources for accessing the symbolic reality of organizations. They are likely to provide important information about organizational expectations and meanings.

Fantasy Theme Analysis

Based on Bales's (1970) work in small group interaction, Bormann and others have refined a technique to analyze messages for fantasy themes (see Ball, 1988; Bantz, 1975b, 1979; Bormann, 1972, 1975, 1980, 1982, 1983, 1985a, 1985b, 1990; Chesebro, Cragan, & McCullough, 1973; Cragan & Shields, 1981; Kidd, 1975). A fantasy theme is the dramatization of events, people, and actions in another time and space (Bormann, 1983). Bales observed that groups engaged in collective dramatizing as a basic element of their interaction, and he incorporated dramatizing as one of his categories for the analysis of group interaction. Bormann (1972, 1975) observed group fantasizing in classroom groups and saw a possible connection between dramatizing in groups and dramatizing as central to rhetoric. This linking of dramatization in ongoing groups and in public communication contributed to Bormann's development of the symbolic convergence theory of communication (1980, 1983, 1985b), which argues that, through the sharing of fantasy themes, members' individual symbolic worlds converge in such a way that a group symbolic reality develops. That is, members of a group have a common view, expressed in language or other symbols of what is "real" in their past or hoped for in their future.

Fantasy themes are "dramatizing message[s] in which characters enact an incident or a series of incidents in a setting somewhere other than the here-and-now of the people involved in the communication episode" (Bormann, 1983, p. 107). The narrative action is set in another time and place than that in which the dramatization occurs (e.g., it is set in the "there and then" as opposed to the "here and now"). This may be a view of the group's past ("We were making big bucks until Bush became president") or the group's future ("We'll make big bucks after the merger"). Fantasies are not mere daydreams but, rather, are shared representations of the past and future. While some are humorous, others are tragic. Kroll (1983) quotes a vivid dramatization centering on the need for collective action among women in Example 7.8:

Example 7.8
Women Unite for Freedom

Sisters for centuries you have struggled with the foot on your neck. Now we will join together and push away the foot. We will stand up and be proud. Be of courage, my sisters. Each of us is unique. Each of us is beautiful. Each of us is meant to be free. Reach for the sky

with one hand and take hold of your sister's hand with the other. Our womanhood has made us all sisters. We must rise together to be free. Women have lived all over the world in bondage. Everywhere men have been and are still the master. . . . We must look to each other for solace. We have been isolated from each other. We must learn about each other and unite for freedom. . . . Together we must create a new society, a new world—where all people are free.
(Kroll, 1983, pp. 144-145)

Such elaborate dramatizations are common in certain public communication genres (e.g., religious and reform speaking, Bormann, 1985a) as well as media news coverage (Bantz, 1975b, 1979; Bormann, 1973). A number of studies have considered fantasy themes in organizations (e.g., Ball, 1988; Cragan & Shields, 1981; Kroll, 1983; Scheibel, 1986, 1990).

As a research technique fantasy theme analysis examines a corpus of messages "for recurrent themes that build to form elements of dramatic structure: scenarios, characters, and plot lines. The critic's job is to forge links among the different words, phrases, sentences, and images to delineate the themes forming the drama" (Bantz, 1979, p. 28; cf. Bormann, 1972, p. 401).

IDENTIFYING FANTASY THEMES

Using fantasy theme analysis to facilitate the understanding of an OCC involves identifying recurrent fantasy themes dramatized in the organization's communicative acts and written documents. To accomplish this the analyst will repeatedly examine the fieldwork journal and documents, looking for instances in which the communicators engage in dramatizing events in the there and then.

Careful gathering of data can help immeasurably. Scheibel (1986, 1990) transcribed the recordings of two rock bands' rehearsals and could thus analyze their talk for fantasy themes. Kroll (1983) gathered newsletters from women's organizations and reviewed them to identify the fantasy themes and types central to the movement (see Ex. 7.8).

As the fantasy themes are identified, the analyst makes note of the location of the theme and may elaborate on the context of the theme (the technique is quite similar to that used in describing topical themes in the message analysis step). In repeated reviews of the message pool the analyst will begin to identify the interrelationships among the dramatizations and should develop "memos" describing the dramatic development of fantasy themes.

INTERPRETING FANTASY THEMES

The manner of interpretation of fantasy theme patterns is driven by the analyst's own approach to the concept. One strategy is to engage in a scriptlike analysis, analyzing the heroes and villains, plot line, and the scenes (Bormann et al., 1982). Bormann, as a practicing dramatist, develops his interpretations through narrative dramatizations that are woven around his own basic argument. Thus, in his first published use of fantasy theme analysis he dramatizes the contrast between the drudgery of everyday life for the pioneering Massachusetts Puritans and the richness of the fantasy themes of their religious life (see Ex. 7.9) to argue that rhetorical fantasies "help people transcend the everyday and provide meaning for an audience" (Bormann, 1972, p. 402).

Example 7.9
Puritan New England

The daily routine of the people was one of back-breaking drudgery. The niceties of life were almost nonexistent; music, the arts, decoration of home or clothing, largely unavailable. A discursive description of the emigration and the daily externals of life would be very grim. But the Puritans of Colonial New England led an internal fantasy life of mighty grandeur and complexity. They participated in a rhetorical vision that saw the migration to the new world as a holy exodus of God's chosen people. The Biblical drama that supported their vision was that of the journey of the Jews from Egypt into Canaan. John Cotton's sermon delivered when Winthrop's company was leaving for Massachusetts was on the text, "Moreover I will appoint a place for my People Israell [sic], and I will plant them that they may dwell in a place of their own, and move no more."
(Bormann, 1972, p. 402).

Bormann (1985a) also employs a dramatistic approach in his book-length treatment of U.S. religious and reform speaking. Other researchers using fantasy theme analysis as a technique have utilized different approaches based on other perspectives (e.g., Kroll, 1983, utilizes feminist theory). The organizational interpreter may then approach fantasy theme analysis from a variety of perspectives that can help broaden the understanding of an organizational communication culture. In particular, the careful matching of a perspective to the organization studied should be consistent with and enhance the interpretation. Thus, Kroll's use of feminist theory to study the women's movement advanced her analysis, since those organizations were explicitly committed to feminism.

Following a dramatistic approach in applying fantasy theme analysis to organizational interpretation, one would examine the actual dramatic content of the fantasy themes and assess their contribution to the symbolic construction of the organizational meanings and expectations. Consider the verbal jabs between members of a rock band named The Grind (see Ex. 7.10) and Scheibel's (1990) interpretation.

Example 7.10
Members of the Rock Band "The Grind" in Rehearsal

Darryl: I don't know how to impress this upon you. I know you've never read the manual *Curt,* but this mem . . . this memory protect button has got to stay *on* on either side. The . . . this was just off!
Curt: Is that a fact?
Darryl: Yeah, it was just off!
Curt: Gosh.
Ed: How did it get that way?
Darryl: I guess it doesn't
Curt: I turn that off . . .
Darryl: . . . matter; just keep it out on the porch . . .
Curt: . . . every . . . every night. I switch a different button every night . . .
Darryl: Yeah, well this was just on.
Curt: . . . I had a screwdriver . . .
Darryl: This was *on.* Memory Protect *on.*
Curt: . . . I had the thing all apart. I was lookin' inside of it . . . it was bitchin.
Darryl: This means every . . . program we got is . . . up!
Curt: . . . you did it again man . . . I tell ya.
Darryl: Yeah, you did.
Curt: That's a nice story. He's gonna tell that story, uh, Sunday night . . . I wrecked the Juno [name of keyboard] . . . anyway, and then we're gonna play "Geisha Girl" [name of a song].

Bob: Don't take the Juno, you'll kill yourself.
Curt: And then, I better turn around and look and double-check
. . .
Darryl: You'd think he'd . . . read the manual . . . no, it's in . . .
English and . . .
Curt: . . . that the keyboard player, like, hasn't left the stage . . .
Darryl: . . . that . . . blows my mind!
Curt: . . . because he might have found out that I ruined his guitar
two weeks before I wrecked the Juno . . .
Darryl: Well, you keep it out in the rain and you know you . . .
Curt: I wonder if he knows about the time that I, like, was playing
catch with the Marshall [name of guitar amplifier]?
Darryl: God! I own part of this thing [the keyboard] . . . why don't
we just chop it in thirds!
(Scheibel, 1990, pp. 160–161)

Scheibel argues that in the exchange Curt makes several attempts to involve Darryl in dramatizing his fantasy of destroying instruments ("I had the thing all apart," "I wrecked the
Juno," "I ruined his guitar," "I was playing catch with the Marshall"). Finally, at the end of the exchange Darryl joins in with
"Why don't we just chop it in thirds!" Scheibel interprets the
fantasy theme as reflective of the conflict within the group:

> The fantasy of destroying various musical instruments can
> be interpreted as a metaphor for the conflict within the
> band. . . . Darryl's comment about chopping the keyboard
> into thirds is a reference to the fact that the keyboard is
> jointly owned by Darryl, Curt, and Ed. The parceling out of
> the fantasized "thirds" of the keyboard is the symbolic de-
> struction of the band. (Scheibel, 1990, pp. 160–161)

By examining the fantasy themes dramatized in the band's rehearsals Scheibel demonstrates how the fantasy themes contribute to the construction of the group's self-definition. The band
members expect one another to take different roles. They expect
conflict to appear over their common property (and, by interpretation, their common identity as a band).

The power of fantasy theme analysis in analyzing messages of
an organization is that fantasy themes are frequently anchored
in the fundamental issues of an organization. Thus, by paying
attention to them it is possible to gain insight into collective constructions of meaning. In the band named The Grind the fantasy
of destruction becomes one of division, which was a critical as-

pect of the band's interpretation of its organization. Conflict and division were central constructs of their organizational meaning. Fantasy themes can provide access to the organization's characterization of relationships, conflicts, heroes, villians, successes, and failures.

Conclusion

This chapter presents metaphors, stories, and fantasy themes as three symbolic forms whose analysis can contribute significantly to understanding organizational communication cultures. Any one of these forms may play the central role in the interpretation of an organization. The organizational interpreter needs to consider the potential contribution of each form in the context of the specific organization being studied. From that consideration one, two, or all three forms may be examined in depth. Furthermore, the interrelationship among the forms may be worthy of consideration, for metaphors may be present in stories and fantasy themes, stories are the source of many fantasy themes, fantasy themes may highlight metaphors, and so on.

The goal of analyzing messages and symbolic forms is to contribute to better understanding organizations, in particular, to provide the basis for inferring organizational expectations and meanings. The examples given in chapters 6 and 7 foreshadow how vocabulary, themes, temporality, and architecture, metaphors, stories, and fantasy themes contribute to understanding expectations and meanings. The following two chapters detail the concepts of organizational expectations and meanings and how they can be inferred from the analysis of messages and symbolic forms.

CHAPTER EIGHT

Inferring Organizational Expectations: Norms, Roles, Agenda, Motives, and Style

Who has the right to do what with whom, when, where, how, how often, and why?
—adapted from D. M. Schneider

Communication involves creating, maintaining, and transforming the co-orientation of behavioral expectations (Chaffee & McLeod, 1968). Expectations are intertwined with meanings, since meaning is the basis on which expectations are constituted. Organizational expectations are manifested as the taken-for-granted patterns of members' coordinated behavior. In order to coordinate their action organizational members develop commonly understood patterns of expectations for organizational behavior. Nearly an infinite variety of expectations for organizational behavior can develop—for example, violence is normal or prohibited, talk is task oriented on Tuesday, Wednesday and Thursday and social on Monday and Friday, executives are frequently transferred and never fired.

This chapter describes the basic patterns of expectations manifested in organizational communication cultures and suggests how those patterns are inferred from message and symbolic form analyses. Such inferences are made before, during, and after the other steps. That is, the process of discerning expectations will begin early in the analysis and continue throughout the project.

Expectations can be characterized in five patterns: norms, roles, agenda, motives, and style. Norms, as discussed below, form the basis of expectations, with the other four hierarchically related to it. The five patterns of organizational expectations include concepts that are widely used in social research (e.g., norms) as well as concepts particular to organizational analysis (e.g., agenda) and concepts that are defined in a different manner than the one typically used (i.e., style). The remainder of this chapter describes each of these concepts, outlines how they may be identified, and illustrates each one from analyses of organizational communication cultures.

Norms

The concept of norm is a venerable social scientific concept that has been articulated by numerous authors (Gibbs, 1965, provides a good review). Following Schneider (1976), norms are patterns for action, with the focus on an imperative: action. Thus, a norm is: (1) a pattern indicating what persons should do in a particular setting, rather than simply reflecting what a person does; (2) "a collective expectation as to what behavior will be; and/or (3) particular reactions to behavior" (Gibbs, 1965, p. 589). In short, norms are expectations for appropriate behavior.

Norms are central to understanding organizational communication cultures. In identifying norms (e.g., male IBMers wearing white shirts, dark suits, dark ties, dark socks, and dark shoes, as in Ex. 7.2) we begin to infer expectations for behavior within a culture. By focusing on expectations for action (cf. Homans, 1950, p. 123) we focus on a fundamental aspect of collective behavior. Friedman (1989), for example, analyzes the 1979 International Harvester labor negotiations and argues that management's violation of interaction norms contributed to a disasterous six-month strike, which was followed by bankruptcy. Even in less serious situations, such as the IBM intern's story (Ex. 7.2), norms and their violations reveal valuable information. Some organizational scholars have used the term *rules* to refer to a similar sense of expected appropriate behavior (e.g., Schall, 1983). An understanding of norms may facilitate both "fitting in" an organization as well as initiating change within it, since an understanding of appropriate behavior enables one to strategically follow or disrupt those expectations.

Norms are fundamental to the four other patterns of expectations, inasmuch as what a person *should* do is central to what roles are taken, what people attribute as reasons for behavior (motives), expectations about how time is structured (agenda), and the style of communication expected. Norms are fundamental to inferring organizational expectations.

The ontological status of norms rests on their inference from messages and symbolic forms. The vocabulary used, the themes presented, and the message's architecture all can provide a basis for inferring norms within the OCC. Additionally, metaphor, fantasy themes, and stories provide a rich portrayal of what constitutes normative behavior and the violations of norms. The analyst discovers norms by interpreting patterns within messages as evidence of expectations of appropriate behavior.

INFERRING NORMS

Norms may be gleaned from the message pool by identifying aspects of messages that constitute appropriate behavior. By noting the prevalence and "approval" or "disapproval" of specific patterns of behavior in the message pool one can begin to identify norms.

Vocabulary analysis is a useful first step in inferring norms. If we note, for example, that the consistent vocabulary usage in addressing a superior is by title (e.g., Captain, Dr., President) and the person's last name, we can use this pattern to identify a form of address norm within the OCC. If violations of this form of address yield "corrections" (e.g., "It is *Captain* Ahab to you!"), then the norm is even more distinct. The genre of vocabulary itself represents normative expectations of the type of discourse within an organization. The colloquial and frequently obscene and scatological vocabulary of the military—as represented in the films *Platoon, Gardens of Stone,* and *Apocalypse Now*—suggests different norms of vocabulary usage than the daily discourse within most religious institutions.

Norms may also be inferred from the message pool by identifying themes that represent appropriate and inappropriate behavior. A theme in television news organizations is speed in accomplishing work; repeated harsh references to a slow-working reporter as "molasses," for example, suggest that rapidity is an important behavioral expectation in television news reporting (Bantz et al., 1980).

Themes may so represent norms by their very occurrence. Themes—that is, repetitive topics in communicative interactions and documents—can be used to gauge to what extent repetition and embedded topicality is appropriate in the organization.

While it would be easy to assume that all organizations define themes as presenting appropriate behavior, organizations differ in the extent to which repetitive topics are appropriate. The American Automobile Association suggests that careful repetition in vocabulary and topics indicates professionalism in quick oil change shops; fast-food restaurants teach employees limited and often repeated themes and vocabulary (not simply for use with customers but also among themselves). Contrast these two organizations with those such as "think-tanks," advertising agencies, and academic institutions, where "lack of originality" is a devastating critique.

Temporal patterns identified in the analysis of messages are valuable bases for inferring norms and often relate to other elements of message and symbolic form analysis. Later we will examine temporal patterns as they relate to agenda.

Architectural analysis contributes to an understanding of norms as patterns of arrangement; violations of those patterns will suggest appropriate behavior. The distinct pattern sequence of talk in some organizations gives evidence of norms. The pattern in meetings of making decisions through the use of "motions," "seconds," "discussion," and "voting," for example, represents a normative expectation built on the architecture of interaction. (This also illustrates how behavior shapes norms and norms shape behavior.) Examining physical architecture will also contribute to understanding norms. For example, after examining an office that has a high counter separating the staff from the customers, including a gate that closes off the open end of the counter and a note on the staff side of the gate which says, "please close the gate" and, on the public side, "employees only" it is easy to infer that appropriate behavior for customers in that office is to remain in front of the counter and not to enter the staff area.

Stories are a rich source for dramatizing appropriate behavior. Stories have long been important in socializing group members to understand "right" and "wrong." Jicarilla Apaches felt storytelling was so central to socialization that, when a child misbehaved, people asked whether the child had been told the stories, which served as a reprimand (Wilkins, 1983, p. 83). The story of IBM chairman Tex Watson, Jr., deferring to the request for proper identification by a security guard can clearly be used to infer appropriate behavior both by management and employees; the story portrays rules that apply to even the highest level of management and that the lowest level of employee is to apply to all (Mumby, 1987, offers an alternative deep-structure intepretation of the story). Frequently, stories will suggest appropriate behavior by dramatizing the success or failure of organizational members. Thus, Example 8.1 presents "Gerri" relating cryptic insider stories of "how far X has gone" by telling how the founder (Merle) and a district manager (Frank) built their way to their current positions.

Example 8.1
Employees of a Medical Products Firm

Gerri: Wasn't always this good. Merle started out in a garage doing all of our jobs every single day. This route is nice that Frank built up. Two years ago Frank was selling coffins, now he's a district manager making six digits out West. What ya think Dave, maybe he'll hire us to clean his house for $50,000 a year? [*laughter*]
Dave: Talk to ya later, Ger.

(Haugen, 1985)

Metaphors can contribute to inferences of norms. Decomposed metaphors may reveal either substantively or structurally appropriate relationships and behavior. The metaphor can constitute a relationship between the focus and frames that demonstrates a norm, such as "leader" and "friendly" (Pepper, 1987). How that relationship is to be interpreted depends upon the prevalence or potency of the metaphor and whether its construction in a discourse constitutes approval. The prevalence of a metaphor gives weight simply by virtue of repetition, whereas its potency provides weight by virtue of the power of a metaphor (e.g., cancer metaphors, see Sontag, 1978).

The constitution of a metaphor within a discourse can dramatically influence the contribution of the metaphor to norms, for the same metaphor can be intended approvingly or disapprovingly. If the metaphor of "friendly leader" is frequently presented in discourse that positively portrays leadership, friendliness, and their metaphoric relationship, then the metaphor can be used to infer that leadership friendliness is normative. Krizek (1990, chap. 4) proposes that one interpretation of the metaphor "He has the X-factor" is that successful players "have heart"—such players will go the extra mile to succeed. Thus, the metaphor implies that here the expected behavior is to work hard in order to succeed.

The complexity of metaphors makes understanding their relationship to the message pool essential. A negatively loaded metaphor (e.g., he is a bear) could be consistently dramatized positively (e.g., he is a bear, but fair) and be seen as evidence of the appropriateness of supervisors who are demanding. Such a metaphor could be steadily dramatized as negative and destructive (e.g., he is a bear foaming at the mouth), which could develop a negative definition of the behavior expected within the organization.

It is possible that metaphors may be dramatized in both a positive and negative light. This variance suggests different expectations about behavior by superiors which need to be located within patterns of expectations held by diverse groups, levels, or special units within the organization. "He is a bear," for example, may be a compliment when spoken by subordinates and a complaint when spoken by top management. Such a finding would lead to the identification of a "metanorm"—that is, a norm with an inconsistent definition, or opposing definitions, of appropriate behavior within the organization. In this case we have institutionalized symbolic conflict, or conflict among expectations and meanings.

Bormann et al. (1978) demonstrate that fantasy theme analysis can suggest group norms. Although working toward a different goal than the one discussed here, Bormann and his colleagues identify fantasy themes for each group in a simulated organization. These themes centered around power, sex, and leadership. Bormann and his associates assess how these fantasy themes became intertwined with the patterns of group development, particularly those concerning leadership. For the group labeled ITE, for example, the occurrence of sexual fantasizing was related to the tension built up around the norm that a female group member exercised de facto leadership through the power of the secretarial role (pp. 133–134). Thus, the fantasizing can, as in this example, cast the norms into relief by providing a break from a behavior that is accepted but not preferred by group members. (Bormann et al. suggest that the sexual fantasizing also reasserted male dominance of females generally and of the secretary specifically.) Fantasizing can also reveal and positively support norms, such as in the group labeled MMC, in which fantasies of a group without game playing and sexist judging of people were related to the emergence of female leadership as appropriate behavior in the group (pp. 129–130).

Norms of appropriate organizational behavior can be inferred from the analysis of messages and symbolic forms as the analyst considers both the constitution of norms through communicative forms (e.g., vocabulary, themes, architecture) and the dramatization of norms within communicative forms (e.g., themes, metaphors, fantasy themes). Inferring norms is critical to understanding the expectations of the organization and roles, agendas, motives, and styles.

Roles

Like norms, roles are a traditional social science concept. In addition to the social science notion, however, the examination of roles has a venerable history in literary analysis, particularly in drama studies. Role has been defined in a variety of ways, reflecting different applications of the concept. A useful working definition is Johnson's (1977) notion that roles are characterized by differential rights and responsibilities.

Roles are important to collective action. Katz and Kahn (1978) argue that organizations are an open system of roles, emphasizing the concept of role behavior instead of the concept of role. For Katz and Kahn role behavior is "the recurring actions of an individual, appropriately interrelated with the repetitive activities of others so as to yield a predictable outcome" (p. 189). In communication research role has been extensively used in group communication theory, which emphasizes those roles that emerge in the group interaction (e.g., Bormann, 1990, chap. 7; Fisher & Ellis, 1990, chap. 8). Group theorists emphasize the dynamic nature of roles by defining them as "that set of perceptions and expectations shared by the members about the behavior of an individual in both the task and social dimensions of group interacton" (Bormann, 1990, p. 161). In organizational communication research roles have been discussed much less explicitly. Organizational communication textbook writers have typically emphasized issues of role conflict and stress based on Katz and Kahn (1978, chap. 7), but devoted much less attention to roles than have group communication authors. An exception is the intense interest by organizational communicational researchers and theorists in superior-subordinate communication (see Jablin, 1979).

Identifying roles is valuable for understanding the patterns of expectations that are present in an OCC. The dramatistic aspect of roles—that is, that roles are something individuals play—is critical to a view that sees organizations as collective creations that are constantly developing and changing. Hence, inferring roles from the message pool utilizing the elements of message analysis and symbolic form analysis is essential.

The inference of roles, like norms, can proceed from the constitution of role in vocabulary, themes, architecture, and temporality as well as the dramatization of roles through the substance of message forms and symbolic forms. In discussing the differential rights and responsibilities that one manifested in communication the inextricable link between norms and roles will become apparent.

ROLES CONSTITUTED

Vocabulary is a useful basis for inferring roles in the OCC. Vocabulary related to roles includes titles (e.g., CEO, President, Queen, Pope) and forms of address (e.g., Sir, Madame, Your Highness, Your Holiness). Such vocabulary usage points to differentiation among members of organizations. By examining both to whom titles and specific forms of address are applied and who uses which titles and forms of address differentiation in the rights of the members becomes visible. The question of who in an organization addresses the chief executive officer by first name, for example, may be indicative of differential role rights (see Peters & Waterman, 1982, p. 75). Whether your superior is a "boss" or a "sponsor" may be an important indicator of different role expectations (see Pacanowsky, 1988, p. 358). Similarly, the use of titles among peers indicates certain role expectations—such as shared formality—in some organizations.

Themes can constitute roles, as repetitive and embedded topics can both enact and substantively reveal differential rights and responsibilities. A commander, for example, by telling a "joke" about recruits who failed boot camp and had to repeat it, reinforces the differences between commanders (who can fail people) and recruits (who can be failed). Similarly, a theme of "taking a break" can be constitutive of role differentiation when it is consistently initiated by the supervisor and followed by those supervised.

In addition to themes enacting roles the substance of themes can indicate roles. The appropriate and inappropriate exercise of rights is likely to be one topic of communication within organizations. Documents will often very specifically develop themes about appropriate role fulfillment (e.g., sales associates should greet every new customer within 30 seconds). Communicative acts will also frequently include themes of members' responsibilities and rights, such as, in the case of a worker's grievance, "You can take it to the union." Because the themes will be plentiful, the analyst's task will be to identify the most salient ones, which will be useful in inferring roles, and to locate interrelated themes to help portray the complexity of roles.

Temporality may help the interpreter infer roles by illuminating (1) for whom the pace of messages varies, (2) who speaks with greater or lesser speed, and (3) for whom message flow stops. Thus, a rapid increase in messages prior to the visit of the CEO and a substantial decrease in messages during the visit illustrate variation in message pace, which contributes to understanding the rights of the organizational members vis-à-vis the CEO. In some organizations speaking rate may be indicative of role, as when subordinates speak quickly, apparently not to take up the superior's time, while superiors speak at a relaxed pace. Finally, the sudden stopping of message exchange when a superior seeks to enter the conversation may point to differences in the rights of organizational members.

Architecture may contribute to roles by fixing the location of various members. The arrangement of space may confer rights of access. Having an office near the highest-ranking person suggests greater ease of access, thus potentially altering roles. Further, space and location (e.g., relative size, floor level) will probably indicate a member's role. DeLorean's description of the fourteenth floor at General Motors illustrates both aspects. Being on the fourteenth floor gave the occupants a greater right of access to one another than to offices on other floors, and the offices were arranged to reflect the executive's specific place in the hierarchy (see Wright, 1979, chap. 2). The architecture of memos may also suggest role relationships—or how roles are changing. Since electronic mail systems provide a template for messages, the change in structure from paper memos to electronic ones will highlight the structure of all types of memos (Kersten &

Phillips, 1992, explore the symbolic dimensions of electronic mail for impression management).

As members use metaphors, these metaphors articulate relationships. Thus, as an organization's message pool is filled with metaphors such as "the CEO is our Moses" or people are metaphorically labeled (e.g., "water walkers," boy or girl "wonders," "high fliers," Kanter, 1977, p. 133), then how members utilize and interpret these metaphors can be inferred, which helps to clarify roles—including the granting of powerful rights, enormous responsibilities, and the expectation of sacrifice. Finding frequent use of military metaphors in an organization would, for example, indicate various roles. The military employs a hierarchy of distinct roles, thus, the use of military metaphors by an organization often implies differential role relationships (such as the company/generals and the employees/troops in Ex. 7.1).

The act of telling stories itself may constitute differential rights, as it reveals the teller's right to relate that information. The telling of "war stories" by oldtimers in an organization, for example, indicates their rights as keepers of the history and reinforces their role as experienced members (e.g., the veteran computer consultant in Ex. 7.6 who demonstrates how to succeed). Stories are also likely to present differential rights and responsibilities. These stories may be officially condoned and distributed, such as the excellence dramatizations discussed in Peters and Waterman (1982). Thus, a story about a Frito-Lay driver servicing an out-of-the-way store and knowing the sale will be small (Peters & Waterman, 1982, p. 164) can be used to infer the sanctioned responsibilities of drivers. In addition to formally distributed stories there are also informal ones. Andrews (1989) reports such stories about Microsoft programmers who work day and night. These stories make clear that such work is part of the responsibilities of being "on the team" (Kidder, 1981, chap. 3, finds a similar pattern at Data General). The "hippopotamus" story told to me by a department chair (Ex. 7.4) clearly suggests that faculty have the right to disagree with the chair and that the chair's power is limited.

The type of dramatic fantasy themes Kroll (1983; also Ex. 7.8) identified in the women's movement exemplifies how fantasy themes can be used to infer organizational roles. The themes of unity, joining together, working together, and supporting each other certainly suggest that rights and responsibilities are shared equally within the collective. Fantasy themes may provide rich dramatizations of the fatal weaknesses of leaders or powerful successes of leaders; they may exalt or denigrate the members. Considering the characterization of different role relationships and role players will assist in interpreting roles within the organizational communication culture.

The inference of roles will build on the inference of norms and concurrently contribute to identifying those norms. As one examines vocabulary, themes, architecture, temporality, metaphors, stories, and fantasy themes to gauge roles, one must, by definition, sense the appropriateness of various behaviors within the OCC. Roles are a specific area of normative behavior—that associated with members' differential rights and responsibilities. Being able to infer those roles depends upon the interweaving of the various elements of messages and symbolic forms. Vocabulary, for example, is essential in thematic development related to roles (e.g., how titles are used in themes), and vocabulary is essential in considering story dramatization (e.g., is the boss in the story called SOB [son of a bitch] or CEO?). The other elements of analysis will interconnect in order to identify roles. Because of this complexity, the discussion above is designed to be heuristic, not exhaustive.

Agendas

Because temporality is central in inferring the agendas of the organization, the discussion of roles and norms has given minimal attention to temporality. Temporality refers to the pacing, frequency, and speed of messages. Agendas are the expectations of patterned sequences of events and are closely related to roles and norms. Temporal sequencing is often accomplished by people in particular roles who construct expectations about behavior related to time. While the sequencing of events in organizations has not been a dominant focus in social science research, several lines of research have considered sequential events. This research includes developmental theories of leadership (e.g., Hersey & Blanchard, 1982), organizing (Weick, 1979), organizational life cycles (e.g., Hannan & Freeman, 1989; Kimberly & Miles, 1980), group phase development (e.g., Poole, 1983), and socialization (see Jablin, 1987).

The identification of temporal patterns within and between messages provides the key to inferring expectations about the structuring of time in an OCC. The rate of speaking in communicative acts, in conjunction with inferred roles, provides the basis for gauging the expectations about how time is structured within an organization. Identifying high speaking rates with grain traders, for example, can contribute to expectations that the pace of events in the trading pit will be rapid. The cryptic conversation between the two workers in a medical products firm (Ex. 6.1) illustrates the expectation of tight time structures as members speak in a rapid-fire, codelike language—the longest speaking turn is only 11 words; the shortest is 1 word. Grenz (1989) observed the frequent use of technical code terms and quick exchanges, both of which support the inference that paramedics expect time to be tightly structured.

The periodicity of organizational messages, such as weekly sales reports, quarterly profit-loss statements, and yearly balance sheets, suggests the structuring of time in organizations. Thus, "annual" versus "quarterly" performance reviews will provide a basis for understanding the differential structuring of time. Many U.S. corporations prepare quarterly financial reports as well as annual reports. Other organizations, especially with the aid of new technology, prepare weekly or even daily reports. Such organizations reveal distinctive time structures (one week, one month, three months, twelve months). All of these temporal markers serve as indicators of expectations about the structuring of time. Employees governed by wage and hour laws, for example, may expect wages to be paid on a weekly basis, while managers may expect bonuses on an annual basis.

The inference of agendas from the analysis of messages and symbolic forms is based primarily on temporality. Vocabulary, themes, architecture, metaphors, stories, and fantasy themes frequently interrelate with temporality, however, to form agendas.

Vocabulary analysis may highlight an organization's attention to time management. When terms such as *timekeeper, planner,* and *just-in-time coordinator* are found, for example, the analyst will want to explore the organization's attention to time management. The labeling of individuals with nicknames related to time is not uncommon in organizations (e.g., Flash, Speedy, Molasses) and can be used to infer expectations about time structuring— for example, that time is precious. Vocabulary can suggest how time is sequenced, as the phrase "just in time" carries the implication that the ordering of parts is timed to the movement of the assembly line.

Themes can provide a basis for identifying agendas in many organizations. Time and its ordering are frequent themes in organizations that structure time rigidly, with frequent and short deadlines. Thus, in tightly scheduled organizations, such as news services, members will frequently make time a topic of conversation (e.g., Cooper, 1989). Similarly, in the medical products firm Haugen (1985) observed (Ex. 6.3) the theme "3:30 zoom" emerged because members expected the day to reach its busiest peak at 3:30 in the afternoon. Even less intensely scheduled organizations exhibit themes related to agendas. Kanter's (1977) classic analysis of "Industrial Supply Corporation" identified mobility as a major theme tied to career development ("Be promoted or perish," p. 131). The themes of mobility helped construct organizational agendas as "rising" executives sought new opportunities by changing jobs frequently, and individuals were judged on how long they stayed in a job—with long tenure being a negative (chap. 6). Organizations that involve boring work will develop themes that contribute to the structuring of time, particularly break time. The clicker room workers Roy (1959–1960) studied had a web of "Time" themes (coffee time, break time, banana time) that broke up the day (and boring work). Ohlendorf (1983) observed the theme "coffee break" structured time throughout a food-processing organization, for *all* employees, from the management level to those working in the field, took common coffee breaks.

In conjunction with temporality architecture can be used to infer agendas in an OCC. Consider the Roman Catholic church as an organization responsible for the construction, across centuries, of numerous great cathedrals or the ongoing multiyear restoration of the Sistine Chapel. This organization's sequencing of time is dramatically different than that of a Phoenix home builder who built three model homes in 1985 and simply tore them down in 1986 when all the houses in the development had been sold. The observation of an organization's physical and spatial architecture across time will reveal dramatically varying agenda. A high-fashion clothing retailer, for example, will remodel every year or two, put out new clothes each season, and redo displays even more often. In contrast, a Rolls-Royce dealership will remodel and change displays much less frequently.

The architectural pattern of written messages can also be a guide to the sequencing of events, as indicated in our terminology for organizational documents. The hypothetical memo in Example 8.2 illustrates an ordering of sales and returns preceding profits, which precede bonuses:

Example 8.2
Memo to Employees

> *To:* All Employees
> *From:* The Boss
>> → Sales are up 40%
>> → Returns are down 10%
>> → Profits are up 50%
>> → There will be bonuses this year

Temporal metaphors occur in organizational messages and may be used to identify expectations about time. Contrast two metaphors such as "his career is a rocket" and "his career is a no-go." Examination of these two metaphors would suggest that careers have direction (up, down) and that they have a temporality (fast/slow/no-go). The prevalence of such metaphors could suggest the career agenda in a given organization. The metaphor's connection to agenda can be more subtle, as in a manager saying "There is a definite weeding out of employees. . . . I think I'm going to have to play 'Grim Reaper' with a couple of employees" (Nolan, 1991, B4). The metaphor of weeding suggests an agenda: The manager goes through the "field" finding and removing "weeds." The commonplace image of weeding is deliberate and inexorable, suggesting that the weeder will eventually get the weeds. This image of agenda is reinforced by the "Grim Reaper" metaphor, which carries a similar inexorable temporal quality but adds a sense of inevitability.

Stories may develop around temporality in some organizations. In news organizations, for example, you can expect to find numerous stories about the importance and consequence of time structuring, which in turn can be used to infer agenda. It was amusing but not surprising, therefore, to hear the story of how, on a particularly difficult day, the graphic artist made up a visual card to put on the air at news time that read: "We have lost the will to continue. Please stand by." What made the story even more poignant was that the storyteller confided that the

card was destroyed because the newsworkers were afraid someone might actually put it on the air. The story effectively dramatized the intensity of expectations in television news that time be
structured (i.e., rush then go on the air) and the importance of
adhering to those structures ("five o'clock will come, ready or
not" was a theme that appeared in these stories). The scenes in
the film *Broadcast News* (Brooks, 1987) showing the reporter June
Craig (played by Holly Hunter) editing a story up to the last possible minute then rushing through the newsroom, sliding under
an open file drawer, popping the video cassette into the re-
corder at the exact moment it was needed, and, finally, celebrat-
ing beating the clock dramatized the intensity of agenda in
television news.

Fantasy themes may display inferences about agenda as
themes can develop around temporality. The development of a
theme about an individual as a manipulator could easily incorporate temporal aspects (controlling the meeting times and
length) and thus be useful in understanding the sequencing of
time in the organization. A theme of "not enough time" sometimes develops into a full-blown fantasy theme in task groups
when members dramatize the mass of pressures, the limits of
time, and the evil of the taskmasters. In this way organizational
agendas are dramatized as being rigidly, unfairly, and arbitrarily
set by superiors without consulting the employees. Given the
salience of fantasy themes, they may be a major contributor to
inferring the organization's agenda. Again in my observations of
television news organizations, members often dramatized how
they "got on the air in spite of . . ." (e.g., a blizzard, equipment
failure, illness). The vivid portrayals of this theme demonstrate
extremely strong expectations that television news operates on
such a strict agenda that nearly anything should be done to meet
those expectations.

Inferring the expectations of time and event sequencing in an
OCC will utilize vocabulary, themes, architecture, temporality,
metaphors, stories, and fantasy themes. Of the elements of analysis typically temporality will be central in inferring agenda. There
will be an interconnection among the various expectations, such as
roles and norms, so that consideration of other expectations will
facilitate identifying agenda. I hope the examples above have suggested, however, that inferring agenda will involve the interplay of
all aspects of analysis and inference, for the structuring of time is
integral to organizational communication.

Motives

Motives and *motivation* have become everyday terms derived primarily from a psychological view of humans. When most people talk of motivation they are referring to some internal psychological drive that "causes" people to behave in a particular way. Such a viewpoint has a firm foundation in psychological theory (e.g., Maslow, 1970). A view of communication as "driven" by internal motivation has been common in communication—especially in interpersonal communication (e.g., Berger & Calabrese's uncertainty reduction theory, 1975). The motivational view has been extremely important in organizational communication; numerous writers have argued that communication must respond to and shape individual motivation in order to accomplish tasks (e.g., Koehler, Anatol, & Applbaum, 1981, chaps. 6, 7).

While viewing motivation as an internal drive is a valuable perspective, it is not the OCC perspective. Rather than looking at motivation as an internal drive, the focus here is on *motives*, which are defined as *expectations about reasons for behavior inferred from messages*. Motives are inferred from messages—not assumed to be inside people's heads. Motives are identified from the members' attributions of reasons for behavior. The concept is communicatively based because expectations for behavior are manifested in the attribution of reasons in messages. That is, organizational members exchange messages that explicitly and implicitly attribute reasons for behavior and indicate the appropriateness of those reasons. This approach locates motives as *publicly exhibited* in the messages of organizational members and is, therefore, a rhetorical view of motives (cf. Burke, 1969a, 1969b; Fisher, 1970; Mills, 1940). Since the focus of an OCC analysis is on collectively constructed expectations and meanings, the question of individual internal motivation is set aside in OCC analysis.

Attribution theory suggests that individuals attempt to make sense of their actions and their world by attributing causality (oftentimes inaccurately, see Nisbett & Ross, 1980; Nisbett & Wilson, 1977). Motives are the attributed expectations of individual causality. Whether those motives are consistent with psychological reality is not the question in a study of an OCC. The question, instead, is how these motives are defined within the OCC—are they appropriate or inappropriate? Motives may vary within various subgroups of an organization. In a sales department, for example, the expectation attributed most consistently might be that salespeople work to achieve personal financial goals, whereas in a human resources department it might be that Equal Employment Opportunity officers help members of discriminated classes.

Messages about appropriate reasons for behavior may be indirect and subtle or direct and dramatic. An example of the latter appeared in the late 1980s, when the British Conservative government proposed to introduce merit pay to British universities. The public response by a group of Cambridge University professors was quite negative. Professor Anthony Snodgrass's description of the proposal as "squalid exaltation of human greed into not merely a motive force, but a virtue" ("Cambridge profs," 1989, p. 705) illustrates a very clear message about organizational motives.

Organizational analysts can infer the direct or indirect attribution of motives from organizational messages. This would include examining the vocabulary, themes, architecture, temporality, metaphors, stories, and fantasy themes. The substance of these elements of messages and symbolic forms needs to be understood within the context of their expression in order to place the motives within the cultural scheme of what constitutes appropriate behavior.

The organization's vocabulary can provide a rich source of reasons for behavior. By noting which individuals are given value-laden labels (e.g., hustlers, saints, cheats, martyrs, "sleazeballs") and what these people are doing, one can infer the motives attributed to those individuals. Identifying the local understanding of those terms will direct the analyst to reasons for acting. It is always essential to use the culture's interpretation of vocabulary when inferring motives, since one organization's "hustler" may be hard-working, achievement oriented, and seeking recognition, while another organization's "hustler" may be lazy, greedy, and working only for personal gain.

Organizational messages are likely to have themes about motives woven into the text. Why people behave as they do is a frequent topic of conversation in organizations (a principal theme in that genre called gossip). A theme such as "meeting your quota," prevalent among sales workers, could be used to infer motives within a sales unit. Grenz (1989) notes that, among emergency medical service (EMS) personnel the priority employees give to patient care and the priority management places on profitability (including paying the employees low wages) are both frequently discussed. The apparent thematic character of working to provide good patient care, in spite of low pay, provides information that is revealing about the motives expected of EMS personnel.

While architecture is not an obvious source of inferring motives, it may provide some useful evidence. When examining the argumentative form of organizational messages one might glean motives by identifying consistent forms. If there are standard acceptable forms, the violation of those forms may indicate motives. If a particular argumentative form is labeled "manipulative," then to say someone used that form is to attribute a manipulative motive to the person's behavior.

Temporality is unlikely to be a major contributor to understanding motives, but it may, like architecture, direct the analyst to attributions. Temporal patterns and their violation may be associated, for example, with reasons for behavior—thus, when a report is not completed within the typical time span the author (whether individual or committee) may be characterized as having violated the temporal pattern for some reason (e.g., stalling to cover up a failure or deficiency).

Metaphors may express motives in organizational messages through their juxtaposition of individuals and behavior. Thus, metaphors such as " 'The Mad Austrian' is a rapist" (adapted from Hirsch & Andrews, 1983, p. 154) or "Auditors are Draculas" can be analyzed to infer the motives attributed within the OCC. Both of these metaphors present the focus (the Austrian, auditors) in an exploitative act (rape, blood-sucking). Thus, the motives attributed by these metaphors are easily characterized as negative, exploitative, self-aggrandizing, and potentially violent. The analysis of metaphors can be a rich source for discovering motives.

Organizational stories frequently dramatize individuals in action, and, consequently, they present a valuable basis for inferring motives. Stories will often characterize individuals as good or evil, heroes or villains, moral or immoral; in so doing they suggest explicitly and implicitly why those characters behave as they do.

The possibly apocryphal story of Seymour Cray (founder of Cray Research and the premier supercomputer designer) telling the telephone company representative that he only wants one telephone at his new facility and that is to be on a telephone pole in the parking lot vividly depicts the work of creative engineers as too important to be bothered by telephone calls. This cue, combined with other data, suggests that at Cray the best reasons for acting are to do creative engineering, not to carry out bureaucratic imperatives.

The story of the successful baseball player J. W. (Krizek, 1990; also Ex. 7.5) presents the motive for honing one's skills through extra practice. The story explicitly tells of the extra dollars J. W. will get in his next contract and demonstrates that those skills helped move J. W. from the minor to the major leagues.

Religious organizations are rife with rich stories attributing reasons to members' extraordinary actions. Thus, the sacrifices of missionaries bringing the "word" to the countryside (e.g., John Wesley and the circuit riders), the martyrdom of youth in the war between Iran and Iraq, the commitment of Mother Teresa to India's poor, and the valiant defense and deadly fall of Masada are all stories that provide rich dramatizations of individuals and a solid basis for inferring the value of motives within their respective religious organizations.

Bormann (1972) argues that fantasy theme analysis provides an avenue for identifying motives within groups. By examining the dramatization in the "there and then" of a fantasy theme the analyst may well find a reflection of the organizational activities in the "here and now," including attributions of motives. Thus, Bormann and his colleagues (1978, pp. 129–130) argue that the MMC group dramatized sexuality as gender, that gender was unrelated to ability, and that game playing was unnecessary. Their analysis can easily be used to infer inappropriate and appropriate reasons for acting in the group (e.g., that sex-role stereotyping would be inappropriate). In the messages of a very different group Bormann (1972; also Ex. 7.9) identifies motives for action in the dramatic fantasy of the Massachusetts Puritans' appointment as the current representatives of the people of Israel. When groups develop such dramatic fantasy themes, with rich and powerfully expressed motives, inferring attributions from them will be quite simple.

By examining the elements of messages and symbolic forms, the analyst has a complex basis for inferring attributions of behavior within an OCC. The major task is to compare the various attributed reasons and to develop a description of motives that reflect not solely an individual's expectations but also those that are understood broadly within the OCC. In so doing the analyst may locate the parameters of subgroups in the OCC, as variation in motives is often a distinct marker of subcultural differences.

Style

The concept of organizational communication style grows out of the notion of communicator style (Bormann, 1980, chap. 3; Norton, 1978). *Style* here refers to the expectations of how people will communicate with one another in a particular organization. The focus is on the tone and feeling of communication in an organization. By emphasizing "tone and feeling" organizational communication style can be seen as analagous to the meteorological metaphor of communication climate (Johnson, 1977, chap. 4, uses the term *climate* in a way very similar to my use of *style*). The power of the meteorological metaphor is that meteorologists don't just describe a day as good or bad; they also have a panoply of bipolar terms such as: *hot/cool, humid/dry, changing/ stable, high pressure / low pressure, polluted / not polluted, clear/ cloudy.* Similarly, organizational communication styles can be labeled as hot/cold, weak/strong, painful/pleasurable, happy/ sad, friendly/unfriendly, task/social, and so forth.

Once again the elements of message analysis and symbolic form analysis provide the basis for inferring the expectations of style. The substance of the elements needs to be considered in the context of their development inside the organization's communication.

Vocabulary and its limits can be useful in identifying communication style. By contextualizing labels and terms, such as the use of *SOB* within a health care organization (Pettegrew, 1982) or *Your Holiness* in a religious organization, the analyst gains a basis for inferring expectations about how members communicate. Thus, finding obscenities used as a common form of address in an army basic-training camp is valuable in understanding patterns of communication style. In Example 3.1 a police officer says "I love [being back at work]" after bantering with four other officers and referring to one's friend as a "hooker" with "needlemarks." Such a response suggests that bantering in street language is pleasurable in a police organization and that such a style of interaction is expected. D. Brown's (1991) study of a hair salon provides a contrast in vocabulary and style. Brown notes that "never does anyone enter without a receiving 'Hi' or leave without receiving a 'Bye' accompanied by the usual name or nickname from those within eyeshot. Regardless of what they were doing, each of the employees took a moment to do this" (p. 7). In such an organization the expected style of communication appears to be "polite cordial."

Organizational themes may directly support inferences about style. Members may develop communication as a theme in conversation, discussing the organization's friendliness, warmth, support, or hostility (e.g., "I love how friendly everyone is around here"). The thematic development may clarify the implications of such labels, as when a statement such as "Everyone always yells at people here" is coupled with "Don't take it personally—it's just the pressure of time." An organization may have a specific stylistic theme, such as "pimping/ripping" (i.e., criticizing and teasing members) and "sharing" (i.e., disclosing personal information to other members). Organizational members talk about how other members communicate, and, as a result, organizational communication style may become thematic. By identifying themes the interpreter can then infer expectations of how members communicate.

Architecture's influence on the ability to communicate makes it important in inferring an OCC's style. The physical arrangement of space and messages can dramatically limit or encourage communication. Therefore, it is vital to carefully examine message architecture to gauge style.

The arrangement of space to limit accessibility to certain areas and facilitate it in others will help clarify the expectations of a closed communication style. Thus, when Kidder (1981) describes Data General's building it is clear that outsiders are shut out of the facility by a plain building with a single entrance, which is supervised by a guard. The engineers in the basement function in an extremely open "bullpen" office setting, while further up the hierarchy the office arrangements become more closed or distant. Recognizing these differences is useful when considering the expectations for how one communicates in the various settings—formal, perhaps curt interaction with outsiders at the entrance to the building; intense, frequent communication among engineers; and variable frequency of communication with managers. Architecture in the form of

structural arrangement and intensity structure is vital to inferring style. The patterned structures of verbal messages also are
important markers of expectations of how one communicates.
Organizations in which communicative interaction consists simply of requests and responses (e.g., in an emergency room one
hears "scalpel," and a scalpel is handed over) is a different style
of organizational communication than one in which titles are exchanged, cards are exchanged, coffee is drunk, small talk is exchanged, requests are made, and answers are given.

The speed and pace of message exchange illustrates how temporality influences expectations about how one communicates.
The expectation of fast or slow message production and fast or
slow speaking rates will form a critical element in an OCC style.
The leisurely pace of a luncheon meeting contrasts with the rapidity of activities at a television studio, a commodity exchange,
or a hockey rink. A television director's messages are rapid, in a
staccato, sometimes brusque, and coded form. Television camera operators expect such a style of communication. Similarly, in
other organizations messages are delivered in a much more leisurely pace, with casualness the expectation, not the exception.
In these contrasting settings the temporality of messages is critical to characterizing style.

Consider the contrast between two commonplace metaphors
"Fred is a shark" and "Fred is a puppy dog." If one of these metaphors were embedded in a characterization of how Fred communicates, then the metaphor could make a substantial
contribution to identifying expectations about how a person
communicates within that organization. Thus, being a shark
could include being viciously argumentative, and being a puppy
dog could mean being friendly and supportive. Clearly, those
metaphors will make a contribution to understanding other expectations, but they do have implications for style as well.

Stories may well dramatize organizational communication
style as they portray patterns of communication directly or indirectly. It is sometimes easy to infer expectations of how one
communicates from many organizational stories. Example 8.3
presents a story told by an employee of a manufacturing company with sales of over a billion dollars a year (Carver, n.d.).
This story demonstrates that a manager will speak disparagingly
about employees to a subordinate. If other such examples are
found, one may infer from the language of "control" and "firing" that arrogance is an acceptable communication style for a

Example 8.3
Manufacturing Company Employee

When I leave _____ I think the only thing I'll always remember is the way they treated people. I've never worked for a company that seemed to care less about its people. I remember one time John told me that he was in Brian's office, Brian was the manager of the division, and he was looking out the glass windows of his office at the people working in the main office. Our division was set up so that all the managers had their offices on the outside wall and everyone else was in the center. Anyway, Brian looks out the window and says to John, "Just look at all those people I can control. If they don't like it, I'll fire them all. It's not their job to think out there."

(Carver, n.d., p. 3)

superior. Such a story offers significant material for gauging how one communicates in that organization. Contrast such a story with the entertaining, humorous, sociable storytelling manner in Roy's (1959–1960) clicker room, where stories were invented about "Danelly's Farm," patterned after "Old McDonald Had a Farm," and "George's daughter's marriage," a teasing story about aspirations for upward mobility.

Fantasy themes may develop around organizational members that include a dramatization of how the individual, or a class of individuals (e.g., supervisors), communicates within the organization. Thus, dramatization of a theme of a supervisor as Machiavellian may include suggestions that the superior communicates in a very cold and calculating manner. The story of Brian the manager and John the supervisor (Ex. 8.3) may develop into a widely shared and dramatized story such that it begins to develop the characteristics of a fantasy theme—including elaborations of Brian's willingness to fire ("he's going to fire us all") and his lowered expectations for employees ("No thinking allowed!"). The story could clearly be dramatized into an oppression theme: "The boss wants no thought, but, if we don't think, things go wrong, and we get blamed. Either way we get fired!" Either interpretation would have a potentially dramatic effect in defining expectations about communicating with the manager.

These elements of analysis can directly or indirectly contribute to inferences about style within an organizational communication culture. The elements may present the style by explicitly referring to communicative behavior, or they may imply aspects of communicative behavior that can be used to infer style.

Interrelationship of Patterns of Expectations

This chapter demonstrates that the five patterns of expectations are not independent concepts. Instead, they are interrelated and reciprocal. The expectations of rights and responsibilities characteristic of roles involve expectations about appropriate behavior (norms). Agendas are developed as expectations about the structuring of time are interwoven with expectations of appropriate behavior and role responsibilities. Motives are embedded in norms and roles and are frequently connected to agendas and style. Thus, in developing an understanding of each of the patterns of expectations the analyst will also develop an understanding of the interrelationship of expectations. These interconnections foreshadow the rich web of organizational meanings that arise in an even more complex pattern than expectations. The next chapter will explore how one can infer organizational meanings in and from analyzing messages and symbolic forms and inferring expectations.

CHAPTER NINE

Inferring Organizational Meanings: Constructs and Relations among Constructs

The world's no blot for us,
Nor blank; it means intensely, and means good:
To find its meaning is my meat and drink.
— Fra Lippo Lippi

Organizational meanings provide the symbolic cement that makes understanding an organization possible. These meanings are identified through the analysis of messages and symbolic forms and the inference of organizational expectations. If we are to understand organizational communication cultures, then we must explore meaning. This chapter prepares us for that exploration by outlining the nature of organizational meanings and describing how those meanings are inferred. The use of examples from previous chapters will demonstrate how deducing organizational meanings is interdependent with message analysis, symbolic form analysis, and the inference of expectations.

Organizational Meanings

The meaning of *meaning* has long been a venerable conundrum for philosophy and rhetoric, anthropology and sociology, literature and history, communication and psychology. While I am not about to answer such a long-standing question here, to understand organizational communication cultures it is necessary to explore "meaning" — specifically organizational meaning (cf. Eisenberg, 1986).

From the OCC perspective it is important to keep in mind that the interest is in *organizational meanings*, not individual meanings. Again, organizational meanings are inferred from the analysis of messages and symbolic forms and the examination of expectations. Thus, while organizational members have individual systems of meaning, they are not of concern to the OCC analyst.

Meaning is operationalized here as two related elements: constructs and relations among constructs (cf. Gray et al., 1985). Both emerge in the collective action of communication, both persist through reconstitution and patterning, and both change through constitution and pattern modification.

CONSTRUCTS

Organizations create constructs by "transforming" entities, actions, and events into organizationally defined entities, actions, and events (Pacanowsky & O'Donnell-Trujillo, 1982). In communication organizational members can transform concepts into organizational constructs. The term *construct* is a literal representation of the collective process of transformation. Members communicating together transform a generalized concept into an organizationally specific referent that is recognizable to members of the organizational communication culture. The process is analogous to the scientist transforming the concept of stage fright into a scientific construct such as communication apprehension. In both cases the transformation is only accomplished if the construct is recognizable within the particular collective (i.e., the organization or research community).

Concepts become constructs as organizational members come to recognize and understand the common referent. Members hear each other refer to the concept in a similar manner, they come to comprehend the reference, and they may (or may not) come to accept the referent. Some constructs are very straightforward. It is common, for example, for an organizational construct to emerge around the "users" of organizations. Thus, "customer" may be a construct in retail stores, "student" may be a construct in educational institutions, "client" may be a construct in law firms, and "patient" may be a construct in hospitals.

Some constructs are more abstract. In a study of an intervention/prevention program for at-risk youth Sass (1991) found the construct of "miracles." Miracles referred to the transformation of lives and the return of life through "improved self-esteem, overcoming drug addiction, finishing high school, stable and productive employment, and improvement in family and personal relationships" (p. 15). In this case the construct refers not simply to a person (although the youth themselves might be labeled "miracles") but also to patterns of change across time. Yet, while the construct is more diffuse than "customer," members in this program used the construct in a manner that suggested that they recognized and understood it, and, most likely, most members endorsed it.

The recognizability of constructs is emphasized here because the question is not that members agree with the substance of a construct but that they recognize and can utilize the construct in a manner understandable within the organization. The distinction between recognizability and agreement, understandable use and consistent use, points toward an important aspect of organizational meaning in the OCC perspective. The collective constitution of a construct does not mean that all the members agree on, accept, or are consistent in using a construct. Thus, when organizational meanings are identified by outsiders and presented to members they may respond with "Of course" or "That's right, but I hadn't thought of it that way" (Carbaugh, 1988c, p. xiv) or even anger at private information having been revealed (cf. Bantz, 1983).

Even the notion of ad hoc collectivity members being able to coordinate their actions with limited disclosure in a transcendent experience (e.g., "jamming," Eisenberg, 1990) involves recognizing collective constructs. Eisenberg describes pickup basketball games and musical groups as sometimes having a jamming experience. He argues that skill, structure, setting, and surrender are necessary for jamming to occur. As Eisenberg demonstrates, such occurrences do not require interpersonal disclosure or significant relational development. What is required, however, and suggested by his concepts of skill, structure, setting, and surrender is a recognition of the constructs of basketball *as played*. If some players do not recognize a move as part of a particular play, then that play cannot be accomplished. The team is limited to playing in a manner consistent with collectively recognized constructs (just as they are limited, argues Eisenberg, by the level of common basic technical skill).

It is possible for members to disagree with, refuse to accept, and inconsistently utilize a construct, yet they and other members may recognize and understand its use within the OCC. Thus, the organizational member who recounted his attempt to be fired by his employer in order to gain substantial severance pay understood very well the constructs "well-dressed" and "efficient." When he systematically violated well-established interpretations of behavior, his violations of the construct "well-dressed" and "efficient" were apparently interpreted as inappropriate but were not sufficiently aberrant to lead to his immediate termination (Woutat, 1983). Thus, in this case individuals understood the constructs and their corresponding expectations, yet they were tolerant of violations.

The collective constitution of constructs reflects the public understanding and use of concepts among members of an organization. It does not require agreement on the value, appropriateness, or ethicality of those constructs. Members may understand, for example, that, within their organization, judgment of individuals based on gender is constituted as "sexual discrimination"; as a result, such judgment is prohibited. Yet understanding that construct does not necessarily mean that members will engage in appropriate behavior.

RELATIONSHIPS BETWEEN CONSTRUCTS

As already implied, constructs do not stand in isolation but, rather, are constituted in relationships through communicative and documentary interactions. These relationships can be labeled as causal and correlative relationships (Weick, 1979, chaps. 3, 5, 7; cf. Gray et al., 1985). The construct of sexual discrimination, for example, could be constituted in a set of relationships with the constructs "illegality," "trouble," "sexism," and "racism," whereby there is a pattern of causal and correlative relationships, as suggested in Figure 9.1. For ease of discussion I will refer to multiple relations among constructs as "constellations" of constructs.

Figure 9.1
A causal chain from the correlates racism and sexism to trouble, showing relations among constructs (#1).

racism | sexism → sexual discrimination → illegality → trouble

In Figure 9.1 racism and sexism are seen as related to one another but are not in a causal relationship; hence, their relationship is identified as correlational (I). Racism and sexism are identified as having a causal effect in increasing sexual discrimination, which in turn causes illegal acts (e.g., harassment), which in turn causes trouble (e.g., lawsuits). This simple linear model suggests causal relationships between the constructs "sexism," "sexual discrimination," "illegality," and "trouble." Each of these constructs would be organizationally established (e.g., the sexism of one organization may not be the sexism of another), and the relations among them would also be organizationally established. Figure 9.2 presents a quite different relationship among these constructs.

Figure 9.2
A causal chain from trouble to the correlates sexism and racism,
showing relations among constructs (#2).

$$\text{trouble} \rightarrow \text{sexual discrimination} \begin{array}{l} \nearrow \ \text{sexism I racism} \\ \searrow \ \text{illegality} \end{array}$$

In Figure 9.2 sexual discrimination is seen as a consequence of organizational trouble (which, in this model, could include economic recession or management failure). Sexism, then, is a consequence of discriminatory action (this logical relationship is similar to the model that assumes behavioral changes precede attitude change). Illegality is a consequence of sexual discrimination. In the Figure 9.2 model the pattern of organizational meanings constitutes a different meaning for sexual discrimination than the model represented in Figure 9.1. In Figure 9.2 sexual discrimination is caused by organizational troubles and causes sexism. In Figure 9.1 sexual discrimination is located in a scheme of causality as an effect of sexism. Organizations with different relations among constructs would have significantly different organizational meanings for specific constructs, such as sexual discrimination.

Organizational meanings are constructs and relations among constructs. These relations may themselves become subsumed by a single construct (see "good work" below). Complex relations among constructs are likely to emerge in organizations. These multirelations are constellations of constructs; there are multiple constructs in multiple relations that are emerging, changing, and disappearing, just as constellations of stars develop, change, and disappear. Patterns of constructs may be simple and direct, complex and indirect, stable and changing. The inference of organizational meanings, then, must incorporate these characteristics of constructs and their relations.

Inferring Organizational Meanings

Inferring organizational meanings is not a formulaic activity. The discussion below is heuristic, not definitional. Inference of constructs and relationships among constructs may be a dramatic insight (an "ah ha!" experience), or it may emerge by carefully working through the various steps in the method. As the following examples illustrate, the working through may involve a series of inferences based on the elements of messages, symbolic forms, or expectations. Thus, in one case I may find that the vocabulary in a story and the story's form help clarify organizational roles, and from that series the meaning of the construct "boss" can be inferred.

Figure 9.3, proposed by Scheibel (personal communication, 1988), helps one to visualize this process of "inferring in" the OCC method. The figure suggests that the organizational intepreter may take a variety of paths to inferring constructs and relations among constructs. In Scheibel's illustration the terms *The Champ, double-quick,* and *winners* are related to the theme of "get the job done." There are stories about the Champ getting the job done and about the role of expediter as it connects to the norm of good work. These stories build into the constructs of professionalism, efficiency, and practicality, as "champs" do good work yet get the job done double-quick. Thus, in some cases the path might be circuitous as one traces vocabulary through temporality to themes leading to the analysis of a fantasy theme, which incorporates an effective metaphor, the combination of which contributes to inferring organizational motives, which in turn contributes to inferring a construct such as "good work."

Other inferences are much more straightforward. The police chief's newsletter column (Caddow, 1986; also Ex. 1.1) labels the accused ("would-be tough guy," "local armed robber") and presents a story of the pursuit and outcome ("returning to his natural habitat"), clearly characterizing the accused in a negative manner. Stein (1991) observed a restaurant in which "doing a

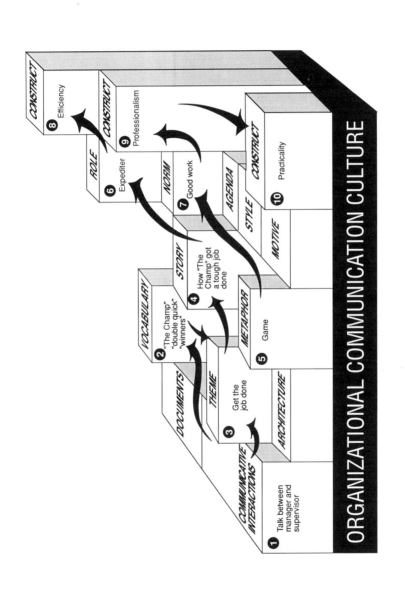

Figure 9.3
The process of inference making in the OCC method.

Source: D. Scheibel
Artist: K. Pepper

good job" was a construct that integrated themes of tipping and income, which in turn were related to agenda, since the structuring of time in a restaurant influences a server's income (i.e., faster service means better tips; faster service means more tables served). Organizations frequently display prevalent constructs, such as "good work," in overt ways. In such cases the examination of vocabulary will begin framing the organization's constructs.

Inferring organizational meanings will be iterative, for identifying a single construct is only one step toward understanding an organization. While some constructs are as accessible as "criminal" is to a police department or "good work" is in Stein's (1991) study, making sense of other constructs will require significant effort. The inference of constructs and their interrelationships requires creative work by the OCC analyst. The overall process will include both simple and complex inferences that build toward understanding the constellation of constructs that form the OCC.

CONSTRUCTS

Vocabulary

The first and fundamental step in identifying constructs is to review the vocabulary identified. Collectively constituted concepts are frequently suggested by terms endemic to the organization. Many constructs are basic to the organizational life, the "taken-for-granteds" of the organization. Different constructions of "customer" illustrate how a common term may actually have different meanings and thus be a different construct in different organizations.

There are no "customers" by birth; people are born; "customers" are a social construction. Organizations collectively transform a biological entity, a person, into a social construction, a customer. People are no longer just "people" when they are labeled customers. Customers are constructed as an organizationally specific entity. By considering the organizational communication the interpreter can begin to identify what a "customer" is for a particular organization.

Consider, for example, businesses in rural areas along interstate highways that cater to the tourist traffic, such as service stations. Such organizations are likely to sell to some individuals repeatedly (e.g., the highway patrol officers assigned to work in the area, neighbors, regular delivery drivers, long-haul drivers who make the same trip weekly), but the majority of their customers are onetime purchasers. The language of the organization may suggest that the repeated purchasers are "friends" or "acquaintances," while the onetime purchasers are "customers." In such an organization the construct "customer" means a person who is an infrequent or one-time purchaser with little likelihood of influencing other purchasers. This could be taken to an extreme in some organizations and, for example, customers might be characterized as "targets," "marks," or "suckers"; themes of "taking customers for a ride" might be heard.

Contrast such a hypothetical organization's concept of "customer" with that identified by Peters and Waterman in many successful businesses (1982, chap. 6). In those organizations customers are seen as the heart of the business, the reason for existence. IBM is frequently cited as having a conception of the customer that makes IBM's business service, not products. The customer—in such organizations as Frito-Lay, IBM, and Boeing—is described as being integral to the organization's development and success. In such organizations the vocabulary referring to customers plus the theme of service and the temporal response to inquiries all contribute to making the construct "customer" significantly different than it would be in the hypothetical interstate highway business.

Numerous other examples can be presented of nouns and phrases that reflect the constitution of people, objects, and behavior. *Newsweek*'s "Buzzwords" column (Ex. 6.2) provides examples for one's coworkers (e.g., *gorillas*), purchasers (e.g., *primate, Bertha, Foamer*), objects (e.g., *Amshack, marriage mail*), and actions (e.g., *pat the can, stabbed*). The use of language modifiers will also be useful in inferring constructs as they help characterize people, objects, and ideas (e.g., *ugly, ineffectual, brilliant, lazy*). Lawrence's (1991) observation of the frequent use of such terms as *thank you* and *please* pointed toward "politeness" as a construct. Thus, vocabulary can help the analyst by labeling, modifying, or exemplifying constructs.

Themes

The repetition of interconnecting topics helps in identifying constructs (and will contribute greatly to inferring relations among constructs). Themes of success or failure may indicate which people are constituted as successful. The theme of conflict we found in a news organization contributed to the construct "good story," which was often (but not exclusively) one that incorporated dramatic oppositions (Bantz, 1985; Bantz et al., 1980). In studying a small advertising agency Drusch (1991) observed conflict as well as discussions about conflict. During her observation employees left, the owners argued, new employees told about past problems, and new employees discussed the conflicts (see Ex. 9.1). Conflict was thematic at JBR Advertising, and Drusch inferred that "conflict" was an organizational construct there.

Example 9.1
JBR Advertising

Lina: Monica, the ad for DC is ready. Does Peppe need to stat it?
Monica: Hold on I will be right there.
Monica: What do I need to do, hold your hand while you do every ad? I told you that I wanted the girl on the stool for this ad. I don't have time to come check on your work every five seconds.
Lina: Monica you told me you wanted the girl standing.
Monica: No, I told you seated. I remember we were standing over by the Xerox machine yesterday. You don't seem to want to listen.

(Drusch, 1991, pp. 9–10)

Owner to new employees:
Monica: Pat, I think we should start off me telling you what happened in the last couple of days. We are a very small agency and we don't have time for stupid mistakes. I expect the employees here to concentrate on what they are doing and to care about the work they are producing. We are attempting to start fresh with all new people because the previous employees didn't care about the work they were doing. If you don't have the loyalty that we are looking for I have to be honest and say that you won't last here just like the others.

(Drusch, 1991, pp. 19–20)

Story about old employees told by new employees:
Cindy: Can you believe that girl just didn't show up to work? I can't

imagine ever doing that.

Gwen: No, I heard she had a courier service drop off her
    resignation letter.

(Drusch, 1991, p. 18)

New employees discussing the owners:

Gwen: Can you believe the way he speaks to her? I have never
    worked in a place where people yelled so much at each
    other.

Cindy: That is nothing. You should have heard them yesterday after
    you left for lunch.

(Drusch, 1991, p. 20)

Temporality

The pacing between and within messages contributes to inferring constructs in several ways. The most obvious is that time
itself becomes a construct. Organizations constitute a sense of
time: Is time a thing? Is the amount of time fixed? Is time con-
trollable (e.g., "Stop the presses!" "It won't matter if we finish
on Monday"), or is it fixed (e.g., "We must be on the air at 5:00
P.M.," "If the bid is not submitted by noon Friday, it will not be
considered")? In both very busy organizations and extremely
slow-paced organizations time may become a construct. In busy
organizations, for example, there may not be enough time, and
its shortage becomes a problem; in slow-paced organizations
there may be too much time, and its plentifulness makes boredom and waiting a problem. Temporality analysis (along with
other analyses, especially concerning agenda) will contribute to
understanding organizational "time."

Beyond "time" itself temporality will help the analyst infer
the temporal dimension of other constructs. The organizationally vital construct "work," for example, has a temporal character: Is it done slowly and deliberately or blazingly fast? Or does
speed have limits (e.g., a great surgeon is a "fast" surgeon but
not a "very fast" surgeon)? Does a good worker finish as many
things as possible or produce a fixed number?

Architecture

The structural characteristics of organizational communication provide assistance to the analyst seeking to infer organizational con-

structs. The construct "superior" is likely to include aspects of space and arrangement, as superiors tend to be located on certain floors, their offices varying in size and furnishings with other offices (e.g., General Motors' fourteenth floor, Wright, 1979).

The architecture of verbal interactions will also contribute to inferring constructs. Emergency Medical Services personnel demonstrated a consistent ordering of messages on accident scenes (Grenz, 1989; also Ex. 6.4). The development of "paramedic" as an organizational construct appears to utilize the architecture of messages, as message flow represents the professionalism and skill of a person licensed to perform medical services in the field.

Thus, all four aspects of message analysis are useful in inferring constructs. While vocabulary is likely to be the basis of much inference, themes, temporality, and architecture also make important contributions.

The identification of constructs continues from the symbolic form analysis. By their very definition symbolic forms are rich stores for the organizational interpreter to browse through when inferring organizational meanings. The symbolic character of metaphor, stories, and fantasy themes offers a valuable resource to the OCC researcher.

Metaphors

The frequent use of military metaphors in organizations (e.g., Ex. 7.1) illustrates how metaphors contribute to inferring constructs. The "superior," or "boss," is constructed with metaphors that differentiate the "troops" from the "generals." To realize the prevalence and taken-for-grantedness of such a metaphor consider its difference from the construct "organizational membership," with the metaphor "managers and members are lovers" (suggested by Brockreide's, 1972, metaphor "arguers as lovers"). Constructing "managers" in a relationship to "members" such that they share a mutuality of loving would be substantially different than finding an organization in which "managers" are metaphorical generals.

The power of metaphors will help shape the interpretation of constructs. A metaphor of light and dark may constitute good and evil (see Osborn, 1967). As Lakoff and Johnson (1980) suggest, orientational and conceptual metaphors may shape the construction of activity (e.g., good is up; going west is inevitable). The complexity of metaphors enables them to interconnect with a variety of aspects of the OCC analysis and suggest constructs. Sass (1991) noted that members referred to their at-risk youth program as a large, forceful, and rapid vehicle (i.e., as a train and as a Mack truck). The metaphor connected temporality and agenda ("The train gets like a heartbeat that moves faster, faster, faster," pp. 36–37) and hints of the "miracles" construct, which are the dramatic changes the program produces in the youth. Careful consideration of the complexity of metaphors can illuminate constructs.

Stories

Stories frequently demonstrate the enactment of constructs. Stories dramatize, for example, tension and its release as they demonstrate what is funny and what is not funny within the organization. Both the "hippopotamus" story (Ex. 7.4) itself and its telling construct the character of both faculty members and department chairs. The three recountings of conflict in the advertising agency (Ex. 9.1) include both older members enculturating "conflict" as an organizational construct and new members performing self-enculturation of "organizational conflict" as a construct. Enculturation stories frequently depict the positive and negative characters of an organization, demonstrating through their telling what "success" is within the organization and how to achieve it. Thus, the baseball coach told the story of J. W. to new recruits (Ex. 7.3), and in Example 9.2 an experienced emergency-call operator, Greg, told a "What *not*-to-do story" to Denise, a newcomer. The emergency operator example is intriguing because its contribution to the construct of "good work" is subtle. The organizational members displayed a great appreciation for humor, not only in Example 9.2 but also in numerous other interactions. Yet the story implies the limits of humor to the new member by signaling that it is not appropriate for her to extend the humor to the public she is serving. The story thus enculturates a newcomer by suggesting to her that the interaction of norms and roles for humor as appropriate behavior is limited to certain organizational roles (i.e., peer-peer).

Example 9.2
Emergency-Call Operators

Denise: We need a few more bush fires.
  Greg: Brush.
Denise: What?
  Greg: They are called brush fires.
Denise: I know. That is what the woman who just called called it.
  Greg: There used to be this guy who worked here who was named
          John. He was the funniest guy. I remember one time a
          woman called and said that there was a burning bush in her
          front yard. He quickly answered, "Ma'am, we try to keep
          those types of stories for Bible school." It was one of the
          funniest things I had ever heard. He was the coolest guy but
          wasn't much into rules and regs though and he only lasted
          here about a year. He sure was funny though. I am sure he
          was fired. I don't know for sure but that was the rumor, and
          I wouldn't put it past him to do something that could get him
          fired.
Denise: Sounds funny, where is he now?
  Greg: After he left I don't know, but he sure was funny.

                                    (LaPointe, 1991, pp. 20–21)

Fantasy themes

In a similar fashion fantasy themes reveal the constitution of characters, scenarios, and plots, as in a dramatization about the women's movement (Kroll, 1983; also Ex. 7.8). What women *are* is
constructed in the fantasy themes as: Women "push away the
foot," "stand up and be proud," "be free," and "look to each other
for solace" (Kroll, 1983, p. 144). For the interpreter spending time
analyzing such fantasy theme dramatizations can be extremely
valuable in inferring constructs and relations among constructs.

Building upon the message and symbolic form analysis, the
inference of expectations will contribute to identifying constructs and, especially, relations among constructs. A brief illustration of each form of expectation and its contribution to
identifying constructs will close this section.

Norms

Expectations of appropriate behavior are integral to the construction of behavior and its meaningfulness. Thus, the type of language-use norm discussed in chapter 8 will be part of the interpretation of constructs that refer to people and settings. The expectation that scatological language is used within locker rooms and "clean" language is appropriate for television interviews may be part of the construction of a "veteran" sports player. In the food cooperative that Lawrence (1991) names "George," there are clear expectations that workers will dress nontraditionally ("one deli worker with bandana and long earrings," 11/10, p. 2; "one deli worker has beard, long braid. Ear ring in one ear. Baseball hat on backwards," 11/10, p. 7), that things are a little tattered (e.g., the office is "junky"; a wall hanging is coming loose at one end), and yet things are very clean. These norms could contribute to a self-definition construct that balances quality with the nontraditionalism prevalent in the food cooperative movement.

Roles

The characterization of roles is often critical to the construction of organizational identities (and vice versa). Identifying "member" and "manager" as constructs utilizes the inferred expectations of rights and responsibilities. As implied in the discussion of metaphors, the construct "manager" would be very different in organizations that expressed the expectation of general-like behavior through the use of military metaphors as opposed to organizations that expressed the expectation of parentlike, siblinglike, or lover-like behavior through the use of related metaphors.

As Example 9.2 suggests, organizations frequently differentiate between appropriate behavior among peers and appropriate behavior with the public. This differentiation of communication is valuable for identifying how both "member" and "the public" are constructed. Sweet's (1991) observation of an exercise club dramatically revealed that the employees labeled, evaluated, and denigrated customers (usually behind the customers' backs), typically using sexually oriented labels. Such a construction of "customer" is quite different than that expressed in Target Stores' (1987) training manual: "We listen to our customers. . . . Each of us is here to satisfy customers. We want you to be friendly to customers" (p. 1). A message about differential rights and responsibilities will contribute to understanding people as constructs within an OCC.

Agenda

In the home construction industry in Phoenix builders routinely promise that a house will be finished in 90 days and deliver on the promise. If a study of such home builders were done, expectations about time such as these might contribute to inferring the constructs "house," "structure," and "to build." The 90-day structuring of time suggests a quite different notion of "to build" than building on interstate freeway or a nuclear power plant, for which the time lines are 10 to 20 years. Similarly, the construct "organized" might vary dramatically among organizations, depending upon their agendas. In Roy's (1959–1960) clicker room a well-organized day appeared to be one in which the materials were available, the output was picked up, and the "times" (e.g., coffee, lunch, banana) occurred as always. In contrast, a well-organized launch day for the National Aeronautics and Space Administration (NASA) is structured down to the minute and even some seconds. The clicker room and NASA are likely to have glaring differences in their construct for "well-organized."

Motives

Expectations about why people behave as they do are rich sources for inferring person constructs. Characterizing an individual or company that seeks to buy another company as a "rapist" (Hirsch & Andrews, 1983, p. 154), describing an ambulance service as not caring enough about patients (Grenz, 1989), or telling a story about how J. W.'s bunting practice led to his improvement and that improvement pays (Krizek, 1990; also Ex. 7.5) help identify what people are in an organization. The rape metaphor suggests that the motives of top management are violent, brutal, offensive, and oppressive of the vulnerable. The theme of an organization as uncaring suggests that management's motives are largely economic, while the paramedics care about people. The story of J. W.'s success through practice also indicates the financial motive of the baseball players.

Style

Like motives, style is primarily valuable in the inference of person constructs. How members communicate is important in understanding what they are within an organization. The sharp-tongued repartee among police officers (Trujillo &

Dionisopoulos, 1987; also Ex. 3.1) more than hints that a police officer is verbally skilled for the give-and-take of the streets. Stories of the communicative style of members, such as a yelling television director and a camera operator, will frequently elaborate the characteristics of individuals and roles. Thus, the appropriateness in some television stations of yelling at a camera operator casts light on "director" as a construct. Similarly, Sweet's (1991) observation of how the staff's communicative style involved the frequent use of obscene language helps characterize the exercise club's construct "staff."

As the discussion of constructs demonstrates, it is difficult to infer single constructs in isolation. Much of the effort spent in identifying constructs will directly contribute to the inference of relations among constructs. Further, constructs emerge, develop, and disappear across time. Thus, examining the interrelationship of constructs across time will make a major contribution to the inference of organizational communication cultures.

RELATIONS AMONG CONSTRUCTS

The identification of constructs is important to inferring organizational meanings, but inferring relations among constructs is equally important. This is true in part because through their relationships the nature of constructs becomes clear. The construct of "customer" is frequently differentiated, for example, by developing a set of relationships with other constructs—such as "good," "friendly," "deadbeat," or "reliable."

Relations among constructs can develop into constellations of constructs that cast light on each construct and each relationship. In addition, these relations reveal the nature of the constellation itself. Constellations are not fixed, the relationships among the constructs develop and change, and the constructs themselves develop, change, and disappear (see Gregory, 1983).

Individual construct relationships and constellations of construct relationships can be inferred by examining individual constructs and by noting message elements, symbolic forms, and expectations that point toward such relationships. The organizational interpreter can review the work done on messages, symbolic forms, expectations, and individual constructs and begin to infer constellations. Following a brief example of how each element of analysis and inference can contribute to identifying relations among constructs, I will again use Scheibel's

(1990) study of two rock bands to illustrate how, by selecting various aspects of the OCC method (as in Fig. 9.3), one can infer a constellation of constructs. (For simplicity in the remainder of this section I will refer to constellations rather than both relations between constructs and constellations of relations.)

Vocabulary

The centrality of vocabulary in identifying constructs suggests that vocabulary may contribute to locating constellations. Members' use of language often labels constellations themselves. As suggested above, one of the most common and powerful such labels is "good work." "Good work" represents a set of relations among a series of constructs. While the series will vary by organization, related constructs could include "work," "quality," "efficiency," "creativity," and "speed." Careful consideration of organizational messages in search of vocabulary that serves as a constellation label can be very productive. Those labels will symbolically frame and interpret the constellation (just as labeling a constellation of stars "the Big Dipper" shapes the observer's scanning of the sky, bounding the constellation and limiting the relationships sought).

Themes

From the complexity of some themes, as they incorporate various organizational elements, and in the powerful symbolism of other themes it is possible to infer constellations of constructs. Studying a modeling school, Brenna (1991) observed thematic complaints about poor organization, lack of professionalism, and lack of discipline. These themes appear to contribute to a set of constructs (e.g., that management is unprofessional; students are not very good; models are unprofessional). Within each of these constructs a conflict is embedded (e.g., management is unprofessional because it does not effectively organize the models' schedules). Furthermore, the three constructs appear to interrelate, thus contributing to a constellation of constructs around conflict and the lack of competence.

Temporality

Temporal analysis will contribute to gauging the pace of change in the constellations and will suggest whether temporality itself is central to the constellations. A good contemporary example of the latter case is high-technology firms, in which the rapidity of new developments, the pressure of competition, and the speed of creating and manufacturing products would direct the interpreter toward a constellation of constructs symbolized by change (Kidder, 1981, emphasizes these aspects of computer manufacturer Data General).

Architecture

While it seems that the analysis of architecture will not be central to the inference of constellations, in some organizations the physical architecture of the organization may be symbolic of constellations. It could be suggested, for example, that the CBS headquarters building ("Black Rock") symbolized a set of organizational constructs including "quality," "style," and "sophistication" present when it was built (cf. Halberstam, 1977, chap. 4; Paley, 1979, pp. 342–345). Further, the architecture of communicative interactions or documents such as memos and reports may also be symbolic of a constellation. In organizations in which the structure of interaction between superiors and subordinates may be fixed (e.g., the military) the rigidity of the structure may symbolize a set of organizational constructs such as "organized," "professional," and "disciplined."

Metaphors

The ability of metaphors to create relationships between foci and frames would suggest that they may contribute to identifying constellations. The use of relational, marital, and familial metaphors in organizations illustrate rich sources for inferring the constellations of constructs integrated in a collective symbol such as organization/marriage/family. Family metaphors may be quite easy to identify but fairly complex in their form. In her study of a unit in a large financial services company ("BiWest"), which had recently been involved in a series of mergers with "Premier," "Metropolitan," and several other unnamed companies, Brinkman (1991) was told the following "analogy":

Example 9.3
Family Metaphors

BiWest are the parents
Premier are the children
Metropolitan are the stepchildren
All the rest are bastards.

(p. 31)

Here the metaphor is clearly familial; unlike many presentations of the family metaphor, however, this one is quite complex. The "BiWest family" includes four direct metaphorical relationships: BiWest-focus, parents-frame; Premier-focus, children-frame; Metropolitan-focus, stepchildren-frame; all the rest-focus, bastards-frame. Further, by using relational family terms there are "meta"-metaphorical relationships among all four foci: BiWest is the parent over all; Premier is the "first born"; Metropolitan has been brought in by marriage; and all the rest are of questionable parentage (not even given names). This is a family in which metaphorical relationships are not only positive but also negative. This is a family in which there are meta-metaphorical relationships, suggesting that multiple constructs are articulated in a complicated constellation of relationships (e.g., parent/child/stepchild/bastard). The analogy presents an emotionally laden multiplex of meanings that are rich resources in interpreting a constellation of constructs.

Stories

Extended stories may help identify constellations, as the emergency-call operator story (Ex. 9.2) points toward the "good work" constellation. Stories of conflict can also represent constellations as multiple actors (e.g., management and labor) are defined in relationship (e.g., cooperation or conflict) toward some goal (e.g., strike or settlement). The repetitive references, for example, to an incident in which models were sent to the wrong address and no one was available at the school to provide the correct information presented the models and school in conflict (Brenna, 1991).

Fantasy themes

As already suggested, fantasy theme analysis can contribute to identifying highly complex relationships. In chapter 10 Pepper presents an extensive dramatization of the fantasy theme "he's outta here!" The theme was integral to a pattern of management bashing by the organizational development team. It was used to express the frustration of the team and involved selecting individuals for poor treatment for a variety of sins. The theme points to a constellation of constructs including the team's self-identity, management's identity, and the lack of progress by the team.

Norms

There exist in some organizations overarching norms that suggest a variety of constructs in a set of relationships. If secrecy is an organizational norm, it suggests that there exists a series of related constructs. To have a norm of secrecy members must know what should be kept secret and what can be told, who can be told what, and what are the consequences of telling someone who should not be told. A set of such constructs (e.g., "secret," "disclosure," "need to know") are necessary for members to recognize when they are doing that which is expected of them.

Roles

Telling someone to behave like a _____ carries the suggestion that the role incorporates a variety of constructs. Roles are relational; hence, in the definition of a role some other role is defined. Working through expectations for one organizational role will illuminate related roles (e.g., superior and subordinate). In the process relationships among the constructs that are integral to those roles will be inferred.

Agenda

The structuring of events is likely to contribute to understanding a constellation of constructs. In studying the modeling school Brenna (1991) noted that chaos reigned at 6:00 P.M. because all the classes started at the same time. The consequence of this agenda symbolized a set of constructs, including the conflicts among management, staff, students, and models as well as disorganization. The earlier example of home builders directs one toward not only constructs but also relations among constructs. The temporal expectation of building homes in 90 days is likely related to constructs of "profitability," "quality," and "sales."

Motives

The emergency medical personnel in Grenz's (1989) study asserted that management was seeking profit at the expense of service. If further analysis supported the attribution of that motive within the organization, then such a motive would direct one toward a constellation of constructs such as "profit," "service," "efficiency," "rewards," and "remuneration." The sales representatives for the modeling school talked about distorting a prospect's chances for modeling in order to sell the school (Brenna, 1991). Such a profit motive could help identify additional aspects of the constellation of constructs beyond those of conflict and disorder. While the complexity of motives will vary among organizations, motives may be particularly valuable in inferring constellations, inasmuch as motives for action may encompass the reasons for multiple activities by many organizational members. Thus motives may interconnect a variety of roles, activities, and norms and their consequent constructs.

Style

Expectations about how members communicate with one another may contribute to inferring constellations of constructs as the interrelationships among differing expectations highlight different conceptions of members. If "workers" are expected to communicate in colloquialisms and incomplete sentences, while "management" is expected to communicate in complete standard English sentences, the relationship between these expectations (growing out of role expectations) may suggest that specific relationships among the constructs "worker" and "management." Given the bias toward standard English, for example, it may be assumed that workers are less "intelligent" than management.

Similarly, Sweet's (1991) observation of a crude, sexually and physically judgmental style by exercise club staff suggests an asymmetrical relationship between staff and customers. The style of communication legitimizes staff making explicit judgments of customers' physical appearance, athletic performance, and sexual attractiveness, typically without the customers' knowledge. From such a style one could infer that the relationship between the constructs "customer" and "staff" in that exercise club is one of staff members providing service to customers while maintaining a superior position through their criticism of the customers.

Constructs

As the last two examples imply, constructs themselves will suggest their relationships. "Management" is likely to be a construct in many organizations. In its construction it suggests a relationship with another construct (whatever term is used for nonmanagement—e.g., *labor, workers, associates*). Similarly, *customer, client, staff,* and *sales representative* all suggest specific types of interrelationships. As noted earlier, identifying constructs will be critical to inferring their relationships.

To close this section of the chapter, I use an example from Scheibel's (1986) study of two rock bands. The example illustrates how interpretation may rest on only a few elements of the method, for they may provide the basis for elaborate inference.

AN EXAMPLE

In his observations Scheibel (1986) noted that on several occasions the conversation of band members included the "marriage metaphor." That metaphor clearly suggested a familial relationship among members, including a sense of obligation, commitment, and, to some extent, long-term affiliation. Scheibel suggests that it is a significant aspect of the symbolic world of the band. To make music bands must coordinate by "playing together," and when they are doing that well they are said to be "tight." This vocabulary, which is thematic among bands, contributes to inferring the meaning of "band" as a unified group.

At the same time bands are made up of individual musicians who play different instruments and who each must have individual talent. Thus, a band is a group made up of individuals. Some players may "stand out" or "outshine" their group members by virtue of technical talent or stage style. The players' individualism was evident not only in their playing but also in whatever conflicts emerged. Several members dramatized a fantasy theme of chopping into thirds their keyboard, which they owned together and which symbolically represented their unity (Ex. 7.10). The dramatization symbolized divorce, splitting up, and destroying that which they shared together. An examination of these three apsects of the band's messages leads to a complex set of relationships among constructs: Bands must be unified (tight). Bands are like families (marriages). Players must be talented individuals. Disagreements can lead to divorce.

This set of relations among constructs—band, players, individual, family, group—offers a complex of meanings whether the "unity" / "family" / "marriage" constructs are ascendant or whether the "individual" / "separate" / "star" / "divorce" constructs are ascendant. By examining these interrelationships the essential character of the organizational communication culture becomes comprehensible to the interpreter.

Constructs, Relations, and Time

The inferences one makes need to incorporate the process of meanings being created, maintained, and transformed. Inferring meanings is always accomplished at a point in time; hence, the interpreter must be sensitive to the *flow* of meanings. This sensitivity can be achieved by recognizing that inferred meanings are created—not always taken for granted—and that meanings will be transformed (possibly even destroyed, see Gray et al., 1985). Analyzing temporality and inferring agenda may help point to the transitional character of organizational meanings.

The nature of the interpretation process leaves the interpretation itself open to change, since organizational meanings undergo change. The retrospective nature of interpretation necessitates recognizing that analysis and inference are constructed from a perspective at a certain place and time, and, as the perspective shifts across time and space, the interpretation will also change. The self-reflexive nature of interpretation, analysis, and inference means that interpretations, like organizational meanings, change across time.

Conclusion

Indeed, it is well said, "in every object there is inexhaustible meaning; the eye sees in it what the eye brings means of seeing."
—Frederick the Great

Organizational interpreters bring various "eyes" to the organizations they seek to understand. The organizational communication culture perspective and method are designed to frame and sharpen those eyes. But the OCC perspective is not a pair of single-vision lenses, nor a pair of bifocals, nor even a pair of trifocals. The OCC perspective is a collection of variable focal lenses that offer choices for interpreters—to match their eyes, to change for differing light, and to challenge their current vision. The measure of success for the organizational communication culture method is not uniformity of reports—for interpreters are not uniform, nor are organizations—but, rather, that interpreters enter into the richness of collective life and understand organizations more fully.

You may seek only to understand your own organizational life; you may seek to represent organizational life to others. Whether the desire is private or public, one's understanding of an organizational communication culture can be represented in a variety of modes. By not prescribing a mode for representation I hope to reinforce that the OCC method is not a fill-in-the-blank scheme (e.g., one measure of vocabulary plus one metaphor . . .). All its elements will not be detailed in each OCC analysis. It succeeds if it enables the interpreter to catch a glimpse of an organization that would otherwise have been obscured, overlooked, or ignored. The organizational communication culture method provides another means of seeing.

The final chapter illustrates the method as a lens as Gerald Pepper shows us his understanding of an organizational development team in a large utility company. In crafting an interpretation for us Pepper selected aspects of the culture, the method, and the reporting and suggests the temporal character of the team. The case of New Public Utility displays a vivid understanding of an organizational communication culture.

CHAPTER TEN

Just Another Day in Abilene, or "When Is a 'Team' Not a Team?": Openness, Accountability, and Identity in an Organizational Development Team

Gerald Pepper

We don't really have goals now, just projects—milestones on the way to nothing. We really don't have any goals to speak of—don't have fewer layers as a goal, don't have fewer people as a goal, whatever. There's never been a target to look at, just a mission statement that says we have a customer focus.
  —member of the New Public Utility Corporate Growth Team

In his classic article "The Abilene Paradox: The Management of Agreement" Harvey (1974) told the story of a family who made a group decision to travel a long, hot road from Coleman, Texas, to Abilene to dine at a restaurant, despite the fact that none of the individuals in the group actually wanted to make the trip. They didn't discover this fact until after the trip was over and the day had been ruined. The critical point made in the article was that often individuals will agree to group goals, resulting in a group decision, when, in actuality, the decision is a false or misleading account of the actual individual inclinations. The Abilene paradox is not about conflict; rather, it is about the inability to manage agreement. It is about members who voice support for ideas that they privately reject, leading to group decisions that may be the opposite of what is actually desired.

The author wishes to thank Charles Bantz for his help in the preparation of this manuscript.

This group consensus, then, is a false agreement made by individuals for any number of reasons, including the fear of reprisals for speaking one's conscience, the ease of following a path of least resistance, the anxiety produced by one's true beliefs may be greater than that produced by agreeing with the group position, and the fear of being labeled a "nonteam player." Whatever the reason, when false consensus characterizes a group it will continually find itself in unintended locations. When it recognizes where it is at the group will tend to respond in predictable ways. First, blaming and victimization will happen. The group will look for an agent responsible for victimizing it, blaming that agent for the group's behaviors (or lack of behaviors). Second, the group will absolve itself from decision-making responsibility. That responsibility will be assigned to the victimizer, reinforcing the issuance of blame.

Unless "Abilene" is avoided, groups will continually find themselves driven by false goals, making decisions that the individuals do not support or understand. As a group, they will continually find themselves laboring to meet "milestones on the way to nothing," as the member quoted at the head of this chapter put it. When groups visit Abilene they truly are teams that are not teams. Beneath their surface appearance of agreement lies a wide diversity of contradictions and disagreements.

Like the family in Harvey's story, the corporate growth team (CGT) to be discussed in this chapter illustrates many of the problems associated with the inability to accomplish true group consensus (i.e., the inability to manage agreement). As an example of what I'm talking about, and as an introduction to the general style of the corporate growth team, I'd like to present an all too common example of decision making in this group. The purpose of the meeting was to begin planning for a team-building retreat to be held about three weeks later. The example is from my field notes.

Example 10.1
CGT Meeting to Clarify the 1991 Agenda

The purpose of the meeting shifted because the team had met with four vice presidents earlier in the day, and they had requested clarification of the team's 1991 agenda along four lines. The meeting now had to be devoted to answering their questions. With almost no discussion they jumped into the process of discussing how to prioritize KRAs (company key result areas, representing corporate-wide goals). They found themselves unable to get to the prioritization however, because they spent about a half-hour simply disagreeing with the whole exercise itself, claiming that it was nothing more than "busy work." The exercise was futile. The eleven members present ultimately decided to split up into groups of three to four each, and divide up the KRAs, so that each group could focus its energies on a limited number of the goals. The groups worked for about an hour, with two of the three groups spending about three-fourths of that time complaining about the absurdity of having to do the exercise in the first place. They then presented their results, and found three totally different approaches to solving the problems raised by the exercise. The question was asked as to how to best reconcile the disparate results into a unified whole. The whole group decided to go with the format advocated by one of the subgroups. A single member volunteered to go into a private room and reconstruct all of the large-group results into that format. The group leader, however, had no input on this because she had been engaged in a phone conversation during that subgroup's presentation. The selected individual left, and returned about one and a half hours later with his report. It was typed up and sent to the vice presidents as the group's response to their inquiries. Nobody in the group except for the person who wrote the draft and the team leader, who had given no input, saw the result that was sent. The group's "consensus," then, actually had little to do with the "group" who, as individuals, had rejected the entire exercise. The result that was sent represented one member's attempt at consolidation of input. The result was never validated by the group; it was simply sent forward on their behalf.

Too many trips to Abilene will have a major impact on any group. The group discussed in this chapter took many such journeys. These journeys, as well as other factors both within and out of the team's control, helped shape its "cultural milieu."

This chapter describes a field research project in which I examined and analyzed the culture of the company growth team of a large, diversified public utility that had been charged with facilitating a corporate-wide organizational development (OD) effort. For this account the company will be referred to as New Public Utility (NPU).

My goal here is to show the sorts of results and understandings that the OCC method makes possible. To give you a feel for the group studied I'm going to begin with an overview of the study's conclusions. I'll then backtrack to the method and work through each dimension, highlighting only a handful of findings that led to three of the critical constructs identified during the research: openness, accountability, and identity. Progressing in this fashion should allow the reader to gain a good feel for what the method can do as well as for how the researcher can use the method. Perhaps most important for this study, progressing in this fashion will demonstrate how the method can facilitate the identification of both contradictions and consensus in organizational cultures.

Before getting to the results, however, it is necessary that you be introduced to the characters and the organization. These introductions will be brief.

Company Growth Team

The Company Growth Team was formed in 1989 for the purpose of coordinating a total system redesign at NPU. The company's overall goal was to restructure in such a way as to accomplish more bottom-up decision making—a more participatory style of management. Since no organizational development group existed, the CGT was created. As the company's chief executive officer (CEO) put it to me one day, the team was brought together because he felt that at some point in the future there may be a need for the employees to be able to perform their work better and more efficiently. If deregulation comes to the utility industry, then supplying low-cost service will require that work be done differently than in today's regulated environment. Employee participation and making decisions at the lowest level are necessary to keep up with the potential developments presented by a somewhat predictable future. The organizational development effort, thus, was the CEO's vision, moving NPU into the future with a flatter, leaner, more competitive organization.

The members were told that their group would exist for two to five years. (Interestingly, at one point I was told that they had a two- to five-year time line, at another point that they had a three-year time line, and the CEO told me that, although the team would formally exist for three to five years, the OD effort would continue after the group disbanded.) The members had to resign their old positions, but were assured that, when the

CGT was dissolved, "a place would be found for them back in the organization." It might be a former position or a newly created one.

The CGT was composed of 14 members, 12 OD consultants, and 2 people serving as the secretarial/support staff. Table 10.1 summarizes the interesting diversity of the group. One of the conditions of my gaining entrance into this group was that participants' names would be kept confidential; therefore, the names in Table 10.1 are pseudonyms. As Table 10.1 shows, length of employment at NPU, education, work background, and age all varied widely. Nine of the OD consultants were men, three (including the team leader) were women, and both secretaries were women.

In addition to the team, seven more characters are important. There were six members of a group called the Senior Executive Team (SET): Phil was the CEO and president of NPU, and Les, Vince, Paul, Bud, and Neil were all vice presidents of the company. Greg, who by then was a manager of a large division of the company (a power generation plant), had been the leader of the CGT for its first year of existence.

Hierarchically, the CGT reported directly to the CEO, which means that they were basically at the same "level" as the SET (senior executives who were also vice presidents). The vice presidents, however, were clearly the CGT superiors; the team reported all of its activities to the appropriate vice president. The CGT's annual budget was about $870,000.

NPU is a diversified public utility. Its core business is supplying electric service to industrial and residential customers in a 26,000-square-mile area. The company also has investments in diverse industries, including coal mining, paper, waste water and sewage treatment, propane gas, and land acquisition. At the time of the research NPU was operating as a highly profitable and financially sound company, with assets over $1.5 billion, operating revenues of approximately $500 million, and 20 years of dividends to shareholders. NPU employs about 2,300 people and enjoys broad-based community support.

LIFE IN THE CGT

To introduce you to CGT life the following "transcript" (with my later comments in brackets) presents a CGT meeting. (I was not

Table 10.1
CGT Membership

Name	Position	Previous position	Years with NPU	Education	Age
Kathy	Full-time secretary	Secretary	8	High school diploma	37
Lisa	Part-time secretary	Secretary	9	High school diploma +	48
Lois	CGT leader	Director level	15	B.A. (accounting) +	49
Grace	Consultant	Manager level	12	B.A.S. (communication disorders) +	38
Sue	Consultant	Secretary	6	High school diploma +	42
Mike	Consultant	Operations analyst	20	High school diploma +	41
Howard	Consultant	Property accounting	12	B.A. +	34
Todd	Consultant	Manager level	22	B.A.	41
Stan	Consultant	Lead lineman	15	High school diploma +	39
John	Consultant	Strategic planner	19	B.A. +	47
Ed	Consultant	Forester	10	B.S.	33
Lee	Consultant	Supervisor level	12	B.S.	38
Art	Consultant	Industrial engineer	15	High school diploma +	38
Carl	Consultant	Control room operator	9	B.A.	32

allowed to tape-record meetings; thus, this transcription is from my field notes and represents the amount of conversation that I was able to record by hand.) This example gives a sense of those in the group and their typical style of exchange. Additionally, many of the issues that will be highlighted in the analysis portion of this chapter are evident in this example.

The setting for this interaction was a large rectangular meeting table, big enough to accommodate 18 to 20 people in relative comfort. The purpose was to process a one-day "team-building" adventure that they had undergone a few days before. During that day they had participated in a number of outdoor activities, including blindfold exercises, lifting and carrying members over obstacles and through mazes, trust falls, and a wall-climbing experience on a rock wall built to teach people the skill of mountain climbing. At the outset of the conversation the members were discussing the fact that about half of them had shown up 20 minutes late for the team-building day.

Example 10.2
CGT Meeting to Process Team-Building Day

Carl: Showing up 20 minutes late was more of a technical than social problem. It's common for us to just pick up and go. [At this point the discussion was tending to get accusatory; people were acting defensive.]

Stan: Instead of overdirecting, we lose the value of someone like Todd who tends to micromanage, but didn't here because "we're so ODish that we reject structure." This is indicative of what we are.

Lois: Except I need it [structure]. I don't look at it as micromanaging, I look at it as helpful.

Stan: Also, we had two hours before we went and everybody sat in their own cubicles and never talked with each other as to what was to happen and what we were to do. [At this point, Carl and others were throwing candy aross the table to each other. Sue reprimanded them in no uncertain terms.]

Sue: Would you guys please stop throwing candy across the table!

John: The problem is, we're all Lone Rangers and we all do our things. We'll figure it out along the way. This is symptomatic of all being volunteers. We feel responsible for ourselves, but not for others. . . .

John: Regarding the blindfold/circle exercise, it was frustrating at the abnormal communication circumstances. It was something of an Abilene experience. Everybody wanted to be grunting and stomping. Instead of directing us where to stand, someone should have directed us how to understand.

Carl: During the human knot exercise, we let everybody lead long enough to get us in trouble, but not long enough to get us out. We failed with a good sense of humor.

Lee: Maybe the message is that we're too big to be a team; maybe we were chosen because we're all leaders who are reluctant to follow.

Stan: Lots of "no, not exactly" we almost never say "that's a good idea, let me build on that."

Lois: We work harder at showing that 12 people can't work together than we do using our abilities to come together and work effectively.

Stan: Maybe it's our sundown [time line]. If it's a choice between bringing the team along or getting the job done, I'm [generic "I"] going to get it done. Shouldn't we be out there doing it?—is our general approach to things.

Lois: I look at it a different way; the CGT can't be composed of Lone Rangers. Shouldn't we be the model of how we are going to fit as team players in the organization that we're trying to build? We're continuously unwilling to do what we're asking the organization to do; however, we're not a bunch of screw ups. . . .

Grace: When I was out there alone, I needed the group; I missed you (crying). [Silence, tissues, joking reference to Sue, who has a reputation of crying during stressful meetings.]

Carl: Too much criticism on what might have been a twist of fate. We're not a lousy team. Honest to Christ, we're pretty good. We talk. We have to quit beating up on ourselves.

Mike: We're OK; we don't have a big problem.

Sue: [Major challenge]: Are you all uncomfortable with this sort of discussion or conversation?

Stan: I felt dumb and competitive. It was frustrating. Do we have competition in the group? I don't see it between groups [subgroups of individuals], maybe between individuals. Is it the desire to excel or to win? I don't see the desire to excel at each other's expense, but it does come at the expense of working together.

Carl: The reality is that some of us might have to go back [to our old jobs and/or departments], and this is our chance. Some of us have already seen and done a lot in the company [reference to Lois], others have not. . . .

Carl: Yes, we let Stan and Ed not find each other and let Sue stand there alone and not take her blindfold off after everyone else did. But so what? It was not malicious. It was good-natured fun. As long as it's shared. Why do we keep killing ourselves on Mondays?

John: Maybe we're reaching our half-life, maybe it's a down cycle, maybe it's summer; but, I think we're all feeling frustration. Our breaks tend to be five minutes on the phone. Where's the balance? So many hot, emotional issues. We have to pick the critical Monday issues more. [At that point the team assigned a subgroup to generate alternatives to the Monday issues.]

Todd: Just in the conversations that go on around here everyday I feel comfortable with what's going on.

Grace: Is there anything here that we haven't discussed yet?

John: Now that's a nice shortcut to the end.

Stan: The ribbon exercise really showed "action versus stop and think." We almost always choose action. Can see it in the group, too. Why plan, let's do.

[The group now decided it will stop; Art and Lois have left, Howard is on the phone. They didn't process the two major events of the team-building day, which was the reason for conducting the afternoon meeting in the first place.]

This interaction highlights many of the crucial dynamics of the company's CGT. Interpretations of abstractions like trust, responsibility, teamwork, openness, conflict, and work were constantly points of dispute in this group. Its members openly discussed their "sundown" (eventual dissolution), their feelings about each other, and their disagreements. They recognized their lack of unity and the fact that they did not model the sort of group that they were asking the organization to become. In short, as a group, the CGT hid almost nothing among themselves; they were totally open with one another. At the same time they consistently failed to allow this openness to converge into a unified identity for themselves (e.g., that CGT is an open team that symbolizes NPU's future). Such an identity would force the group to be accountable in ways that it is unwilling to be.

The absence of such an identity sent the team to Abilene constantly. Surface unity covering underlying disagreements was one of its trademarks. Other indications that the whole team-building day was an Abilene experience are evident in Example 10.2, including the presence of accusations, blaming, disagreement over identity, discomfort with self-analysis, and perceived shared agreement as a driving force behind behavior.

Beginning with conclusions, the remainder of this chapter will focus on these three central constructs: openness, accountability, and identity. By limiting the focus to these three, the reader should be able to get a good, if limited, feel for the organizational communication culture of the Company Growth Team at New Public Utility.

Organizational Meanings at CGT

A number of key constructs emerged as critical to the daily meanings and experiences of the CGT members. Based on the analysis, the most evident constructs were: consensus; procedures and procedural issues; the "turd on the table"; problem identification (if not always problem solving); the approximately three-year time line; identification and accountability issues; personal agendas and issues of self-presentation, self-reliance, the acceptability of others, project ownership, team, teamwork, and restraints; the role of the OD consultant; SET and leadership issues; meetings and the general format of business; the center table and space/design issues; key result areas; the "bottom line"; and faith.

What is important to note when looking at these constructs is that each one represents a slice of shared group reality. Each one, in and of itself, represents a whole domain of experiences and understandings. None, however, in isolation, offers a composite picture of the culture of the NPU Company Growth Team. For that picture we turn to the relations among constructs.

Based on the identification and analysis of relevant constructs, six critical sets of relationships emerged: *openness issues, accountability and identity issues, agenda issues, leadership issues,* the *bottom line,* and *individual faith in the company.* For this chapter only two of these relationships will be explored: openness (O) and accountability/identity (AI).

OPENNESS

This was one of the most interesting constellations of constructs. The CGT consciously chose an unusual architectural layout for its office space. When initially formed the group was housed in a traditional office clustering. Two members shared offices with doors that opened onto hallways, and so on. For their new office space, however, they chose a large, open room that afforded individuals virtually no privacy. The large central meeting table, meant to encourage meeting participation by anyone interested; the use of space in the room; the lack of privacy; the fact that, in order to have privacy, individuals must go to a separate room where most will then notice that they are working on their own;

and the fact that the CGT consciously chose this sort of design are all interesting components of the openness construct.

Further, the way that the team conducted itself was a continuation of how it used space. Its meetings were open, its room was open, members were continually in contact with the outside world via the phones and "voice mail," its conflicts were open, its successes and losses were open, its budget was open, and the member's personal agendas were open. This amount of openness could easily lead to a tendency to retreat into oneself, to reject the group and to feel invaded. Such reactions were clearly not the case here. The level of openness resulted, instead, in a bonding and a clear sense by members of reliance on the group for support and self-affirmation. The members had abundant faith in one another and described themselves as pulling in the same direction.

This, of course, highlights one of the team's biggest internal contradictions. The group rallied around its openness; the members drew strength from their participation in such an environment. At the same time a number of the members confided that they went along with the group so that they did not make waves. Then, when left to their own projects, they did whatever they wanted.

Their sense of openness, then, allowed the members to publicly express a consensus that actually did not exist. Their personal agendas often contradicted those of the team. The "team" was not a team, except in Abilene.

ACCOUNTABILITY AND IDENTITY

Accountability (A) and identity (I) issues are the most complex of all the constructs uncovered. Conceptual issues that contributed to this constellation of constructs included the following: a finite time line (A); the knowledge that the group would be dissolved three to five years after it was formed (A); the development of personal agendas (A); the tendency of members to view projects as personal possessions and the tendency of the group to legitimize this view in its treatment of individuals and their project successes and losses (A); the inability of the group to establish a sense of group identity (I); the commonly presented vision of the CGT members as Lone Rangers, Mavericks, and high achievers and risk takers and how these self-definitions affected the members' tendencies to "go it alone"—to rely primarily on themselves as individuals first and on the group second (I); the impact of member concerns about the time line, their working relationships, their team structure, and their personal agendas on the group's ability to form and function as a team, to engage in "teamwork," to view teamwork as something other than a constraint, and, indeed, to even reach agreement on what a "team" is (I); and, finally, the inability of the team to agree about the role of consultant (I).

The analysis showed clearly that the CGT failed to establish a consistent group identity for itself. Individual definitions of *self*, *group*, *team*, *teamwork*, and *consultant* still conflicted after two and a half years of being together. This lack of identity was fueled by two critical factors. First, the team's leaders changed after one year, and the styles and philosophies of the leaders were extremely different. Second, the group was constantly under the pressure of a finite time line for "completing" a task that was not easily labeled as ever being completed. Lack of identity has contributed more than anything else to the group's lack of accountability. The group does not take responsibility for the OD effort partly because to do so would force it to make distinct decisions about identity, decisions it is unwilling or unable to make.

The above summaries highlight many of the general cultural features of the CGT. To understand how these features were uncovered, I'll now work through the methodological steps themselves, focusing exclusively on data that led to conclusions about O and AI.

Messages

As with any culture study, two key message forms were examined: documents and communicative interactions. Both are briefly summarized below.

KEY DOCUMENTS

Since documents are enduring, they can be referred to any number of times by the researcher. Great care needs to be taken in the examination of documents, however, for, unlike interactions, documents tend to be heavily scripted. In other words their appearance is usually crafted toward some sort of goal. The researcher, then, needs to view documents for what they tell about the group being studied as well as for what they tell about the crafters of the documents (if they are different than the group being studied).

The primary documents that I examined included hundreds of pages of internal documents; the many posters, wallboards, and flip charts throughout the office; the OD room/office itself and the proximity of the CGT room to the NPU general office building; organizational development and effectiveness surveys; and internally produced video magazines, brochures, magazines, articles, and books about NPU and the utility business generally.

Interestingly, despite the fact that this group had been charged with the primary responsibility of facilitating an entire corporate redesign, it consistently refused to allow itself to be profiled in any internal videos or publications, for fear that such a treatment would focus too much attention on the group and its efforts. This attitude was carried to an extreme when one of the members developed a series of cartoons that were printed in an internal newsletter. The cartoons put forth the positive benefits of organizational development in a humorous way. The author chose a pseudonym for the strips, however, rather than use his real name, so that the strips would not be identified with the CGT.

The only internal or external documents I found that referred specifically to the CGT were the general announcement of its formation and a series of three videotaped interviews with the CEO. In these he answered questions about the NPU restructuring and, occasionally, mentioned the formation and role of the CGT to facilitate the change process.

KEY COMMUNICATIVE INTERACTIONS

As message sources, communicative interactions pose a particularly difficult challenge for the researcher. First, the transient nature of interactions means observers typically depend upon note taking and memory to gather the messages. This means the data from communicative interactions are likely to be less complete and detailed than documentary messages. Second, the researcher must be constantly aware of the impact of her or his own presence on participants' responses. This is especially important to note while the researcher is still being assimilated into the group. Until she or he becomes a "fly on the wall"—or, as I was referred to once, "a beetle in the dung heap"—the researcher must always assume that the interactions have been influenced by her or his presence.

The following interactions played a central role in this study: formal one-on-one interviews with all CGT members; formal one-to-group interviews with the whole team as well as with subgroups; over 300 hours of observation during all facets of the group's work between March 1 and July 29, 1991; observation of the group during two team-building "advances" (the group preferred to call them advances rather than retreats); formal participation in a variety of the group's projects; eight hours of formal interviews with the former and current team leaders; and a formal interview (and informal observations) with the NPU chief executive officer.

Before proceeding to the analysis of messages some final notes about the gathering of information need to be presented. All researchers will face a different set of problems and will be greeted with different sets of advantages during the course of their studies. I was no different. For advantages, the CGT gave me a desk among them, a phone and voice mail, access to any and all information I wanted, and their time and patience. They also included me in some of their work. I did evaluations of corporate-wide surveys, participated in a two-day team-building advance, observed and then processed a one-day "outdoor and wall climbing" team-building experience, and took part in the planning of a number of projects with various team members. All of this made me feel accepted and trusted. I was fully socialized into their group.

As for disadvantages, the problems I faced may seem minimal, but they did have a cumulative effect. I was allowed admittance into this group only after courting them for over three months. They were suspicious of my presence at the outset; indeed, I doubt that I would have gained access if two of the members had not met me previously in a professional setting. In any case, I definitely was not "welcomed with open arms" at first. Additionally, I was not allowed to audio- or videotape interactions, which was especially problematic, given the OCC's emphasis on symbolic forms. The result was a more intense effort at note taking and journaling, and a greater effort at reconstructing conversations and stories. It turned out to be a trade-off, of course: I became a more adept listener and observer/recorder and gained more precisely quoted stories and anecdotes.

The issue of culture research trials and tribulations, raptures and joys, ultimately raises questions about the quality of results. The basic question will always be: Are the results that are being reported an adequate reflection of the "culture" of the group studied? To this question I can confidently answer yes. All results reported in this chapter were fed back to the CGT for validation, and the group has given me the go-ahead for adequacy and thoroughness. In other words, when they saw my results they acknowledged they saw themselves.

This is not to say that the team enjoyed my results. Indeed, members wished the results were different—that they would be "portrayed" in a different light. They described my findings as a "negative" portrayal, yet they did not deny the legitimacy of my observations. I am confident, therefore, that these results can be trusted.

Analysis of Messages

In this section I will touch briefly on some of the key findings that allowed me to draw conclusions about openness (O), and about accountability and identity (AI). Data will be presented in the areas of vocabulary, themes, temporality, and architecture as well as about metaphors, stories, and fantasy themes. This brief presentation is intended to give the reader a taste for these important dimensions of the CGT culture and a feel for the OCC method in an actual application.

The presentation to follow may cause two problems. First, it will give the impression that the OCC method is a linear process for gathering and analyzing data. This is not the case at all. The results of this study are being presented in a "step-by-step" fashion for the sake of demonstrating the method in an actual application. Culture study results usually tend to focus on conclusions rather than on the process of doing the research. In this chapter, however, conclusions are used to illustrate the process.

Second, because the results are being presented in such a linear fashion, much of the initial data may appear too cryptic for the reader to understand. You may wonder, for example, about the vocabulary phrase "the turd on the table." The ambiguity of results presented out of context is unavoidable. As you keep reading, however, progressing through the method, the vague terms will become increasingly clear until, ultimately, a composite understanding emerges that represents a vision of the CGT culture.

KEY VOCABULARY

One of the most interesting, yet frustrating, tasks for any culture researcher is learning the vocabulary of the group studied. Recording vocabulary is certainly the first significant activity performed by the researcher, for vocabulary represents an immediately obvious clue to group understanding. For the CGT the following vocabulary consistently referenced O and AI issues: consensus, the "turd on the table," time line, personal agenda, "light bulbs and drinking fountains," team, teamwork, consultant, client, SET (the senior executive team, or "groupies," as they were called, denoting their status as NPU vice presidents), and micromanagement.

KEY THEMES

The vocabulary of a group often encompasses or points at key themes. Themes are more difficult to locate than vocabulary, for they must be repeated, and they must be meaningful. The following represent some of the key themes expressed in the CGT, that had a clear bearing on O and AI constructs: (1) team (teamwork, group work), identity (refers to the amount of self-reflection, plus the group's perceived image of itself to outsiders), individuality, autonomy, life after OD, personal agendas, consultant role, and leadership (management bashing, loyalty).

The tie between vocabulary and themes is a strong one. In their efforts at self-definition, for example, members would commonly ask the question, "Are we more than light bulbs and drinking fountains?" The meaning behind the question was that the group wasn't interested in facilitating "cosmetic" changes (installing drinking fountains and changing light bulbs); rather, they saw their role as corporate (and culture) change agents.

This identity theme was found in a lot of the team's vocabulary, including the use of *team, teamwork, consultant*, and *client*. The relationship between vocabulary and themes is sometimes clear, as with the light bulbs example, and sometimes subtle.

The point is that in an OCC analysis vocabulary will add up to identifiable themes.

KEY TEMPORALITY ISSUES

Temporality is one of the more difficult things for the researcher to observe. The rhythm and pacing of group life is seldom commented upon by the members themselves, and when the researcher is participating with the group, these issues of timing are easily overlooked. Interestingly, many of these temporality issues represent differences in the general philosophies and team-building approaches of the two leaders the CGT has experienced.

In its two years of existence the CGT had undergone two leaders, both appointed by senior management. Two more different leadership styles would have been hard to find. The difference was once described to me as follows: while holding his hand outstretched, palm up, John (CGT member) said, "If this were Greg [the first CGT leader], then this would be Lois [palm turned down]." In an interview with Greg I asked him if he would have given me the same access to the group as Lois did. He answered absolutely not, because my presence would only serve to legitimize the group, giving it an identity. He believed that having an identity would hurt the group, make it self-conscious, and force an internal (self-growth) maintenance focus instead of an external ("get the job done") focus.

The following represent key O and AI temporality issues: the length, pacing, and frequency of meetings generally and the long Monday meetings especially; the regular debates and disagreements over the appropriate amount of time spent on internal self-development (team-building) tasks versus an external focus, which would move the OD effort out into the organization; the tendency and apparent preference to do rather than plan; telephone interruptions as an artificial pace setter; the tendency to respond to client solicitations for development help rather than to initiate OD efforts (as was the preference under the first leader); and the team's three- to five-year time line.

KEY ARCHITECTURAL DIMENSIONS

The first thing a culture researcher notices is the architectural design of the space occupied by the group studied. Unfortunately, architecture is most likely the first important feature taken for granted by this same researcher. Physical space is only one dimension of architecture. Equally important are psychological and communicative space.

The following represent some of the key O and AI architectural issues of the CGT: as the focal architectural feature of the office, a large meeting table made virtually all meetings more or less open forums; the room design itself (a single large office divided into cubicles, spaced around the center table); the lack of privacy; a separate private meeting room within the large room; open cubicles as private space; the OD hierarchy (confusion over who, ultimately, was responsible for OD efforts); time structuring; the group's general rejection of planning; the use of space generally (personal touching, such as shoulder rubs, flip charts, wall posters); and subgroup decision making.

Symbolic Forms

Part of the message analysis process of the OCC is the identification and analysis of symbolic forms. To any outsider symbolic forms will represent the most cryptic messages available. All groups use the communicative shorthand of symbolism, and their representations become so common that they are often used out-of-awareness. Clearly, the identification and interpretation of these symbols is important in cultural analysis.

Without audiotaping it is more difficult to study communicative interactions to determine their symbolic import. Yet, given the amount of time I spent with CGT members and the diversity of activities in which I took part, metaphors, stories, and fantasy themes clearly did emerge.

KEY METAPHORS

Metaphors represent a complex meshing wherein we attempt to comingle domains of experience, both real and imagined. The result is an understanding that goes beyond the boundaries of either single domain. Within the CGT and as regards O and AI, the following represent some of the more important metaphorical conceptions of experience: this team is a bunch of Lone Rangers; teamwork is a restraint; this is the "turd on the table"; projects are personal possessions; the fifth floor (of the general office building, where senior management is located) is a wilderness; and the question of whether CGT is the driver or a passenger on the "OD train." Most of these metaphors are illustrated in examples throughout this chapter.

KEY STORY ISSUES

Stories are sometimes told in full, at single sittings, revealing detail and insight. More often, however, they are told in parts, unfolding over the course of time, disclosed to the researcher as she or he becomes more and more accepted into the group. The full impact of stories can only be captured through recording devices that were unavailable to me. Because of the continued (and continuous) nature of the stories of the CGT, however, I was able to identify and elaborate upon a number of important stories within the group as a whole. Each elaborates upon a variety of the O and AI issues. Two stories will be discussed here: CGT's relationship with SET and the vision (or lack thereof) that justifies the CGT's efforts and existence. These two stories overlapped in interesting ways. The CGT developed an essentially adversarial relationship with the SET, the group to which the CGT directly reported. Their relationship is demonstrated in the quality of their meetings.

Five of the six (the sixth member was located out of state) members of the SET had allotted one hour every two weeks to meet with the CGT. After a year and a half of these meetings neither group felt as though the meetings were productive. So, instead of addressing issues such as meeting content (CGT wanted detail-rich, disclosive content; those in the SET were unwilling to disclose in front of one another and the CEO), format (SET wanted high structure and efficiency; CGT wanted free-flowing, "go where you will" agendaless discussions), or even what the groups expected of each other during the course of one meeting, the two groups decided to stop meeting as a whole, preferring instead one-on-one meetings.

Having observed the CGT for about two months by that point, this decision did not surprise me. The level of antagonism between the groups was one of the most frequently discussed "small-talk" topics. It usually came out in the form of jokes about the SET. Before meeting these executives for the first time, for example, I was told to look closely at their neck muscles. They were very overdeveloped from nodding "yes, Phil [the CEO], yes, Phil" so much.

Another time one member commented that, "when Phil stubs his toe and says "Shit," the whole fifth floor [location of senior management] starts to stink." Again, while on my way to interview the CEO one day, I had some time before the meeting, so I headed to a sporting goods store nearby to make a purchase. Three members noticed that I was going to the store first, and one remarked, "Yeah, you wouldn't want to wander up to the fifth floor without a compass and a knife."

Most of this antagonism was embedded in a general frustration by CGT and SET over "who owns the OD effort." The effort was initiated by the CEO, not the SET. The CGT was created to fulfill the CEO's mandate, but reported to the SET. The CGT orginally set out to "sell" the OD effort at the lowest levels of the organization but received too little support from middle and senior management, so it redesigned its efforts toward the upper-management levels. Unfortunately, it never successfully convinced those who it felt had to be most responsible for any success of the effort in the first place: the SET. Thus, the CGT held the SET accountable for the development effort's success or lack thereof, the SET held the CGT accountable, the CEO simply tried to sell his vision to all parties concerned, and the company as a whole has no idea where to place accountability for the many OD redesign efforts that they were being asked to undertake.

The second important O and AI-related story has to do with the ultimate fate of the CGT. These members resigned their old positions under the "promise" that, when the CGT was dissolved, a place would be found in the company for each of them. At some point during the second year the members were told to "watch the board" for postings of openings into which they would fit. They would be expected to compete for internal openings, just like everyone else in the company. Some of the team members began to question their original faith in the company and its plans for them.

Then, in the budget prepared for the team's third year, money was allocated under the assumption that there would be two to three fewer members. Everyone began wondering if that meant termination or voluntary movement. Many discussions occurred about the possibility of returning to positions and areas from which the members came. They generally agreed that, in virtually every case, this was not an option. Either the old jobs were no longer attractive, or the old coworkers were no longer receptive. Also, the members had to simultaneously look for work and do their work, while at the same time battling both outside rumors of preferential placement options ("greasing the skids") and internal pressures against "featherbedding."

The members wondered if they deserved more than they were getting. Their time line was coming to an end. As one member put it: "It was easier to take the risk two years ago. I can run toward the cliff when it's 500 yards away, but when it's 20 yards I begin to think twice." To compound the difficulty of their assumed dissolution they had largely distanced themselves from the organization as a whole, its rules and expectations and ways of doing things. They were different now, they argued. One member put the issue this way: "Can you imagine what it would be like to go out into the organization today? Get those time cards away from me."

KEY FANTASY THEMES

Like stories, the analysis of fantasy themes is best facilitated by the use of recording devices. In the absence of such tools, the researcher must be particularly careful to listen for consistent symbolic references that may not seem to make sense at the time but which most of the group members seem to "just understand." Fantasy themes are not explained along the way, like stories may be. Rather, they are symbolic creations of the reality that the members may actually believe they see.

In the CGT three fantasy themes that highlighted O and AI constructs were consistently played out and were important. First was the fantasy theme of the "emperor's new clothes." This fantasy referred to the lack of a clear identity for the CGT and the OD effort itself. Because it was advocated by the "king" (NPU chief executive), everybody was expected to see it. This theme would be triggered by spoken cues such as mention of the "emperor's new clothes" and questions such as "Are we more than light bulbs and drinking fountains?" and "Is this another trip to Abilene?"

The second key fantasy theme is called getting the "turd on the table." This refers to calling something what it actually is and not covering up and pretending that things are what the group wants them to be. This reference usually occurred before group conflict episodes. It grew out of a statement one day when, in making a point, one of the members offered the following scenario: "If you look at the middle of the table and see this big brown thing, and it looks like a turd, and it smells like a turd, then it ain't no Baby Ruth [candy bar]." From that point on, whenever any member felt as though another member was somehow covering up or being less than totally straightforward, she or he simply called for putting the turd on the table. Indeed, the image became so strongly held that a large poster-sized picture of a Baby Ruth candy bar became a permanent fixture in the CGT office.

While this fantasy theme had an obvious impact on openness, it also played a key role in the AI construct. The member who created this fantasy was an accomplished artist and cartoonist. At one point he decided to create a series of comics that would present, in a subtle yet both serious and humorous way, the positive impact that OD could have on the work lives of NPU members. His superiors and the public affairs department approved of the strips and agreed to publish them in the company's monthly newsletter. The name chosen for the author of the comic was Tourdonne de Taibel, pronounced "turd on da [the] table." The comic could thus not be traced to any CGT member or the team itself.

The third major fantasy is encompassed in the phrase "he's outta here." This call refers to the imaginary process of removing perceived obstacles in CGT's way. This process is most reflected in the common practice of "management bashing." Management bashing, or making fun of upper management, was one of the more consistently demonstrated forms of cohesiveness building I observed within CGT. One significant instance needs to be shared here.

While attending a team-building advance with the CGT, I sat in on a late evening work session in which the members were individually selecting their primary projects for the coming year. As the process wound down, I was able to watch a remarkable session (and a more extreme form than ever witnessed again) of management bashing. The example (10.3) is from my notes.

Example 10.3
CGT Fantasy Theme: "He's Outta Here"

At this time, the members were sort of sitting around wondering if they should leave the room and play elsewhere, or do something there in the room. Carl took the lead, and began relating stories of past experiences he thought were funny. Others jumped on the wagon and started relating "Carl-isms," funny stories about Carl, as well as imitations and stories about management and others, especially upper management and vice presidents. Imitations were offered and stories abounded, mostly for my sake as the outsider and for the sake of any others not acquainted with the characters in question. About a half-hour into this routine, the phrase "he's outta here" emerged, and become a rallying cry denoting the explusion of anyone who does not meet the work and/or relational demands of the group. Carl, again, led this discussion, and was enjoying it so much that he moved to the front of the room so that he could write the names of these expelled individuals for all to see. Virtually all of the group present (Carl, Mike, Todd, Art, Lois, Grace, Ed, Howard, Stan) joined in and Lois made the list early. She took it well, and it became a goal of the group members to make the list. Soon after the activity began, it was decided that one list was insufficient; a second was begun to indicate those who should be beaten or otherwise hurt before being expelled, and a pillar in the CGT office was designated as the pillar of pain. Many who were put on that list were beaten, whipped, castrated, put in head locks and given "nuggies," had their nuts cut off, crucified, and other punishments. I almost made the list twice, and my punishment was a lifetime of Monday meetings. Carl drove this activity and loved it; it prompted lots of laughter and statements like "well, it hasn't been all that bad," and "we never would have made it without a sense of humor."

This was true fantasy sharing. Carl clearly emerged as a "legend," and this event, because of its extremity, will become legendary. Interestingly, though this event happened during my first month of being with the group, it was seldom mentioned again (in my presence). The event lasted for over one and a half hours, until about 10:30 P.M., at which point it broke up, and members moved to Howard's room to party and play cards, eventually calling the evening quits at about 1:00 A.M.

Inference of Organizational Expectations

From the analysis of messages (actually, while conducting the message analysis) the OCC researcher will be able to identify those patterns of group life that are observable and meaningful. The method calls for the examination of norms, roles, motives, agenda, and style. Key dimensions of each are discussed below.

Again, the results presented here are only those that were particularly relevant in understanding openness and accountability/identity.

SIGNIFICANT NORMS

Norms refer to behavior that is accepted as appropriate by group members. When behavior becomes normative it is available for comment and observation; thus, even dysfunctional norms can be changed. The following represent some of the significant openness and accountability/identity norms of the CGT: speaking for others ("jumping in" to clarify a point); subgroup decision making rather than by the whole team; groups composed of whoever is available rather than according to who would make the most reasonable or most competent member; long (sometimes as long as eight hours) and tiring Monday meetings; conducting one's affairs as if nobody else were around; a distant relationship with SET (treating SET members with kid gloves when in their presence then bashing them when apart); being willing to give feedback to the CEO but not to the SET; physically touching each other; and rejecting planning and documentation as unnecessary tasks or something of a waste of time.

As a brief example of how some of these norms were observed, consider the following description of 15 minutes of a regular Monday meeting attended by the whole CGT and four of the six SET members. Both groups recognized their longstanding conflict over the issue of expectations. The CGT expected the SET to take the visionary lead in the OD effort, and, indeed, the CGT went to great pains to distance itself from being identified with the vision of the effort itself. The SET, on the other hand, had little vision or enthusiasm for the effort.

This particular meeting included an agenda item "expectations." A CGT member raised the question: "What do you want the CGT to do?" The SET response was interesting and totally in line with its character: "Do you want some sort of list—more or less a keep-or-throw-it-out sort of thing?" This response was met by a period of uncomfortable silence, until Mike [a CGT member] offered some clarification: "Do we need a fairly regular way to keep track of each other?" To that Todd [another CGT member] offered further clarification, and Mike, in turn, attempted to elucidate Todd's version.

After some additional "back-and-forth," Lois, the CGT leader, attempted to redirect the discussion back to the question of what the two groups expected of each other. One vice president suggested that, although he didn't mind the group meetings, he preferred a one-on-one format. The members of the SET agreed, arguing that they didn't understand how groups could have relationships with one another in the first place. The suggestion was raised that these biweekly hour-long meetings between the two groups charged with the responsibility of carrying out a total organizational restructuring be stopped. Having already left for Abilene, nobody objected, and, for the only time in all of my hours of observing these groups, the SET members left a meeting early.

Their early exit caught everybody in the CGT by surprise, but later they commented that it was a sign of health in their relationship with the SET, that those in the SET could now feel comfortable leaving early. And, so, a two-year tradition of holding one-hour meetings every two weeks was ended during a 15-minute discussion, in which neither side understood what the other was getting at nor, apparently, cared that they didn't understand. Both sides could now be more comfortable knowing that these awkward meetings were no longer expected.

SIGNIFICANT ROLES

Roles refer to behaviors that are expected in light of other's behaviors (i.e., differential rights and responsibilities). So, although norms are not necessarily roles, roles are certainly normative. Of the many roles played by the CGT as a whole, and by members individually, I'll comment on three that concisely highlight O and AI issues. The first role can be labeled "low profile." The CGT chose to act as followers of the OD initiative, without assuming an identifiable leadership role. While this low profile allowed the group to shift accountability to the SET, it meant that, in cases of success, its members paid the price of being unable to accept credit without guilt. Were they to accept credit, then they would have to assume a degree of responsibility that they chose to avoid.

Second, within the team itself, members were allowed, and usually expected, to perform their own individual roles. In the performance of these roles the members were almost never criticized, even when the performances appeared dysfunctional.

One member, for example, was the agreed-upon devil's advo-
cate, another was expected to cry often under stress, and a third
was expected to be able to ferret out the "feeling" dimension of
activities. These roles were often discussed by the members
themselves.

   Third, the CGT assumed the role of truth revealers, or wise
counsel and, as such, positioned itself (and talked about itself)
as though it were not like other groups. It was "beyond all of
that," having a wisdom and an understanding that set it apart
from other groups and from the organization as a whole. It
should not be forced to follow normal rules and policies, and the
SET should be tolerant of the CGT on its own terms. This, of
course, was a very interesting role to adopt (obviously developed during a trip to Abilene), given that the SET didn't even
understand how it could maintain a working relationship with
the CGT.

SIGNIFICANT MOTIVES

As made clear earlier in this book, the search for motives as part
of the OCC method, is based on observable behaviors and references, not the inference of psychological motivation. To get at
motives I conducted formal interviews on the subject with every
member about their reasons for joining the group, in the first
place, and for staying, in the second place. I then watched
closely for specific references to motives that were consistently
repeated among the CGT members.

   The following represent some of the important motives behind group actions and behaviors: (1) The members expressed a
"rebel" self-image. This was the desire to make the SET take the
CGT on its terms only. Members also often described themselves as corporate rebel "types" in explaining why they joined
the group. (2) Members expressed simultaneous group and individual self-promotion and humility. This complex motive was
a reflection of the awkward position in which members found
themselves. They felt compelled to put projects before personal
success. They tended toward self-deprecation (e.g., "It was
more to the credit of the client than to anything that we did")
and deflected credit. Still, every member openly discussed her
or his thoughts and goals concerning upward mobility and impressing the CEO. (3) Members expressed a desire for safety.
This refers to "safe" topics, which were considered to be at a

premium. In their meetings with the SET they felt that SET executives preferred discussing safe topics rather than being questioned by the group. The CGT chose to end its biweekly meetings with the SET rather than confront the group on this issue. (4) Members articulated a preference for action rather than reflection and projects rather than goals. This was the tension constantly reflected in the debate over whether it was better to be out of the office "working" or in the office "planning," which was seen by about half of the group as "not really working." (5) The short time line was a significant motive for the members. Each person knew that she or he was in for a three- to five-year commitment, after which that person would be moving on to another part of the company.

Finally, a number of individual motives emerged during discussions about why members terminated their old positions to join the CGT in the first place. Despite being almost uniformly ignorant about what the job would entail, for example, most members believed in the cause of organizational development at NPU. They saw their move as a significant challenge, and they were quick to accept the ambiguous terms of employment because of a sense of loyalty and faith in the company, loyalty to Greg (the first formal leader of CGT), and general dissatisfaction with their old positions.

SIGNIFICANT AGENDA ISSUES

To most it is clear how a written agenda can drive an interaction, such as a meeting. Less clear, however, are the sorts of impacts that ambiguous or unspoken agendas can have on how work gets done. O and AI in the CGT were influenced by many agenda issues, including: (1) a vague three- to five-year time line coupled with the general belief that "you can't go back." The members shared an overwhelming sense that they had burned their bridges by joining CGT. This was now their chance to move forward in the company because the OD effort would outlive the CGT. (2) The group was guided by a preference for getting work done rather than spending time on self-reflection. This agenda issue revolved around a general hesitancy by the group to examine itself as an identifiable corporate entity. The members were split on the issue of how work should be done and on the balance between "work" and team development. (3) The meeting-participation format was another important agenda issue. The CGT—emphasis here on *team*—worked as an elaborate system of groups and subgroups, coming together as a single group only for Monday meetings. For the most part they worked on specific projects individually and in small groups. Thus, members belonged to the large group, headed up development projects of their own within the company, and belonged at the same time to any number of groups working on other members' projects. Additionally, whenever new work came to the CGT or special short-term projects needed attention, members could expect to find themselves in new subgroups.

Even with all of this potential confusion the team, as a whole, consistently rejected the leader's efforts at structuring, planning, tracking, and documenting work. Indeed, CGT had held its long Monday meetings for over a year before instituting a formal agenda or system of keeping minutes.

SIGNIFICANT STYLE ISSUES

In the OCC method style, like motives, must be observable. A group's style is much easier to observe than its motives. Regarding the qualities of openness, accountability, and identity, three style issues dominated interactions within the CGT: (1) Individual variations in style were readily accepted, meaning that nobody's "style" was compromised. (2) A "fishbowl" atmosphere was the regular working environment of this group. (Members did not hesitate to comment openly and to criticize one another as they met and worked. There was a continuous coming and going of members and outsiders into meetings and into the OD room; the phones rang and the voice mail messages arrived constantly. Group members shouted across the room to one another; and flip charts and wallboards showed the status of ongoing work, "wise sayings," vacation plans, and even personal details about members' private lives.) (3) Dyads and groups were the primary communicative contexts. In these small formats, the members found themselves in lots of meetings. And, as discussed earlier, efforts at coordinating and documenting these meetings were consistently rebuffed.

COMPOSITE CULTURAL IMAGE

Taken together, the data presented above serve as clues about the culture of the CGT. Figure 10.1 shows how they build upon one another.

As impossible as it is to visually demonstrate any communication process, the point of Figure 10.1 is to highlight the cumulative process of uncovering the culture(s) of an organization or group.

Figure 10.1
A splattering of openness, accountability, and identity constructs.

Artist: K. Pepper

Culture analysis is not linear. The researcher does not start at Go and proceed around some predetermined game board until she or he has collected a required amount of information, then getting to draw conclusions. On the contrary, culture research looks a lot like the Jackson Pollack paintings mentioned earlier in the book. As a process itself, it seeks to uncover the process of meaning construction among a group of people. The researcher may suspect when a project first begins what she or he will ultimately find, or the researcher may leave the project feeling as though the underlying cultural dimensions of the studied group were never uncovered.

The OCC method looks like a linear prescription for culture research. It cannot help that. It is bound by the constraints of language, which is a linear form of communication. The researcher, however, must not be misled by the method's linear presentation. The categories suggested by the method as useful compartments for filing information should be understood as layered guidelines. This layered nature of the research and results is suggested in Figure 10.1. Approaching the figure, or a culture, from a different angle will uncover a new meaning. A new insight will emerge, embedded in the energy of the total picture.

The implications of this research agenda are that, as the reader already knows, culture research does not follow a straight line, with a beginning and end. Recognizing its complexity is useful because the process can be quite unclear and confusing. Just when the researcher thinks she or he "has it," "it" changes. The main reasons for this confusion, of course, are that culture researchers inevitably begin as outsiders to the groups they study and because organizational communication cultures are not simple and uniform. Outsiders have to be taught as well as become one of the group.

Being taught is the relatively straightforward process by which any outsider is "shown the ropes" in an unfamiliar situation. How long the process takes is less important than how comprehensive the insiders let it be. The important issue for the researcher to keep in mind is that this kind of overt teaching is always scripted: the members are putting on a play of sorts. They are choosing which qualities about themselves they will disclose and which they will keep secret. All culture researchers must get beyond this level of being taught to the more informative process of becoming a member of the group being studied.

Becoming one, "going native," is both a blessing and a big problem of culture research. Until the researcher has become one of the group she or he cannot claim to know much about that group. On the other hand, if the researcher has gone native, then it is fair to assume that she or he is no longer observing the group with the goal of making an objective assessment. Rather, that researcher is writing with the subjectivity and bias of the group built in. "New" is no longer new once the outsider becomes an insider.

When the balance between outsider and insider has been reached the researcher might truly be able to present novel insights about the group being studied. And, given that balance, the group should be able to receive these insights, both positive and negative ones, as though they were acts of self-criticism, rather than the reactions of an uninformed outsider. The group should see itself in the researcher's conclusions.

At this point, without repeating myself too much, I'm going to retrace the reasoning that has resulted in my conclusions about openness, accountability, and identity. By drawing the previous examples together, I hope to show the "sense" of this part of my painting of the CGT.

Openness

The most obvious indicators of openness revolve around the group's use and construction of its own physical space. Beyond that the analysis showed how the group's physical space impacted its relational openness. The group chose an open office structure, developed around a center table. The room/office had a separate private meeting room in it and was bordered by open cubicles. Throughout the room were flip charts, posters, signs, drawings, and diagrams displaying everything from calendars and ongoing project status reports to the latest jokes and significant quotations. All of these physical artifacts encouraged openness. The physical setting discouraged privacy, calling the matter up for discussion whenever it was sought; the setting invited members of the team to put the turd on the table.

Given such a work environment, it is little wonder that team members acted openly within it. Seeing teamwork as a restraint ("you lose your openness and individuality when you become part of a team"), searching for an open relationship with the SET, having free-flowing meetings, being open about personal agendas, bashing management, speaking for others, making decisions within subgroups, participating in meetings, and accepting style variations can all be seen as outgrowths of the group's fishbowl working environment.

As a central constellation of the CGT culture, openness represented both its greatest strength and its greatest weakness. The group was the product of its own design. It crafted itself according to its own rules and its own ways of thinking and was more than willing to let others know what it thought, what it wanted, and what it knew. The CGT wanted to work with the company in an open, creative way.

On the other hand, this self-creation resulted in an elitism on the part of the group. Its members were charged with facilitating a corporate redesign of immense magnitude, yet they did not solicit clients, demanding instead that work groups come to them for help. The CGT saw itself as being exempt from the rules and regulations affecting others within the company ("too constraining"); it was unwilling to meet senior management on that group's terms, insisting that management recognize the team's unique purpose and style.

In other words, the group manufactured a working environment that began to characterize its members' working relationships and, eventually, began to profoundly impact their group culture. They were a culture of openness that, paradoxically, was quite closed to outsiders.

Accountability and identity

The AI constellation, unlike openness, does not offer obviously observable physical artifacts. This cultural element was determined only after many clues had come together. Among the primary clues were the shift in leaders (two leaders, both appointed, in two years); the constant debate over how much time should be spent on internal definitional issues versus external "getting the work done" issues; the three- to five-year time line; the Lone Ranger / maverick self-image; the "emperor's new clothes" feelings about the OD effort; the "He's outta here" approach to working with the SET; members' refusal to take primary responsibility or accept an identifiable role in accomplishing the effort; the constant efforts and debates over "team" and "teamwork"; the group's low profile and self-perceived differences between it and other groups; its belief that it needs to stick to safe topics with the SET; and its preference to get work done rather than theorize about it.

What these clues show is the paradoxical nature of the AI construct. Although we seek information about a group's culture it is always dangerous to speak of culture as if each group had only one. As illustrated by the three- to five-year time line issue, the AI construct is really a number of conflicting scenarios.

One scenario is that the finite time line may imply ultimate accountability, in the sense that the group will live as long as the project takes. Team and project, then, become one; the team's identity becomes the project. In another scenario the time line might also imply a lack of accountability, in the sense that the group will dissolve no matter what happens. The project transcends the group, so the group is no more responsible for it than is any other group in the company. A third scenario is also possible for the effect of the time line: Some might suggest that the time line itself is so big that it actually makes the job more ambiguous, while simultaneously focusing the team's identity. Rather than clarifying the relationship between the job and the group, the time line may act a source of confusion because most people are not used to working within such broad parameters; identity and accountability become impossible to fix within such a range. At the same time group identity is pulled in the opposite direction by the time line, which serves as a basis upon which to anchor the type and amount of work the group undertakes.

The above conclusions represent a portion of a group's reality. I believe that my analysis accomplished the necessary balance between outsider objectivity and insider knowledge; at least, that's what the group's members told me. I discovered a group composed of hard-working organization members, brought together under vague circumstances, forced to forge their own identity, abandoned by their original leader (after he had sat in a meeting and promised that he would see the project through to its end), working as change agents in a company that had no apparent reason to change other than the CEO's belief that it could be better.

These members had faith in a company they believed was in some ways betraying them. They appreciated the efforts of their new leader yet fought her initiatives to establish structure and provide definition every step of the way. They believed in themselves as individuals more than they believed in the group; they called themselves a team yet had no consistent definition or profile of team against which to measure themselves. They had to work with a senior executive team that was not committed to the OD initiatives of the CEO, had a totally different working style than the CGT, allocated only one hour of formal meeting time twice a month with the CGT, and ultimately asked that these group-to-group meetings end because they did not see a reason for them to continue.

These paradoxical and contradictory descriptions could go on and on. A group's culture is most likely the result of both planning and accident. Groups will try to create identities for themselves, and, as the members grow in relation to one another, unique and unplanned circumstances will arise. Organizational communication cultures are themselves rich symbolic worlds that are contradictory and sometimes confusing.

The world of the CGT was no different. The group realized, to some degree, its contradictory stance between openness and accountability. And, in its many efforts to bypass Abilene, it confronted the paradoxical nature of this problem — that, on the one hand, it was a totally open group, inviting inspection and challenge, while, on the other hand, it rejected accountability. In this case, then, most detours still led to Abilene. Problems were addressed but seldom deeply enough to find the level of submerged, individual disagreement.

Researchers should be cautious when taking a method into a culture study, realizing that they may not find the seamless reality some expect. The OCC method proved its value in this study. Its categories are specific enough to direct the researcher's attention, yet they are also broad enough to allow for a diversity of findings. Using this method, I was able to look for certain things, and, especially at the early stages of the research, when everything was new, the method offered (in the form of categories) some degree of explanation for the things I was observing.

Epilogue

At this writing, eight months after my formal observations of the CGT, a great deal has happened to the group. The group still does good work, the redesign at NPU is still going on, and, for now at least, the team's sundown is still on the horizon—but many changes have also occurred.

First, about four months before I wrote this case study the group received word informally that upper management was interested in seeing the CGT dissolved. Being an expensive group to fund, some top managers felt that it was time for the consultants to take their knowledge out into the organization. While the team was away on a two-day planning advance, about half of its members were left voice-mail messages telling them that they should be putting their résumés together in anticipation for the group's dissolution. The message, apparently, was an "accident," an error made by the human resources department. Since then, however, morale has plummeted and has stayed low, and members are more suspicious than ever of their relationship with management.

A second interesting change in the group has been in its leadership. Lois received a major promotion to a corporate officer level, which left the team without a "leader." During a trip to Abilene upper management decided that, instead of going with a single leader, it would appoint two individuals to serve as co-leaders. It chose Grace and Carl. Thus, the team by now has lost two leaders in less than three years and must now adjust to a leadership form that is difficult at best and certainly untested, especially in this sort of environment.

Other than Lois, no one else has left the group yet, though Sue has put in a bid on another position within the company, and others are actively looking. The general attitude is that the group is being phased out, and nobody really wants to be the one who has to turn out the lights. There is still some belief in the idea that a core crew of OD consultants will remain on indefinitely. For the most part, though, in talking with the members one can sense their feelings of discouragement and resignation that their end truly is inevitable.

REFERENCES

Adoni, H., Cohen, A. A., & Mane, S. (1984). Adolescents' perception of social conflicts in social reality and television news. *Journal of Broadcasting, 28,* 33–49.

Adorno, T. W., & Horkeimer, M. (1972). *Dialectic of enlightment.* New York: Herder and Herder. (Original work published 1944.)

Agar, M. H. (1980). *The professional stranger: An informal introduction to ethnography.* New York: Academic Press.

Alberts, J. K. (1988). An analysis of couples' conversational complaints. *Communication Monographs, 55,* 184–197.

Allaire, Y., & Firsirotu, M. E. (1984). Theories of organizational culture. *Organization Studies, 5,* 193-226.

American Psychological Association. (1973). *Ethical principles in the conduct of research with human participants.* Washington, DC: Author.

Andrews, P. (1989, April 23). Inside Microsoft. *Seattle Times,* Pacific, p. 8.

Apple, W., & Williams, M. (Prods.). (1979). The adventures of Garry Marshall [television program]. Chicago: Television City Production.

Aristotle. (1954). *The rhetoric.* (W. R. Roberts, Trans.). New York: Modern Library / Random House.

Austin, J. L. (1962). *How to do things with words.* Cambridge, MA: Harvard University Press.

Bales, R. F. (1970). *Personality and interpersonal behavior.* New York: Holt, Rinehart & Winston.

Ball, M. A. (1988). *A descriptive and interpretive analysis of the small group decision-making culture of the Kennedy and Johnson administrations regarding the decisions concerning the expansion of the Vietnam War.* Unpublished doctoral dissertation, University of Minnesota, Minneapolis.

Ball, M. A. (1990). A case study of the Kennedy administration's decision-making concerning the Diem coup of November, 1963. *Western Journal of Speech Communication, 54,* 557–574.

Bantz, C. R. (1972). Fantasy theme analysis and its limits. Unpublished manuscript, University of Minnesota, Minneapolis.

Bantz, C. R. (1975a). *Organizing as communicating: A critique and experimental test of Weick's model of organizing.* Unpublished doctoral dissertation, Ohio State University, Columbus.

Bantz, C. R. (1975b). Television news: Reality and research. *Western Speech, 39,* 123–130.

Bantz, C. R. (1979). The critic and the computer: A multiple technique analysis of the *ABC Evening News, Communication Monographs, 46,* 27–39.

Bantz, C. R. (1983). Naturalistic research traditions. In L. L. Putnam & M. E. Pacanowsky (Eds.), *Communication and organization: An interpretive approach* (pp. 55–71). Beverly Hills, CA: Sage.

Bantz, C. R. (1985). News organizations: Conflict as a crafted cultural norm. *Communication, 8,* 225–244.

Bantz, C. R. (1987, August). *Understanding organizations: Analyzing organizational cultures.* Paper presented at the Alta Conference on Interpretive Approaches to Organizational Communication, Alta, Utah.

Bantz, C. R., McCorkle, S., & Baade, R. (1980). The news factory. *Communication Research, 7,* 45–68.

Bantz, C. R., Scheibel, D. F., & Harrell, B. (1990, June). *Measuring organizational communication modes and motives.* Paper presented at the annual meeting of the International Communication Association, Dublin, Ireland.

Bantz, C. R., & Simpson, S. (1990, June). *Communication satisfaction, job satisfaction, and motives for written organizational communication.* Paper presented at the annual meeting of the International Communication Association, Dublin, Ireland.

Bantz, C. R., & Smith, D. H. (1977). A critique and experimental test of Weick's model of organizing. *Communication Monographs, 44,* 171–184.

Barnett, G. A. (1988). Communication and organizational culture. In G. M. Goldhaber & G. A. Barnett (Eds.), *Handbook of organizational communication* (pp. 101–130). Norwood, NJ: Ablex.

Barnlund, D. C. (1962). Toward a meaning-centered philosophy of communication. *Journal of Communication, 11,* 198–202.

Basso, K. (1970). "To give up on words": Silence in Western Apache culture. *Southwestern Journal of Anthropology, 26,* 213–230.

Bauman, R. (1983). *Let your words be few: Symbolism of speaking and silence among seventeenth-century Quakers.* Cambridge: Cambridge University Press.

Beach, W. A. (1985). Temporal density in courtroom interaction: Constraints on the recovery of past events in legal discourse. *Communication Monographs, 52,* 1–18.

Beach, W. A. (Ed.). (1989). Sequential organization of conversational activities: A special issue. *Western Journal of Speech Communication, 53,* 85–246.

Becker, H. S. (1951). The professional dance musician and his audience. *American Journal of Sociology, 57,* 136–144.

Becker, H. S., Geer, B., Hughes, E. C., & Strauss, A. L. (1961). *Boys in white: Student culture in medical school.* Chicago: University of Chicago Press.

Becker, S. L. (1968, May 4). Toward an appropriate theory for contemporary speech-communication. In D. H. Smith (Ed.), *What rhetoric (communication theory) is appropriate for contemporary speech communication?* (pp. 9–25). Proceedings of the University of Minnesota Spring

Symposium in Speech-Communication. Minneapolis: Department of Speech, Communication, and Theatre Arts, University of Minnesota.

Becker, S. L. (1983). *Discovering mass communication.* Glenview, IL: Scott, Foresman.

Benedict, R. (1934). *Patterns of culture.* Boston: Houghton Mifflin.

Berger, C. R., & Calabrese, R. J. (1975). Some explorations in initial interaction and beyond: Toward a developmental theory of interpersonal communication. *Human Communication Research, 1,* 99–112.

Berger, P. L., & Luckmann, T. (1967). *The social construction of reality: A treatise in the sociology of knowledge.* Garden City, NY: Anchor Books. (Original work published 1966.)

Berlo, D. (1960). *The process of communication.* New York: Holt, Rinehart & Winston.

Bernard, C. (1968). *The functions of the executive.* Cambridge, MA: Harvard University Press. (Original work published 1938.)

Bettman, J. R., & Weitz, B. A. (1983). Attributions in the board room: Causal reasoning in corporate annual reports. *Administrative Science Quarterly, 28,* 165–183.

Birdwhistell, R. L. (1972). *Kinesics and context: Essays on body motion communication.* New York: Ballantine. (Original work published 1970.)

Blecha, S. (1982). *Interpreting an organizational culture.* Unpublished manuscript and fieldnotes, University of Minnesota, Minneapolis.

Blumer, H. (1969). *Symbolic interactionism: Perspective and method.* Englewood Cliffs, NJ: Prentice-Hall.

Blue, M. (1991). Research paper. Unpublished manuscript and fieldnotes. Arizona State University, Tempe.

Bormann, E. G. (1965). *Theory and research in the communicative arts.* New York: Holt, Rinehart & Winston.

Bormann, E. G. (1969). *Discussion and group methods: Theory and practice.* New York: Harper & Row.

Bormann, E. G. (1972). Fantasy and rhetorical vision: The rhetorical criticism of social reality. *Quarterly Journal of Speech, 58,* 396–407.

Bormann, E. G. (1973). The Eagleton affair: A fantasy theme analysis. *Quarterly Journal of Speech, 59,* 143–159.

Bormann, E. G. (1975). *Discussion and group methods: Theory and practice* (2nd. ed.). New York: Harper & Row.

Bormann, E. G. (1980). *Communication theory.* New York: Holt, Rinehart & Winston.

Bormann, E. G. (1982). The symbolic convergence theory of communication: Applications and implications for teachers and consultants. *Journal of Applied Communication Research, 10,* 50–61.

Bormann, E. G. (1983). Symbolic convergence: Organizational communication and culture. In L. L. Putnam & M. E. Pacanowsky (Eds.), *Communication and organization: An interpretive approach* (pp. 99–122). Beverly Hills, CA: Sage.

Bormann, E. G. (1985a). *The force of fantasy: Restoring the American dream.* Carbondale: Southern Illinois University Press.

Bormann, E. G. (1985b). Symbolic convergence theory: A communication formulation. *Journal of Communication, 35* (4), 128–138.

Bormann, E. G. (1988). "Empowering" as a heuristic concept in organizational communication. In J. A. Anderson (Ed.), *Communication yearbook 11* (pp. 391–404). Newbury Park, CA: Sage.

Bormann, E. G. (1990). *Small group communication: Theory and practice* (3rd ed.). New York: Harper & Row.

Bormann, E. G., Howell, W. S., Nichols, R. G., & Shapiro, G. L. (1982). *Interpersonal communication in the modern organization* (2nd ed.). Englewood Cliffs, NJ: Prentice-Hall.

Bormann, E. G., Pratt, J., & Putnam, L. (1978). Power, authority, and sex: Male response to female leadership. *Communication Monographs, 45,* 119–155.

Braithwaite, C. A. (1990). Communicative silence: A cross-cultural study of Basso's hypothesis. In D. Carbaugh (Ed.), *Cultural communication and intercultural contact* (pp. 303–320). Hillside, NJ: Lawrence Erlbaum Associates.

Breidenstein-Cutspec, P. (n.d.). *A view from within: The management of storytelling behavior from the organizational actor's point of view.* Unpublished manuscript, Department of Theatre and Communication Arts, Memphis State University, Memphis.

Brenna, J. (1991). *OCC method paper.* Unpublished manuscript, Arizona State University, Tempe.

Brinkman, J. (1991). *Emerging culture within BiWest Company.* Unpublished manuscript and fieldnotes, Arizona State University, Tempe.

Brockriede, W. (1972). Arguers as lovers. *Philosophy and Rhetoric, 5,* 1–11.

Brockriede, W., & Scott, R. L. (1970). *Moments in the rhetoric of the cold war.* New York: Random House.

Brooks, J. L. (Prod. & Dir.). (1987). *Broadcast news* [film]. Livonia, MI: CBS / Fox Video.

Brown, D. (1991, December). *An OCC analysis of a small salon.* Unpublished manuscript and fieldnotes. Arizona State University, Tempe.

Brown, M. H. (1981, August). *The tanks: Stories from the county jail.* Paper presented at the Alta Conference on Interpretive Approaches to Organizational Communication, Alta, Utah.

Brown, M. H. (1985). "That reminds me of a story": Speech action in organizational socialization. *Western Journal of Speech Communication, 49,* 27–42.

Brown, M. H. (1990). Defining stories in organizations: Characteristics and functions. In J. A. Anderson (Ed.), *Communication yearbook 13* (pp. 162–190). Newbury Park, CA: Sage.

Brown, M. H., & McMillan, J. J. (1991). Culture as text: The development of an organizational narrative. *Southern Communication Journal, 57*, 49–60.

Brown, R. H. (1987). *Society as text: Essays on rhetoric, reason, and reality.* Chicago: University of Chicago Press.

Browning, L. D. (1978). A grounded organizational communication theory derived from qualitative data. *Communication Monographs, 45,* 93–109.

Browning, L. D. (1989, November). *Lists and stories as organizational communication.* Paper presented at the annual meeting of the Speech Communication Association, San Francisco.

Bruyn, S. T. (1966). *The human perspective in sociology: The methodology of participant observation.* Englewood Cliffs, NJ: Prentice-Hall.

Burgoon, J. K., & Jones, S. B. (1976). Toward a theory of personal space expectations and their violations. *Human Communication Research, 2,* 131–146.

Burke, K. (1969a). *A rhetoric of motives.* Berkeley: University of California Press. (Original work published 1950.)

Burke, K. (1969b). *A grammar of motives.* Berkeley: University of California Press. (Original work published 1945.)

Burrell, G., & Morgan, G. (1979). *Sociological paradigms and organisational analysis.* London: Heinemann.

Buzzwords. (1989, December 11). *Newsweek,* p. 10.

Buzzwords. (1990a, March 5). *Newsweek,* p. 8.

Buzzwords. (1990b, March 26). *Newsweek,* p. 8.

Caddow, V. (1986). *Suburban police department.* Unpublished manuscript and fieldnotes, Arizona State University, Tempe.

Cambridge profs piqued at merit pay. (1989, August 18). *Science, 253,* 705.

Campbell, K. K., & Jamieson, K. H. (Eds.). (n.d.). *Form and genre: Shaping rhetorical action.* Falls Church, VA: Speech Communication Association.

Carbaugh, D. (1985). Cultural communication and organizing. In W. B. Gudykunst, L. P. Stewart, & S. Ting-Toomey (Eds.), *Communication, culture, and organizational processes* (pp. 30–47). Beverly Hills, CA: Sage.

Carbaugh, D. (1986). Some thoughts on organizing as cultural communication. In L. Thayer (Ed.), *Organization, communication: Emerging perspectives I* (pp. 85–101). Norwood, NJ: Ablex.

Carbaugh, D. (1988a). Comments on "culture" in communication inquiry. *Communication Reports, 1,* 38–41.

Carbaugh, D. (1988b). Cultural terms and tensions in the speech at a television station. *Western Journal of Speech Communication, 52,* 216–237.

Carbaugh, D. (1988c). *Talking American: Cultural discourses on DONO-HUE*. Norwood, NJ: Ablex.

Carver, C. R. (n.d.). *Interview assignment*. Unpublished manuscript, University of Minnesota, Minneapolis.

Chaffee, S., & McLeod, J. (1968). Sensitization in panel design: A coorientational experiment. *Journalism Quarterly, 45*, 661–669.

Cheney, G. (1991). *Rhetoric in organizational society: Managing multiple identities*. Columbia: University of South Carolina Press.

Cheney, G., & Tompkins, P. K. (1988). On the facts of the text as the basis of human communication. In J. A. Anderson (Ed.), *Communication yearbook 11* (pp. 455–481). Newbury Park, CA: Sage.

Chesebro, J. W., Cragan, J. F., & McCullough, P. (1973). The small group techniques of the radical revolutionary: A synthesis of consciousness raising. *Speech Monographs, 40*, 136–146.

Conquergood, D. (1983). Communication as performance: Dramaturgical dimensions of everyday life. In J. I. Sisco (Ed.), *The Jensen lectures: Contemporary communication studies* (pp. 24–43). Tampa: University of South Florida, Department of Communication.

Conrad, C. (1983). Organizational power: Faces and symbolic forms. In L. L. Putnam & M. E. Pacanowsky (Eds.), *Communication and organizations: An interpretive approach* (pp. 173–194). Beverly Hills, CA: Sage.

Conrad, C. (1985). *Strategic organizational communication*. New York: Holt, Rinehart & Winston.

Conrad, C., & Ryan, M. (1985). Power, praxis, and self in organizational communication theory. In R. D. McPhee & P. K. Tompkins (Eds.), *Organizational communication: Traditional themes and new directions* (pp. 235–257). Beverly Hills, CA: Sage.

Cooper, E. M. (1989). *Storytelling in the newsroom: The oral tradition of a writing profession*. Unpublished master's thesis, Arizona State University, Tempe.

Corman, S. R. (1990). A model of perceived communication in collective networks. *Human Communication Research, 16*, 582–602.

Coughlin, P. (1981). *Organizational communication field study*. Unpublished manuscript and fieldnotes, University of Minnesota, Minneapolis.

Coupe, C. M. (1986). *High technology manufacturing company*. Fieldnotes, Arizona State University, Tempe.

Cragan, J. F., & Shields, D. C. (1981). *Applied communication research: A dramatistic approach*. Prospect Heights, IL: Waveland.

Deal, T. E., & Kennedy, A. A. (1982). *Corporate cultures: The rites and rituals of corporate life*. Reading, MA: Addison-Wesley.

Deetz, S. A. (1982). Critical interpretive research in organizational communication. *Western Journal of Speech Communication, 46*, 131–149.

Deetz, S. (1988). Cultural studies: Studying meaning and action in organizations. In J. A. Anderson (Ed.), *Communication yearbook 11* (pp. 335–345). Newbury Park, CA: Sage.

Deetz, S. A. (1992). *Democracy in an age of corporate colonization: Developments in communication and the politics of everyday life.* Albany: State University of New York Press.

Deetz, S. A., & Kersten, A. (1983). Critical models of interpretive research. In L. L. Putnam & M. E. Pacanowsky (Eds.), *Communication and organizations: An interpretive approach* (pp. 147–171). Beverly Hills, CA: Sage.

Deetz, S., & Mumby, D. K. (1990). Power, discourse, and the workplace: Reclaiming the critical tradition. In J. A. Anderson (Ed.), *Communication yearbook 13* (pp. 18–47). Newbury Park, CA: Sage.

Denzin, N. K. (1987). Under the influence of time: Reading the interactional text. *Sociological Quarterly, 28,* 327–341.

Devito, J. A., & Hecht, M. L. (Eds.). (1990). *The nonverbal communication reader.* Prospect Heights, IL: Waveland.

DeWine, S. (1988). The cultural perspective: New wave, old problems. In J. A. Anderson (Ed.), *Communication yearbook 11* (pp. 346–355). Newbury Park, CA: Sage.

Donnellon, A., Gray, B., & Bougon, M. G. (1986). Communication, meaning, and organized action. *Administrative Science Quarterly, 31,* 43–56.

Douglas, J. D. (1976). *Investigative social research: Individual and team field research.* Beverly Hills, CA: Sage.

Douglas, J. D., & Rasmussen, P. K. (1977). *The nude beach.* Beverly Hills, CA: Sage.

Drusch, J. A. (1991). *An analysis of the communication culture at JBR advertising.* Unpublished manuscript and fieldnotes, Arizona State University, Tempe.

Duncan, H. D. (1967). The search for a social theory of communication in American sociology. In F. E. X. Dance (Ed.), *Human communication theory: Original essays* (pp. 236–263). New York: Holt, Rinehart & Winston.

Ehninger, D., & Brockriede, W. (1978). *Decision by debate* (2nd ed.). New York: Harper & Row.

Eisenberg, E. (1986). Meaning and interpretation in organizations. *Quarterly Journal of Speech, 72,* 88–96.

Eisenberg, E. M. (1990). Jamming: Transcendence through organizing. *Communication Research, 17,* 139–164.

Eisenberg, E. M., & Riley, P. (1988). Organizational symbols and sensemaking. In G. M. Goldhaber & G. A. Barnett (Eds.), *Handbook of organizational communication* (pp. 131–150). Norwood, NJ: Ablex.

Ellis, D. (1991). *From language to communication.* Hillsdale, NJ: Lawrence Erlbaum Associates.

Ellis, D. G., & Donohue, W. A. (1986). *Contemporary issues in language and discourse processes.* Hillsdale, NJ: Lawrence Erlbaum Associates.

Ellis, D. G., & Fisher, B. A. (1975). Phases of conflict in small group development. *Human Communication Research, 1,* 195–212.

Etzioni, A. (1964). *Modern organizations.* Englewood Cliffs, NJ: Prentice-Hall.

Ewart, J. J. (1985). *The dynamics of the organizational "engineering" of a newcomer to crew member: A descriptive analysis of the socialization process in local television news stations.* Unpublished doctoral dissertation, University of Minnesota, Minneapolis.

Faules, D. F., & Alexander, D. C. (1978). *Communication and social behavior: A symbolic interaction perspective.* Reading, MA: Addison-Wesley.

Filstead, W. J. (1970). *Qualitative methodology: Firsthand involvement with the social world.* Chicago: Markham.

Fine, G. A. (1984). Negotiated orders and organizational cultures. *Annual Review of Sociology, 10,* 239–262.

Fine, E. C., & Speer, J. H. (1977). A new look at performance. *Communication Monographs, 44,* 374–389.

Fisher, B. A., & Ellis, D. G. (1990). *Small group decision making: Communication and the group process* (3rd ed.). New York: McGraw-Hill.

Fisher, B. A., & Hawes, L. C. (1971). An interact system model: Generating a grounded theory of small group decision making. *Quarterly Journal of Speech, 58,* 444–453.

Fisher, W. R. (1970). A motive view of communication. *Quarterly Journal of Speech, 56,* 131–139.

Fisher, W. R. (1984). Narration as a human communication paradigm: The case of public moral argument. *Communication Monographs, 51,* 1–22.

Fisher, W. R. (1985). The narrative paradigm: In the beginning. *Journal of Communication, 35* (4), 74–89.

Fisher, W. R. (1987). *Human communication as narration: Toward a philosophy of reason, value, and action.* Columbia: University of South Carolina Press.

Flaherty, M. G. (1987). Multiple realities and the experience of duration. *Sociological Quarterly, 28,* 313–326.

Follett, K. (1983). *On wings of eagles.* London: Collins.

Friedman, R. A. (1989). Interaction norms as carriers of organizational culture: A study of labor negotiations at International Harvester. *Journal of Contemporary Ethnography, 18,* 3–29.

Frost, P. J., Moore, L. F., Louis, M. R., Lundberg, C. C., & Martin, J. (Eds.). (1985). *Organizational culture.* Beverly Hills, CA: Sage.

Frost, P. J., Moore, L. F., Louis, M. R., Lundberg, C. C., & Martin, J. (Eds.). (1991). *Reframing organizational culture.* Newbury Park, CA: Sage.

Frye, N. (1981). The bridge of language. *Science, 212,* 127–132.

Garfinkel, H. (1967). *Studies in ethnomethodology*. Englewood Cliffs, NJ: Prentice-Hall.

Geer, B. (1964). First days in the field. In P. E. Hammond, *Sociologists at work*. New York: Basic Books.

Geertz, C. (1973). *The interpretation of cultures*. New York: Basic Books.

Geist, P., & Chandler, T. (1983). Account analysis of influence in group decision-making. *Communication Monographs, 51*, 67–78.

Glaser, B. G. (1965). The constant comparative method of qualitative analysis. *Social Problems, 12*, 436–445.

Glaser, B. G., & Strauss, A. L. (1967). *The discovery of grounded theory: Strategies for qualitative research*. Chicago: Aldine.

Gibbs, J. P. (1965). Norms: The problem of definition and classification. *American Journal of Sociology, 70*, 586–594.

Giddens, A. (1979). *Central problems in social theory*. Berkeley: University of California Press.

Giddens, A. (1984). *The constitution of society: Outline of the theory of structuration*. Berkeley: University of California Press.

Goffman, E. (1959). *The presentation of self in everyday life*. Garden City, NY: Doubleday.

Goffman, E. (1961). *Encounters: Two studies in the sociology of interaction*. Indianapolis: Bobbs-Merrill.

Goffman, E. (1974). *Frame analysis: An essay on the organization of experience*. New York: Harper & Row.

Gold, R. L. (1958). Roles in sociological field observations. *Social Forces, 36*, 217–233.

Goodall, H. L., Jr. (1990). A theater of motives and the "meaningful orders of persons and things." In J. A. Anderson (Ed.), *Communication yearbook 13* (pp. 69–94). Newbury Park, CA: Sage.

Gray, B., Bougon, M. G., & Donnellon, A. (1985). Organizations as constructions and destructions of meaning. *Journal of Management, 11*, 83–98.

Gregory, K. L. (1983). Native-view paradigms: Multiple cultures and culture conflicts in organizations. *Administrative Science Quarterly, 28*, 359–376.

Grenz, S. L. (1989). *Communication in emergencies: The organization of verbal interaction among emergency medical services personnel*. Unpublished master's thesis, Arizona State University, Tempe.

Gronn, P. C. (1983). Talk as the work: The accomplishment of school administration. *Administrative Science Quarterly, 28*, 1–21.

Gudykunst, W. B., & Kim, Y. Y. (1984). *Communicating with strangers*. Reading, MA: Addison-Wesley.

Habermas, J. (1971). *Knowledge and human interests* (J. Shapiro, Trans.). Boston: Beacon Press.

Halberstam, D. (1977). *The powers that be*. New York: Knopf.

Hall, E. T. (1959). *The silent language*. Garden City, NY: Doubleday.

Hall, E. T. (1966). *The hidden dimension.* Garden City, NY: Doubleday.

Hammond, B. (1989, January 15). *Duffy.* (Copyright Universal Press Syndicate.)

Hannan, M. T., & Freeman, J. (1989). *Population ecology.* Cambridge, MA: Harvard University Press.

Hanson, G. J. T. (1987). *Corporate community involvement: The intraorganizational communication and employee perception of a corporate value.* Unpublished doctoral dissertation, University of Minnesota, Minneapolis.

Harvey, J. B. (1974). The Abilene paradox: The management of agreement. *Organizational Dynamics, 3* (1), 63–80.

Hattenhauer, D. (1984). The rhetoric of architecutre: A semiotic approach. *Communication Quarterly, 32,* 71–77.

Haugen, T. (1985). *Medical products firm.* Fieldnotes, University of Minnesota, Minneapolis.

Hawes, L. C. (1973). Interpersonal communication: The enactment of routines. In J. J. Makay (Ed.), *Exploration in speech communication* (pp. 71–90). Columbus, OH: Charles E. Merrill.

Hawes, L. C. (1974). Social collectivities as communication: Perspectives on organizational behavior. *Quarterly Journal of Speech, 60,* 497–502.

Hawes, L. C. (1976). How writing is used in talk: A study of communicative logic-in-use. *Quarterly Journal of Speech, 62,* 350–360.

Hersey, P., & Blanchard, K. (1982). *Management of organizational behavior: Utilizing human resources.* Englewood Cliffs, NJ: Prentice-Hall.

Hirsch, P. M., & Andrews, J. A. Y. (1983). Ambushes, shootouts, and knights of the roundtable: The language of corporate takeovers. In L. R. Pondy, P. J. Frost, G. Morgan, & T. C. Dandridge (Eds.), *Organizational symbolism* (pp. 145–155). Greenwich, CT: JAI Press.

Hochmuth, M. (1954). Lincoln's first inaugural. In W. M. Parrish & M. Hochmuth (Eds.), *American speeches* (pp. 21–71). New York: Longmans, Green.

Homans, G. (1950). *The human group.* New York: Harcourt, Brace & World.

Hummel, R. P. (1977). *The bureaucratic experience.* New York: St. Martin's Press.

Hymes, D. (1974). *Foundations in sociolinguistics: An ethnographic approach.* Philadelphia: University of Pennsylvania Press.

Jablin, F. M. (1979). Superior-subordinate communication: The state of the art. *Psychological Bulletin, 86,* 1201–1222.

Jablin, F. M. (1987). Organizational entry, assimilation, and exit. In F. M. Jablin, L. L. Putnam, K. H. Roberts, & L. W. Porter (Eds.), *Handbook of organizational communication* (pp. 679–740). Beverly Hills, CA: Sage.

Jablin, F. M., & Sussman, L. (1983). Organizational group communication: A review of the literature and model of the process. In H. H. Greenbaum, R. L. Falcione, & S. A. Hellweg (Eds.), *Organizational communication: Abstracts, analysis, and overview* (Vol. 8, pp. 11–50). Beverly Hills, CA: Sage.

Jacobs. S. (1988). Evidence and inference in conversation analysis. In J. A. Anderson (Ed.), *Communication yearbook 11* (pp. 433–443). Newbury Park, CA: Sage.

Jacobs, S., & Jackson, S. (1983). Strategy and structure in conversational influence attempts. *Communication Monographs, 50,* 285–304.

Jamieson, K. H., & Campbell, K. K. (1988). *Interplay of influence: Mass media and their publics in news, advertising, and politics* (2nd ed.). Belmont, CA: Wadsworth.

Jefferson, G. (1972). Side sequences. In D. Sudnow (Ed.), *Studies in social interaction* (pp. 294–338). New York: Free Press.

Johnson, B. McD. (1977). *Communication: The process of organizing.* Boston: Allyn & Bacon. (Reprinted American Press, 1981.)

Johnston, J. (1985). *Luxury car dealership.* Fieldnotes, University of Minnesota, Minneapolis.

Kahn, R., & Mann, F. (1952). Developing research partnerships. *Journal of Social Issues, 8,* 4–10.

Kanter, R. M. (1977). *Men and women of the corporation.* New York: Basic Books.

Katriel, T. (1986). *Talking straight: "Dugri" speech in Israeli Sabra culture.* Cambridge: Cambridge University Press.

Katriel, T., & Philipsen, G. (1981). "What we need is communication": "Communication" as a cultural category in some American speech. *Communication Monographs, 48,* 300–317.

Katz, D., & Kahn, R. L. (1978). *The social psychology of organizations* (2nd ed.). New York: John Wiley.

Katz, E., Blumler, J. G., & Gurevitch, M. (1974). Utilization of mass communication by the individual. In J. G. Blumler & E. Katz (Eds.), *The uses of mass communications: Current perspectives on gratifications research* (pp. 19–32). Beverly Hills, CA: Sage.

Kersten, L., & Phillips, S. R. (1992, February). *Electronic identities: The strategic use of email for impression management.* Paper presented at the annual meeting of the Western States Communication Association, Boise, ID.

Kessing, R. M. (1974). Theories of culture. *Annual Review of Anthropology, 3,* 73–97.

Kidd, V. (1975). Happily ever after and other relationship styles: Advice on interpersonal communication in popular magazines, 1951–1973. *Quarterly Journal of Speech, 61,* 31–39.

Kidder, T. (1981). *The soul of a new machine.* Boston: Atlantic–Little, Brown.

Kimberly, J. R., & Miles, R. H. (Eds.). (1980). *The organizational life cycle.* San Francisco: Jossey-Bass.

Knapp, M. L. (1978). *Nonverbal communication in human interaction* (2nd ed.). New York: Holt, Rinehart & Winston.

Koch, S., & Deetz, S. (1981). Metaphor analysis of social reality in organizations. *Journal of Applied Communication Research, 9,* 1–15.

Koehler, J. W., Anatol, K. W. E., & Applbaum, R. L. (1981). *Organizational communication: Behavioral perspectives* (2nd ed.). New York: Holt, Rinehart & Winston.

Kreps, G. L. (1990). Stories as repositories of organizational intelligence: Implications for organizational development. In J. A. Anderson (Ed.), *Communication yearbook 13* (pp. 191–202). Newbury Park, CA: Sage.

Krizek, R. L. (1990). *The socialization of baseball rookies: A focus on the communicative activities of organizational insiders.* Unpublished master's thesis, Arizona State University, Tempe.

Kroll, B. S. (1983). From small group to public view: Mainstreaming the women's movement. *Communication Quarterly, 31,* 139–147.

Lakoff, G., & Johnson, M. (1980). *Metaphors we live by.* Chicago: University of Chicago Press.

Lapointe, J. (1991). *The emergency company cultural analysis.* Unpublished manuscript and fieldnotes, Arizona State University, Tempe.

Lawrence, K. S. (1991). *Organizational communication culture: A study of a food cooperative.* Unpublished manuscript and fieldnotes, Arizona State University, Tempe.

Lewis, J. D., & Weigert, A. J. (1981). The structures and meanings of social time. *Social Forces, 60,* 432–462.

Lincoln, Y. S. & Guba, E. G. (1985). *Naturalistic Inquiry.* Beverly Hills, CA: Sage.

Lofland, J. (1971). *Analyzing social settings: A guide to qualitative observation and analysis.* Belmont, CA: Wadsworth.

Lofland, J., & Lofland, L. H. (1984). *Analyzing social settings: A guide to qualitative observation and analysis* (2nd ed.). Belmont, CA: Wadsworth.

Louis, M. R. (1980). Surprise and sense-making: What newcomers experience in entering unfamiliar organizational settings. *Administrative Science Quarterly, 25,* 226–251.

McCall, G. J., & Simmons, J. L. (Eds.). (1969). *Issues in participant observation: A text and reader.* Reading, MA: Addison-Wesley.

McCorkle, E. (1987). Unpublished manuscript, Arizona State University.

McMillan, J. J. (1990). Symbolic emancipation in the organization: A case of shifting power. In J. A. Anderson (Ed.), *Communication yearbook 13* (pp. 203–241). Newbury Park, CA: Sage.

Maines, D. R. (1987). The significance of temporality and the development of sociological theory. *Sociological Quarterly, 28,* 303–311.

Maines, D. R. (1989). Culture and temporality. *Cultural Dynamics, 2,* 107–120.

Martin, J. (1982). Stories and scripts in organizational settings. In A. H. Hastorf & A. M. Isen (Eds.), *Cognitive social psychology* (pp. 255–305). New York: Elsevier / North Holland.

Martin, J., & Meyerson, D. (1988). Organizational culture and the denial, channeling, and acknowledgement of ambiguity. In L. R. Pondy, R. J. Boland, Jr., & H. Thomas (Eds.), *Managing ambiguity and change* (pp. 93–125). New York: John Wiley.

Martin, J., Feldman, M. S., Hatch, M. J., & Sitkin, S. B. (1983). The uniqueness paradox in organizational stories. *Administrative Science Quarterly, 28,* 438–453.

Maslow, A. H. (1970). *Motivation and personality* (2nd ed.). New York: Harper & Row.

Mead, G. H. (1934). *Mind, self, and society: From the standpoint of a social behaviorist.* Chicago: University of Chicago Press.

Mehrabian, A. (1971). *Silent messages.* Belmont, CA: Wadsworth.

Merton, R. K. (1957). *Social theory and social structure* (rev. & enlarged ed.). Glencoe: Free Press.

Mills, C. W. (1940). Situated actions and vocabularies of motive. *American Sociological Review, 5,* 904–913.

Miller, G. R., & Burgoon, J. K. (1982). Factors affecting the assessments of witness credibility. In N. Kerr (Ed.), *The psychology of the courtroom* (pp. 169–194). New York: Academic Press.

Miller, S. M. (1952). The participant observer and "over-rapport." *American Sociological Review, 7,* 97–99.

Miller, G. R., & Steinberg, M. (1975). *Between people: A new analysis of interpersonal communication.* Chicago: Science Research Associates.

Mintzberg, H. (1973). *The nature of managerial work.* New York: Harper & Row.

Monge, P. R., Farace, R. V., Eisenberg, E. M., Miller, K. I., & White, L. L. (1984). The process of studying process in organizational communication. *Journal of Communication, 34* (1), 22–43.

Moore, L. F., & Beck, B. E. F. (1984). In J. G. Hunt, D. Hosking, C. Schriesheim, & R. Stewart (Eds.), *Leaders and managers: International perspectives on management behavior and leadership* (pp. 240–252). Oxford : Pergamon Press.

Morgan, G. (1980). Paradigms, metaphors and puzzle solving in organization theory. *Administrative Science Quarterly, 25,* 605–622.

Mumby, D. K. (1987). The political function of narrative in organizations. *Communication Monographs, 54,* 113–127.

Nisbett, R., & Ross, L. (1980). *Human inference: Strategies and shortcomings of social judgment.* Englewood Cliffs, NJ: Prentice-Hall.

Nisbett, R. E., & Wilson, T. D. (1977). Telling more than we can know: Verbal reports on mental processes. *Psychological Review, 84*, 231–259.

Nofsinger, R. (1975). The demand ticket: A conversational device for getting the floor. *Speech Monographs, 42*, 1–9.

Nofsinger, R. (1991). *Everday conversation*. Newbury Park, CA: Sage.

Nolan, K. (1991). *Organizational communication culture analysis: The Sandwicherie*. Unpublished manuscript and fieldnotes, Arizona State University, Tempe.

Norberg-Schulz, C. (1980). *Meaning in Western architecture*. New York: Rizzoli.

Norton, R. W. (1978). Foundations of a communicator style construct. *Human Communication Research, 4*, 99–112.

Ogden, C. K., & Richards, I. A. (1923). *The meaning of meaning: A study of the influences of language upon thought and of the science of symbolism*. New York: Harcourt, Brace & World.

O'Keefe, D. J. (1975). Logical empiricism and human communication. *Communication Monographs, 42*, 169–183.

Ohlendorf, D. L. (1983). *Interpreting organizational culture*. Unpublished manuscript and fieldnotes, University of Minnesota, Minneapolis.

Olson, J. (1985). *Collection agency*. Unpublished manuscript and fieldnotes, University of Minnesota, Minneapolis.

Osborn, M. (1967). Archetypal metaphor in rhetoric: The light-dark family. *Quarterly Journal of Speech, 53*, 115–126.

Pacanowsky, M. (n.d.). *The organizational culture fieldwork journal*. Unpublished manuscript, University of Utah, Salt Lake City.

Pacanowsky, M. E. (1983). A small-town cop: Communication in, out, and about a crisis. In L. L. Putnam & M. E. Pacanowsky (Eds.), *Communication and organizations: An interpretive approach* (pp. 261–282). Beverly Hills, CA: Sage.

Pacanowsky, M. (1988). Communication and the empowering organization. In J. A. Anderson (Ed.), *Communication yearbook 11* (pp. 356–379). Newbury Park, CA: Sage.

Pacanowsky, M. E., & O'Donnell-Trujillo, N. (1982). Communication and organizational cultures. *Western Journal of Speech Communication, 46*, 115–130.

Pacanowsky, M. E., & O'Donnell-Trujillo, N. (1983). Organizational communication as cultural performance. *Communication Monographs, 50*, 126–147.

Pacanowsky, M. E., & Putnam, L. L. (1982). Organizational communication and culture: A special issue. *Western Journal of Speech Communication, 46*, 115–208.

Paley, W. S. (1979). *As it happened: A memoir*. Garden City, NY: Doubleday.

Pearce, W. B., & Cronen, V. E. (1980). *Communication, action, and meaning: The creation of social realities*. New York: Praeger.

Pepper, G. L. (1987). *A procedure for assessing and contrasting the metaphoric and literal perceptions of leadership within an organization.* Unpublished doctoral dissertation, University of Minnesota, Minneapolis.

Peters, T. J., & Waterman, R. H., Jr. (1982). *In search of excellence: Lessons from America's best-run companies.* New York: Harper & Row.

Pettegrew, L. S. (1982). Organizational communication and the S.O.B. theory of management. *Western Journal of Speech Communication, 46,* 179–191.

Pettigrew, A. M. (1979). On studying organizational cultures. *Administrative Science Quarterly, 24,* 570–581.

Philipsen, G. (1975). Speaking "like a man" in Teamsterville. *Quarterly Journal of Speech, 61,* 13–22.

Philipsen, G. (1976). Places for speaking in Teamsterville. *Quarterly Journal of Speech, 62,* 15–25.

Philipsen, G., & Carbaugh, D. (1986). A bibliography of fieldwork in the ethnography of communication. *Language and Society, 15,* 387–398.

Pilotta, J. J., Widman, T., & Jasko, S. A. (1988). Meaning and action in the organizational setting: An interpretive approach. In J. A. Anderson (Ed.), *Communication yearbook 11* (pp. 310–334). Newbury Park, CA: Sage.

Pondy, L. R., Frost, P. J., Morgan, G., & Dandridge, T. C. (Eds.). (1983). *Organizational symbolism.* Greenwich, CT: JAI Press.

Poole, M. S. (1983). Decision development in small groups II: A study of multiple sequences in decision making. *Communication Monographs, 50,* 206–232.

Poole, M. S. (1985). Communication and organizational climates: Review, critique, and a new perspective. In R. D. McPhee & P. K. Tompkins (Eds.), *Organizational communication: Traditional themes and new directions* (pp. 79–108). Beverly Hills, CA: Sage.

Poole, M. S., & McPhee, R. D. (1983). A structurational analysis of organizational climate. In L. L. Putnam & M. E. Pacanowsky (Eds.), *Communication and organizations: An interpretive approach* (pp. 195–219). Beverly Hills, CA: Sage.

Power-Ross, S. J. (1984, November). *The information acquisition style and decision-making mode of high-level managers in an information rich environment.* Paper presented at the annual meeting of the Speech Communication Association, Chicago.

Putnam, L. L. (1982). Paradigms for organizational communication research: An overview and synthesis. *Western Journal of Speech Communication, 46,* 192–206.

Putnam, L. L. (1983). The interpretive perspective: An alternative to functionalism. In L. L. Putnam & M. E. Pacanowsky (Eds.), *Communication and organizations: An interpretive approach* (pp. 31–54). Beverly Hills, CA: Sage.

Putnam, L. L., & Pacanowsky, M. E. (1983). *Communication and organizations: An interpretive approach.* Beverly Hills, CA: Sage.

Puzo, M. (1969). *The godfather.* Greenwich, CT: Fawcett.

Qualis Research Associates. (1987). *The ethnograph* [computer program]. Boulder, CO: Author.

Rapoport, A. (1982). *The meaning of the built environment: A nonverbal communication approach.* Beverly Hills, CA: Sage.

Richard, S. (1983). *Enterprise high school.* Fieldnotes, University of Minnesota, Minneapolis.

Riley, P. (1983). A structurationist account of political culture. *Administrative Science Quarterly, 28,* 414–437.

Rombough, R. K. (1991). *Organizational communication culture method.* Unpublished manuscript and fieldnotes. Arizona State University, Tempe.

Rosengren, K. E., Wenner, L. A., & Palmgreen, P. (Eds.). (1985). *Media gratifications research: Current perspectives.* Beverly Hills, CA: Sage.

Roy, D. F. (1959–1960). Banana time: Job satisfaction and informal interaction. *Human Organization, 18,* 158–168.

Sackmann, S. (1989). The role of metaphors in organization transformation. *Human Relations, 42,* 463–485.

Sacks, H. (1972). An initial investigation of the usability of conversational data for doing sociology. In D. Sudnow (Ed.), *Studies in social interaction* (pp. 31–74). New York: Free Press.

Sacks, H., Schegloff, E. A., & Jefferson, G. (1974). A simplest systematics for the organization of turn-taking for conversation. *Language, 50,* 696–735.

Sanjek, R. (Ed.). (1990). *Fieldnotes: The makings of anthropology.* Ithaca, NY: Cornell University Press.

Sass, J. (1991). *Youth intervention program.* Unpublished manuscript and fieldnotes, Arizona State University, Tempe.

Schall, M. S. (1983). A communication-rules approach to organizational culture. *Administrative Science Quarterly, 28,* 557–581.

Scheflen, A. E. (1976). *Human territories: How we behave in space-time.* Englewood Cliffs, NJ: Prentice-Hall.

Scheibel, D. F. (1986). *Communicative organizing activities and the organizational culture of a rock and roll band.* Unpublished master's thesis, California State University, Northridge.

Scheibel, D. F. (1990). The emergence of organizational cultures. In S. R. Corman, S. P. Banks, C. R. Bantz, & M. E. Mayer (Eds.), *Foundations of organizational communication* (pp. 154–164). New York: Longman.

Scheibel, D. F. (1991). *Organizational communication cultures and the social worlds of local rock music.* Unpublished doctoral dissertation, Arizona State University, Tempe.

Schein, E. H. (1985). *Organizational culture and leadership: A dynamic view.* San Francisco: Jossey-Bass.

Schneider, D. M. (1976). Notes toward a theory of culture. In K. H. Basso & H. A. Selby (Eds.), *Meaning in anthropology* (pp. 197–220). Albuquerque: University of New Mexico Press.

Schroeder, L. (1985). *Health Care Inc.* Fieldnotes, University of Minnesota, Minneapolis.

Schwartzman, H. B. (1983). Stories at work: Play in an organizational context. In S. Plattner & E. M. Bruner (Eds.), *Text, play and story: The construction and reconstruction of self and society* (pp. 80–93). Washington, DC: American Ethnological Society.

Searle, J. (1969). *Speech acts: An essay in the philosophy of language.* Cambridge: Cambridge University Press.

Sharf, B. (1978). A rhetorical analysis of leadership emergence in small groups. *Communication Monographs, 45,* 156–172.

Shaver, P. M., & Shaver, L. D. (1992, February). *Signs in the organization: Architectural changes as organizational rhetoric in a public health facility.* Paper presented at annual meeting of the Western States Communication Association, Boise, ID.

Shibutani, T. (1966). *Improvised news: A sociological study of rumor.* Indianapolis: Bobbs-Merrill.

Smircich, L. (1983). Concepts of culture and organizational analysis. *Administrative Science Quarterly, 28,* 339–358.

Smircich, L. (1985). Is the concept of culture a paradigm for understanding organizations and ourselves? In P. J. Frost, L. F. Moore, M. R. Louis, C. C. Lundberg, & J. Martin (Eds.), *Organizational culture* (pp. 55–72). Beverly Hills, CA: Sage.

Smith, D. H. (1972). Communication research and the idea of process. *Speech Monographs, 39,* 174–182.

Smith, R. C., & Eisenberg, E. M. (1987). Conflict at Disneyland: A root-metaphor analysis. *Communication Monographs, 54,* 367–380.

Sontag, S. (1978). *Illness as metaphor.* New York: Farrar, Straus & Giroux.

Speer, A. (1971). *Inside the third reich* (R. Winston & C. Winston, Trans.). New York: Avon. (Original work published 1969.)

Spradley, J. P. (1979). *The ethnographic interview.* New York: Holt, Rinehart & Winston.

Stein, J. (1991). *The organizational communication culture method: A study of "Eddie's."* Unpublished manuscript and fieldnotes, Arizona State University, Tempe.

Stohl, C., & Redding, W. C. (1987). Messages and message exchange processes. In F. M. Jablin, L. L. Putnam, K. H. Roberts, & L. W. Porter (Eds.), *Handbook of organizational communication: An interdisciplinary perspective* (pp. 451–502). Newbury Park, CA: Sage.

Sundstrom, E. (1986). *Work places: The psychology of the physical environment in offices and factories.* Cambridge: Cambridge University Press.

Sweet, A. (1991). *Organization communication culture method: Work-out world*. Unpublished manuscript and fieldnotes, Arizona State University, Tempe.

Sykes, R. E., & Brent, E. E. (1983). *Policing: A social behaviorist perspective*. New Brunswick, NJ: Rutgers University Press.

Talk of the town. (1990, May 21). *New Yorker*, pp. 27–28.

Tanen, D. (1990). *You just don't understand: Women and men in conversation*. New York: William Morrow.

Target Stores. (1987, June). *You and Target*. (Available from Target Stores Division, Dayton Hudson, Minneapolis, MN.)

Texaco, Inc. (1988, January 29). Second amended disclosure statement pursuant to section 1125 of the bankruptcy code. U.S. Bankruptcy Court, S. Dist. N.Y. (87.B.20142).

Ting-Toomey, S. (1985). Toward a theory of conflict and culture. In W. B. Gudykunst, L. P. Stewart, & S. Ting-Toomey (Eds.), *Communication, culture, and organizational processes* (pp. 71–86). Beverly Hills, CA: Sage.

Tompkins, P. K. (1985, November). *Symbolism as the "substance" of organization*. Paper presented at the annual meeting of the Speech Communication Association, Denver, CO.

Tompkins, P. K., & Cheney, G. (1983). Account analysis of organizations: Decision making and identification. In L. L. Putnam & M. E. Pacanowsky (Eds.), *Communication and organizations: An interpretive approach* (pp. 123–146). Beverly Hills, CA: Sage.

Tompkins, P. K., Fisher, J. Y., Infante, D. A., & Tompkins, E. L. (1975). Kenneth Burke and the inherent characteristics of formal organizations: A field study. *Communication Monographs, 42,* 135–142.

Trujillo, N. (1983). "Performing" Mintzberg's roles: The nature of managerial communication. In L. L. Putnam & M. E. Pacanowsky (Eds.), *Communication and organizations: An interpretive approach* (pp. 73–97). Beverly Hills, CA: Sage.

Trujillo, N., & Dionisopoulos, G. (1987). Cop talk, police stories, and the social construction of organizational drama. *Central States Speech Journal, 38,* 196–209.

Tuchman, G. (1978). *Making news: A study in the construction of reality*. New York: Free Press.

Turner, V. (1980). Social dramas and stories about them. *Critical Inquiry, 7,* 141–168.

Uttal, B. (1983, October 17). The corporate culture vultures. *Fortune*, pp. 66–72.

Van Maanen, J. (Ed.). (1983). *Qualitative methodology*. Beverly Hills, CA: Sage.

Van Maanen, J. (1988). *Tales of the field: On writing ethnography*. Chicago: University of Chicago Press.

Vonnegut, K., Jr. (1967). *Player piano*. New York: Avon. (Original work published 1952.)

Wagner, R. (1975). *The invention of culture.* Englewood Cliffs, NJ: Prentice-Hall.

Warren, C. A. B., & Rasmussen, P. K. (1977). Sex and gender in field research. *Urban Life, 6,* 349–369.

Watzlawick, P., Beavin, J. H., & Jackson, D. D. (1967). *Pragmatics of human communication: A study of interactional patterns, pathologies, and paradoxes.* New York: Norton.

Weber, M. (1947). *The theory of social and economic organization* (A. M. Henderson & T. Parsons, Trans.). New York: Free Press.

Weick, K. E. (1969). *The social psychology of organizing.* Reading, MA: Addison-Wesley.

Weick, K. E. (1979). *The social psychology of organizing* (2nd ed.). Reading, MA: Addison-Wesley.

West, N. (1983). *The circus: MI5 operations 1945–1972.* New York: Stein and Day.

White, D. M. (1950). The "gatekeeper": A case study in the selection of news. *Journalism Quarterly, 27,* 383–390.

Wieder, D. L. (1988). From resource to topic: Some aims of conversation analysis. In J. A. Anderson (Ed.), *Communication yearbook 11* (pp. 444–454). Newbury Park, CA: Sage.

Wilkins, A. L. (1983). Organizational stories as symbols which control the organization. In L. R. Pondy, P. J. Frost, G. Morgan, & T. C. Dandridge (Eds.), *Organizational symbolism* (pp. 81–92). Greenwich, CT: JAI Press.

Word, C. (1992, February). Organizational cultural performance: An ethnographic study of "on the job" communication of psychiatric nurses. Paper presented at the annual meeting of the Western States Communication Association, Boise, ID.

Woutat, R. (1983, February 27). A dissatisfied man finds a challenge at work: Getting fired. *Minneapolis Star and Tribune,* p. 13A.

Wright, J. P. (1979). *On a clear day you can see General Motors: John Z. De Lorean's look inside the automotive giant.* Grosse Pointe, MI: Wright Enterprises.

Zerubavel, E. (1987). The language of time: Toward a semiotics of temporality. *Sociological Quarterly, 28,* 343–356.

Zimbardo, P., & Ebbesen, E. B. (1969). *Influencing attitudes and changing behavior.* Reading, MA: Addison-Wesley.

Zimmerman, D. H. (1988). On conversation: The conversation analytic perspective. In J. A. Anderson (Ed.), *Communication yearbook 11* (pp. 406–432). Newbury Park, CA: Sage.

INDEX